THE FORMAL PRINCIPLE
IN THE NOVEL

Also by Austin M. Wright

The American Short Story in the Twenties

NOVELS:
Camden's Eyes
First Persons
The Morley Mythology

The Formal Principle
in the Novel

Austin M. Wright

Cornell University Press

ITHACA AND LONDON

First published 1982 by Cornell University Press.
Published in the United Kingdom by Cornell University Press Ltd.,
Ely House, 37 Dover Street, London W1X 4HQ.

International Standard Book Number 0-8014-1462-8
Library of Congress Catalog Card Number 81-70711
Printed in the United States of America
*Librarians: Library of Congress cataloging information
appears on the last page of the book.*

*The paper in this book is acid-free, and meets
the guidelines for permanence and durability of
the Committee on Production Guidelines for Book
Longevity of the Council on Library Resources.*

*To the students who have worked
with me in graduate seminars at
the University of Cincinnati
through the years, this book
is affectionately dedicated.*

Contents

[7]

Contents

Preface

It used to be considered obvious that if an art of the novel existed, distinct and different from other arts, it would have as a central concept the principle of formal unity. By "formal unity" I mean what holds a fiction together, what makes it one. Critics took such a principle for granted as they tried to explain particular works. So did novelists, who, aside from any other aims, were always trying at least to write novels, not short stories or poems or histories, and expected to find at last the right place to stop.

This book is about formal unity. The idea comes from Aristotle, who, studying tragedy, found the unity in the *plot*. But many modern novelists do not care for plot, and modern critics do so even less. Aristotle's idea, even when liberated from plot, is often put down as irrelevant, useless, obsolete, even destructive. What once seemed obvious is no longer so.

In spite of such a change in critical fashion, I have, through years of teaching and writing, found the concept (introduced to me originally at the University of Chicago) becoming no less necessary to me. It has showed a problematical sort of indispensability, curious not only because of what modern novelists are doing, but also because almost any statement about formal unity seems to need an armor of definitions, since its terms are so variously understood. Conceptual difficulties keep cropping up. What's more, the whole issue looks different when I write novels myself.

I discovered I had to write this book when I took stock of the many modifiers, silent assumptions, and reservations that had attached themselves to this indispensable concept. If it is to con-

tinue useful, I realized, capable of dealing not only with familiar but with original and experimental fiction, then these qualifiers must be explored and made explicit. The continuing value of the concept depends on them; they are the adaptations or solutions to problems that could otherwise destroy it—that have done so, for many readers.

The book is divided into three parts. The first eight chapters (Part 1) are theoretical. They look for assumptions upon which the idea of formal unity rests and develop a description of the principle: how the concept must be understood in their light and how in a practical sense it can be characterized. The discussion moves from general artistic considerations in the first three chapters to specifically novelistic ones in the rest. I redefine "plot" and clarify the terms for its analysis. My aim is to test the claim of formal unity to importance—to centrality—in the novel's art. The novel does not exist in isolation. It has connections with all arts, nonliterary as well as literary, which can often help us understand it. Its links with the modern short story are close indeed, and I have not hesitated to use short stories for illustration when there was no danger of violating the clear distinction between the two.

The next four chapters are concerned with application: practical studies of the formal principles of four celebrated modern American novels, each of which presents a particular challenge. The final chapter (Part 3) approaches the whole question from a third viewpoint, that of my own experience as a writer of novels. From this angle the whole question of formal unity indeed looks different. There are good theoretical reasons for the hostility between critic and novelist, even in the same person; I offer my writing experiences to illuminate these differences and provide some useful antitheoretical perspective.

I am indebted to the Taft Foundation at the University of Cincinnati for grants that have given me time to complete this book. It is a pleasure also to recognize here my debts to so many individuals who have in ways general or specific, both long ago and recently, helped toward the making of this book. There is a deep original debt to my teachers at the University of Chicago, both the so-called neo-Aristotelians and those who did not wish

Preface

to be so called—especially Walter Blair, the late R. S. Crane, Elder Olson, Theodore Silverstein, and the late Napier Wilt—who in their various ways introduced me to the questions that have been absorbing me ever since. There are debts to friends and colleagues in those long ago days when I was a graduate student and first beginning to teach, contracted in many discussions about criticism and theory, never forgotten: to my first literary friend, Preston T. Roberts; to Edward Rosenheim, who chaired the first humanities course I ever taught; to James Schroeter, Herman Sinaiko, Richard G. Stern, and Kenneth Telford. There is my more recent debt to my colleague at the University of Cincinnati, Thomas LeClair, who engaged with me in an exchange of letters debating questions of contemporary theory. I am indebted to Norman Friedman of Queens College, New York, who read the manuscript in an early stage and gave me helpful comments. I feel an especially deep obligation to Wayne C. Booth of the University of Chicago, James K. Robinson of the University of Cincinnati, and Edgar M. Slotkin of the University of Cincinnati, each of whom read the manuscript and gave time and effort, generously and without reward, to detailed criticism and advice. Their suggestions have helped to make this a better book than it would have been otherwise, and of course my failure to meet some of their criticisms is not their fault. Finally, I must mention my deepest debt, to my wife, Sally, who has made herself felt in this book everywhere through the influence on my thinking of our years of talk about books, music, movies, the arts in general, and life itself.

AUSTIN M. WRIGHT

Cincinnati, Ohio

THE HIERARCHY
OF FORM

[1]

The Problem of Wholeness

Consider what it means to call a novel an organic whole. The term is heavy with authority: we remember Henry James, who "delight[ed] in a deep-breathing economy and an organic form," and before him Coleridge (although he was thinking not of novels but of poems). The metaphor is admonitory: you feel guilty if you question it, as if you did not believe in life. To fail to see a work's organic form (the words imply) is to miss everthing, its vitality, its breath, its heart, its soul. By stressing organism, the interdependence of living tissues, the words hint that analysis is impossible: at best, it is autopsy, at worst, murder. Surely such a term is meant to stop discussion. Yet how can it be denied, since what it names is so evident and clear, so obvious and beautiful?

If we look closely—past the biological metaphor—the meaning of the words is not so clear. If we try to discuss the matter with others, we soon find out that people mean a great variety of things by the "wholeness" of a novel, just as they do when they use the word "form." The term conceals differences; it does not resolve them. We can expose some of these differences by asking what the quality of wholeness actually is, how it can be described, others by asking what relative importance it has among the qualities a novel may possess. The two questions are not altogether independent, to be sure; our answer to one usually limits our responses to the other.

On the importance of wholeness, opinion among critics (and novelists as well) ranges all the way: for some it is a trivial or even a negative quality; for others it embraces everything that makes the novel worthwhile. The judgment of insignificance comes

often from politically oriented critics and others who think of literature as useful, serving ends outside itself, who will often dismiss an interest in form as "pedantic," "reactionary," or "mere narrow formalism." Teachers worried about the relevance of literature to the lives of their students often take such a view, as when a presidential address to the Modern Language Association several years ago attacked traditional kinds of literary study: "I spend less time on form and more on the values embodied in the work. I ask my students to compare their lives to those in the novels, poems, autobiographies, or histories we read. I ask them to listen to the voices in essays and describe the persons they hear."[1]

For many others—novelists as well as critics—the quality of wholeness (unified, rounded, complete) is a virtue, an attraction in a novel, but it is not essential and may be antagonistic to other more important qualities. In Ian Watt's account of the rise of the novel, the development of a unified whole was a necessary step, but it was not the first, and indeed the driving interests which led to the development of the novel were originally hostile to the unity or structure of the whole. Thus Defoe "merely allowed his narrative order to flow spontaneously from his own sense of what his protagonists might plausibly do next. In so doing Defoe initiated an important new tendency in fiction: his total subordination of the plot to the pattern of the autobiographical memoir is as defiant an assertion of the primacy of individual experience in the novel as Descartes's *cogito ergo sum* was in philosophy."[2] According to Watt, although unity, or structure, was a necessary quality in a fully developed novel, it was not attained until Richardson, and then not completely until *Clarissa*.[3]

Even for Henry James—who among novelists most vigorously defended unity—the quality was apparently not absolutely essential, no matter how desirable it might be. In the same passage

---

[1] Florence Howe, "Literacy and Literature," *PMLA* 89 (May 1974), p. 436.

[2] Ian Watt, *The Rise of the Novel* (Berkeley, 1967), p. 15.

[3]"In *Clarissa*, even more completely than in *Pamela*, Richardson resolved the main formal problems which still confronted the novel by creating a literary structure in which narrative mode, plot, characters and moral theme were organised into a unified whole" (Watt, *The Rise of the Novel*, p. 208).

in which he delights "in a deep-breathing economy and an organic form," he recognizes the vitality of "loose baggy monsters"—even as he disapproves of them "artistically":

> A picture without composition slights its most precious chance for beauty, and is moreover not composed at all unless the painter knows *how* that principle of health and safety, working as an absolutely premeditated art, has prevailed. There may in its absence be life, incontestably, as "The Newcomes" has life, as "Les Trois Mousquetaires," as Tolstoi's "Peace and War," have it; but what do such large loose baggy monsters, with their queer elements of the accidental and the arbitrary, artistically *mean?*[4]

The monsters do have life, however, and there were many readers, in James's own time and after, who made the same distinction and regarded life as the preferable virtue. It is true that James did slip life back into his idea of unity—*organic* form, after all—yet others did not: E. M. Forster, for instance, in his criticism of James: "The longer James worked, the more convinced he grew that a novel should be a whole— ... it should accrete round a single topic, situation, gesture, which should occupy the characters and provide a plot, and should also fasten up the novel on the outside.... A pattern must emerge, and anything that emerged from the pattern must be pruned off as wanton distraction. Who so wanton as human beings?"[5] The human beings sacrificed by James are characters, which in a novel are life. Forster asks if a "rigid pattern" can be "combined with the immense richness of material which life provides"[6]— and concludes that it cannot be, agreeing with H. G. Wells "that life should be given the preference, and must not be whittled or distended for a pattern's sake."

Forster's distress about the weak endings of most novels illustrates in another way the conflict between unity (here expressed by plot) and life: "Nearly all novels are feeble at the end. This is because the plot requires to be wound up. Why is this necessary? Why is there not a convention which allows a novelist to stop as

---

[4]Henry James, *The Art of the Novel* (New York, 1946), p. 84.
[5]E. M. Forster, *Aspects of the Novel* (New York, 1927), pp. 230-31.
[6]Ibid., p. 233.

soon as he feels muddled or bored? Alas, he has to round things off, and usually the characters go dead while he is at work, and our final impression of them is through deadness."[7] Then he asks: "After all, why has a novel to be planned? Cannot it grow? Why need it close, as a play closes? Cannot it open out? Instead of standing above his work and controlling it, cannot the novelist throw himself into it and be carried along to some goal that he does not foresee? . . . Cannot fiction devise a framework that is not so logical yet more suitable to its genius?" "Modern writers say that it can," he tells us, using Gide's *Les faux monnayeurs* as the modern example that provides "a violent onslaught on the plot as we have defined it."[8]

Among modern critics, some structuralists and their successors go further still, to find the effect of unity actually undesirable in a literary work as it interferes with the perception of what is really important. Thus Jonathan Culler argues that "it may well be misleading to speak of poems as harmonious totalities, autonomous natural organisms, complete in themselves and bearing a rich immanent meaning." Instead, "in this cultural context it is important to reflect on what has been lost or obscured in the practice of an interpretive criticism which treats each work as an autonomous artefact, an organic whole whose parts all contribute to a complex thematic statement."[9] And *S/Z*, Roland Barthes's model for the close study of fiction, sharply distinguishes, in the search for the text, between its "difference" (desirable) and its "individuality." The latter is disparaged ("what names, signs, finishes off each work with a flourish"),[10] because it is thought to limit that multiplicity of meanings which Barthes most values.

It is possible, however, to regard a novel's wholeness in a different way, to see it indeed as prerequisite to artistic success of any kind. Toward this idea we see James regularly pushing; he *almost* embraces it again and again, in spite of the life in loose baggy monsters, and we find the notion fully implicit in the metaphor of organic form. We see it clearly when someone de-

[7]Ibid., pp. 142–43.

[8]Ibid., p. 145.

[9]Jonathan Culler, *Structuralist Poetics: Structuralism, Linguistics, and the Study of Literature* (Ithaca, 1975), pp. 116, 119.

[10]Roland Barthes, *S/Z*, trans. Richard Miller (New York, 1974), p. 3.

scribes a work of art as an expressive or symbolic form or an indivisible intuition—the conception is there. Belief in the essential prerequisite wholeness is implicit in Coleridge's view of the imagination as the great synthesizing power. It is aggressively put forward by Croce. It is evident in Susanne Langer's elaborately developed conception of form. Less absolutely, it is present in modern Aristotelian criticism—at least when the critic postulates a hierarchy of elements in a poem or insists that each work is the creator of a genre peculiar to itself. For if the work is sui generis, the principle of unity is equivalent to the genre, which governs everything. Such theories, addressed not to the novel alone but to "all art" or "all poetry," not only stand at the furthest extreme from those of the critics of ideas, social purpose, and relevance but are at odds with some of the most vigorously asserted claims in the field of contemporary poetics.

Even if we could agree on the importance of wholeness in a work, we would still be likely to disagree as to how to describe it. Roughly speaking, there seem to be four common ways. The first is merely *assertive*. The assumption is that the unity of a work is not analyzable or describable beyond the mere act of pointing to its presence. The term "organic form" is itself an example. Unity is described—if at all—by metaphors and analogies, figures emphasizing the integrity of the whole but not usually distinguishing it from other wholes. Details may be said to fit in, but what they fit or how or why remains unspecified.

The second way is *aggregative*. Unity is described by the enumeration of a series of recurring or limiting features found in the work. A pattern of images can be called a unifying principle in the sense that it contributes to our impression that the work hangs together. Such a pattern will never be the only such principle; a critic taking this position will want to add other patterns. Themes and motifs are unifying principles; so is a narrative point of view, a limitation on the setting, a verse pattern in a poem. So, too, is language itself, and the critic trying to demonstrate the wholeness of the work will try to gather as many common strands together as possible, to build a composite picture.

Such a procedure is common in practical criticism. An accumulation of strands can make an impressive-looking demon-

stration of a sort. Yet if a whole is greater than the sum of its parts, as the saying is, such a method will fail, since the totality that it describes is exactly the sum. And though the combination of "unifying principles" collected may imply a whole greater than a total, still the critic's own enumeration remains a process only of adding, not of integrating.

A third way of describing the unity of a work is *reductive*. Some relatively simple element with an obviously indivisible structure is abstracted from the work and is postulated as its unifying principle, which the critic then simply shows to be inherent in the work, connecting the element to as many details as possible. Forster's analysis of *The Ambassadors*, again, can illustrate:

> *The Ambassadors*, like *Thais*, is the shape of an hour-glass. Strether and Chad, like Paphnuce and Thais, change places, and it is the realization of this that makes the book so satisfying at the close. The plot is elaborate and subtle. . . . Everything is planned, everything fits. . . . The final effect is pre-arranged, dawns gradually on the reader, and is completely successful when it comes. Details of intrigue . . . may be forgotten, but the symmetry they have created is enduring.[11]

Here the abstracted pattern is geometrical, made easier to grasp by embodiment in the image of an hourglass. The pattern may be a principle of change, a unity of action, to use Aristotle's phrase, or a principle of character or change in a character, of centrality (as when James speaks of unifying a novel by making a character its "center of consciousness"), or an archetype. It may be anything, if only the quality of singleness is evident in it.

This way of abstracting can be so effective that sometimes, we feel, nothing need be added about the wholeness of a work. Still, the method does not individualize; it joins rather than divides. *The Ambassadors* differs from other hourglasses in the particulars, the details in which the pattern is embodied. Our unifying principle cannot differentiate if its description does not include this difference. The problem is present whenever we attempt to reduce the unity of a work to an abstract statement. We think of form as peculiar to a given work—the ultimate expression of its very

[11]Forster, *Aspects of the Novel*, pp. 218-19.

individual identity—and especially if we think of the work as an organic whole—yet any abstract principle we use to describe that unity will miss its distinctiveness, will only tell us how this particular case resembles others.

There remains a fourth way to describe wholeness, which attempts to discover (or impose) a principle of unity within a hierarchy of elements in the work. This *hierarchical* method uses the second and third techniques described above and arranges them in some order. The variety of separate and equal unifying elements seen in an aggregative analysis will reappear here, along with some abstracted principle(s) of singleness from a reductive analysis, but all will be arranged in a relationship to each other. In the composite will be found that which makes the work a single, unique thing.

The hierarchical method appears to be a more serious means of tackling the problem than the others I have mentioned. It would seem to be the only way in which a critic could really examine the unity of a work effectively so as to show, for instance, how this or that part really belonged or what damage removal would cause. The power of the formal principle as a critical concept seems to depend on the assumption of a hierarchy of parts.[12]

Yet even this conclusion meets with problems. In the ordinary kind of analytical hierarchy—what I shall call a *simple hierarchy*—the larger (or higher) structures are always more abstract, more general, than the smaller, or lower. Such is the hierarchy in Northrop Frye's analysis of symbols in literary works, for example: each of the five successive phases, moving up from the literal and descriptive through the formal to the archetypal and the anagogic, provides a structure more general and comprehensive than the one below.[13] So, too, with the "larger structures," or "metastructures," in the analyses by the

---

[12]See, for example, the concept of "the dominant" as formulated by Roman Jakobson: "The dominant may be defined as the focusing component of a work of art: it rules, determines, and transforms the remaining components. It is the dominant which guarantees the integrity of the structure." ("The Dominant," trans. Herbert Engle, in *Readings in Russian Poetics: Formalist and Structuralist Views*, ed. Ladislav Matejka and Krystyna Pomorska [Cambridge, Mass., 1971], p. 82).

[13]Northrop Frye, *Anatomy of Criticism* (New York, 1967), pp. 71–128.

structuralists. Plot, for example, is often conceived by them as a structure *shared* by and abstractable from a number of works. Such a hierarchy, though it can tell us more than a simple aggregative or reductive analysis, cannot, after all, help us much in defining the unique formal principle of an individual work.

If that unique principle is to be analyzed hierarchically—and I cannot imagine how it could be analyzed in any other way—it will have to be some other kind of hierarchy. Let me postulate a *compound hierarchy,* in which the largest structure would be conceived not as the most abstract or general but as the governing principle and therefore unique to the particular work. Some such hierarchy seems to be implied in the writings of the so-called Chicago critics. R. S. Crane, for example, regards the plot of *Tom Jones* as peculiar to *Tom Jones.* It is the governing principle, "the particular temporal synthesis effected by the writer of the elements . . . that constitute the matter of his invention."[14] The specific comic effect of the novel is the "form of the plot," which in turn is the form of the novel's action, character, and thought, which in their turn are the form of the remaining elements. The result resembles a compound hierarchy because the larger structures incorporate the smaller ones that they control.

Unfortunately, a compound hierarchy (or at least an exact and complete definition of one) seems to be a logical impossibility because the governing principle in the hierarchy can only be, in its uniqueness, identical to the formal principle itself, that is, to the wholeness it is supposed to help us describe. In Crane's analysis, the plot of *Tom Jones* is identical to *Tom Jones;*[15] his description of that plot is a reduction from it. Yet his example does indicate how the concept of a compound hierarchy can be useful and suggests its limitations. We can approach a compound hierarchy as a fictitious possibility, a hypothesis, in much the same way that the differential in calculus approaches the

[14]R. S. Crane, "The Concept of Plot and the Plot of *Tom Jones*," in *Critics and Criticism,* ed. Crane (Chicago, 1952), p. 620.

[15]Or it would be if *Tom Jones* were (for Crane) a perfectly unified work. Crane's analysis admits of blemishes in the novel, by virtue of which the work falls a little short of the full realization of its form. To that extent Crane's "plot" is the compound hierarchy for an ideal *Tom Jones* rather than the actual novel. See the discussion of disunity in chapter 5. See also chapter 6, n. 11.

infinitely small. Though the governing principle will be an abstraction, and therefore a reduction, we can take pains to include in this abstracted principle some account of the control it exerts over the other contributing principles in the work, which in a simple hierarchy are likely either to escape notice or to appear simply as "given" (independent) elements. (My description here is itself highly abstract; its meaning when applied to a novel will emerge in later chapters.) We can work around and toward the unique governing principle, not allowing ourselves to forget how much it has to account for. At the same time, since any principle we describe, no matter how complexly articulated, will continue to be a reduction, we can be sure that something will be left out. Our hypothesis will be subject to the competition of rivals; it stands in danger of becoming obsolete. This we must expect.

If a novel is an organic whole, our understanding of its nature will depend intimately upon the kind of compound hierarchy we invent to describe its form. We shall look further into the conceptual difficulties of a compound hierarchy in a later chapter. Before we do so, however, we must consider: what makes this idea of organic wholeness, or form, seem so important to us? Why should it be defended? On what assumptions (about the art of the novel, its values, its purposes, and its nature) is the claim to importance based? The place to begin our inquiry is with such questions as these.

[2]

The Idea of Form in Art

In what conception of the novel does the idea of form play the most important role? I ask the question in this peculiar backward way in order to find the assumptions underlying that idea's claim to importance.

In the first place, should we begin a definition of the novel by classifying it as a specialized use of *language* or as a kind of *art*? Is it more significantly related to histories, biographies, editorials, advertisements, and treatises, *or* to paintings, operas, dramas, movies, statues, and string quartets? Obviously it resembles both in some ways, and definitions starting from either point may be equally true. Yet their emphases may differ because of the different assumptions from which they start.

Most contemporary poetics and practical criticisms define the novel as a use of language. This is the first principle of structuralist fictional theory, as it was with the New Critics. It is plausible and has led to powerful results. With the advance of linguistics as well as the increased recognition of the extent to which language shapes our thinking, this definition has become even more dominant; it appears *almost* to have carried the day.

If I prefer to begin this inquiry from a different starting point, it is not from a (foolish) notion that such language-based theory is wrongheaded or futile. To rediscover or rehabilitate the concept of form in the novel, we may find it most fruitful to begin elsewhere. To be sure, if we initially assume that the novel is a specialized use of language and we examine it through linguistic

analysis, principles of art will be forced on our attention by the linguistic differences between the novel and other uses of language. But the definition of art so discovered will be conditioned by what we have already assumed about language, and we cannot penetrate beyond that conditioning unless we bring into view ideas about art independent of our notions about language.

The idea of form as wholeness is not necessarily or intrinsically implicated in approaches that begin with language, especially if language is defined as a means (or the means) of communication. Linguistic analysis tends to proceed upward from its smaller units; there is nothing intrinsic to the idea of communication that would require it to do otherwise.

The linguistic approach to literature has led to some valuable insights that a nonlinguistic formal theory can also use, reaching them from different directions and placing them in a different context. One of these is the recognition that the ability to understand and respond to literature (what Jonathan Culler calls *literary competence*) is comparable to what the linguists call linguistic competence and can therefore be organized into a structure like that of the language. The analogy makes plain the complete dependence of literature upon conventions—a point which is, as we shall see later, also essential to our proper understanding of formal theory.

Another valuable discovery from the linguistic approach is that literary art (both poetry and fiction) is language that calls attention to itself as language. The ideal is described in certain metaphors: the language in a literary work is "thickened," or it becomes "opaque." That is, instead of seeing through it transparently to some external reality, we see only the language itself. The image describes something important, yet it is ambiguous. The difficulty is that opacity is also generally attributed to governmental and other kinds of jargon as well as to clichés and dead language. The desirable opacity is not, I believe, a blocking of meaning but the reverse—a calling of attention to the power of language to convey a multitude of meanings. The ambiguity is compounded by different opinions regarding the scope of the concept. Is the language of poetry more opaque, for instance, than that of prose? Is language opaque in a classic novel by Jane Austen? If the theory replies no—if it says that the ideal of

opaque language was not reached in fiction until contemporary times—then of course it is not a theory of fiction but a manifesto of taste.[1] If, on the other hand, the answer is yes—Jane Austen's language is indeed opaque in the proper way—then (since it cannot be that the readers of almost two centuries were mistaken in thinking the novels dealt with characters and actions) opaque language must be only another metaphor for fiction itself. No doubt fiction (fictional world, characters, action, and so forth) does manifest the power of language to refer to and describe in general without referring to or describing anything "actual"; in this sense fiction might be considered a means by which language calls attention to itself, but the notion could be stated less equivocally, more simply.

The idea that literature is language calling attention to itself relates closely to the more general (and very powerful) notion that any work of art is an artifact that calls attention to itself. Unlike that idea, however (which I shall have more to say about shortly), language calling attention to itself does not necessarily signal wholeness, completeness, or unifying form. For this reason, too, I prefer to start by considering the novel not as a kind of language but as a kind of art.

Art itself can be defined in various ways, and again we shall have to choose. Most criticism and theory depend—either directly, explicitly, or in some narrowed version, implicitly—upon one of the following definitions, which differ according to what is considered the "end."[2] First, art is *expression,* as in Benedetto Croce or Susanne Langer; it eternalizes, materializes, objectifies, transmutes, or in some way brings out the artist's vision. Art primarily serves the artist in making possible vision, knowledge, or mastery of the self; the value to the reader lies in identification with the artist and duplication in some way of the ar-

---

[1] So Roland Barthes in *S/Z* (trans. Richard Miller [New York, 1974]) implies when he criticizes the "parsimonious plural" of the classic text.

[2] This analysis derives partly from the teaching of R. S. Crane and Elder Olson and partly from the famous four-part distinction of kinds of literary criticism made by M. H. Abrams in *The Mirror and the Lamp* (New York, 1958), chap. 1. Essentially Aristotelian, Abrams's distinctions provide, in my view, the most useful broad way to begin differentiating among critics, since Abrams's divisions are less hierarchical and less prejudicial than are those of a critic like Frye. I have modified the distinctions here, however, and have altered the four parts to six.

tist's experience. Second, art is *kinetic, operative,* or *functional,* as in Matthew Arnold or F. R. Leavis: it acts upon its readers, to benefit them or change their behavior or satisfy their needs, to heal, to teach, to persuade or, on a larger scale, to influence society or the world. The value of art consists in whatever benefit it gives to the audience. Again, art is *mimesis,* as in Percy Lubbock or E. M. Forster: it imitates or represents images of life, real or imagined, abstract or concrete, ranging from the most specific and individualized to the most universal and archetypal. Works tend to be judged by the "truth" of what they depict—the vividness of the resemblance of their images to either real or imaginable life. Studies of narrative point of view usually fall into this category, as do those that distinguish between realism and fantasy or examine fictional heroes, women in fiction, fictional worlds, and kinds of archetypes (the archetype itself being usually a category of mimetic images, whatever psychological [expressive] significance the critic may also find for it). Another definition holds that art is ultimately *communication:* it acts as a bridge between artist and audience, conveying the ideas or meanings held by the one more or less accurately to the other. The value lies in the joining of artist and audience together, in their sharing of meaning. The critic's emphasis may be on the communicated meaning itself, as in studies of theme in the novel and of the novel in the history of ideas, or on the communicative process, as in studies by the New Critics and the structuralists. Theories of the novel conceived as a kind of language, as discussed above, usually regard art as a kind of communication. Finally, there is the idea that art is essentially indefinable: there is no common ground between the various phenomena that have laid claim to the name of art, and anything is art if one says it is.

In each of these theories the concept of *form* tends to differ in meaning and importance, as does the concept of genre and hence of the novel as a genre. These differences will also depend on how the primary assumptions are developed and qualified by particular critics. Thus, for example, the notion of the unified work tends to assume greater importance in expressive theories than in kinetic theories. The idea of genre is rejected by one expressive critic such as Croce and defended by another such as Langer. Genre tends to be disregarded by communicative critics

like I. A. Richards and the New Critics; it is central in the thinking of others, like Tzvetan Todorov.

We shall find it convenient for our purposes to begin our search for the importance of form with still another view, simpler than the others, that art is *making*: it gives us products which may be called artifacts, works of art, products of craft. Such creations may be tangible or intangible, permanent or ephemeral, spatial or temporal, and they may or may not (depending on the critic) be subdivided into categories of the useful and the self-contained.

This view is distinctive in that it imposes no limits upon the ends that may be suitable to art; it is more comprehensive, freer, than any of the other conceptions noted except the idea that art is indefinable. Artistic questions are, strictly speaking, always questions of the adaptation of means, but to unlimited ends. Hence the primary distinctions are between ends themselves, and the distinctions next in importance identify different ways of attaining them. Criticism of this kind never denies that art may be expressive or useful or communicative or mimetic; it may be (perhaps usually is) most or all of these things, but none is a necessary prerequisite for art.

Among the definitions I have mentioned, the idea of art as making leads us most immediately and inevitably to a conception of unity in the work of art. Therefore, and because I suspect also that many critics starting from a different point implicitly assume this definition when they emphasize formal unity in expression or communication or mimesis, it seems appropriate to begin our inquiry here. I do so not merely because form becomes most important in this view but also because this definition of art is broadest, most general, least likely to exclude eccentric or unusual or special kinds of art, least committed to some particular scheme of values, some special narrowing view of behavior. It best meets the objections of those who say that art is indefinable.

ART AS MAKING

The view of art as the process of making things is the oldest we have. This idea does not romantically distinguish between art

The Idea of Form in Art

and craft; it does insist, however, that "making" of this sort is not just a random and accidental process but involves a reasoned, orderly, or skilled and purposeful procedure. Such an attitude is unpopular with modern artists committed to spontaneity or freedom or the unconscious. Their objections might be accommodated, however, if we interpret "skilled and purposeful" broadly and do not attempt to specify how the artist may think or work.

According to this view, "art" is the process in which skill (broadly understood) is employed to bring about some specific end. The activity is adapted to that end by the exercise of skill, which implies knowledge of the problems that must be faced and the ways in which they can be solved. The end, "the work of art," need not be a tangible object: the traffic cop makes traffic flow; the violinist persuasively interprets the composer's music. No distinction is made in the beginning between useful and so-called fine arts, so that at the outset this idea of art does not look obviously different from the kinetic. But kinetic definitions all start with a *specific* function (for example, that poetry must teach and delight) and turn to art as the means, whereas the idea of art as making *in general* leaves ends unspecified.

When attention focuses on the making rather than on the end, however, the subsequent distinction between the fine and the useful immediately becomes possible. This distinction—normally understood to separate arts in which the making serves a functional purpose from those in which the making of the work is an end in itself—requires us to accept some further assumptions. What do we mean when we say that a work of art is an "end in itself"? Not that we may not find uses for such a work, but only that they are no part of its intrinsic—its *artistic*—value. A painting is worth money, but this is not part of its artistic value. Nor is the instruction or entertainment or therapy which it may give us. Nor can a work "designed to please" be regarded as an end in itself. Pleasure may be the consequence of a work prized for its own sake—a sign of our recognition of value—but that value cannot be defined in terms of the pleasure it produces. All external ends are by-products of the intrinsic artistic values which a work of art possesses if we esteem it in itself. This, at any rate, is what we seem to mean when we speak of self-

contained, or fine, art. But the description is negative. Can it be put in positive terms? Can we describe intrinsic artistic values as real in our actual experience of art?

Perhaps we can make such values more palpable by considering what they may be *before* we make a distinction between useful and fine. What, then, do we mean when we admire some well-constructed or ingenious practical object as a "work of art"? We are praising more than the thing's practical value: its ingenuity, its ornamentation, or simply the evidence of great care taken in its construction. We are appreciating the evidence that the object has been made deliberately with attention and skill. If the art is in the making, then the aesthetic quality is the evidence of this making.

The aesthetic object is "excellently," "skillfully" made. One would think that the most excellently made practical item would be the one whose parts were most efficiently adapted to its particular end, whatever that might be. To a true rail buff, however, a steam locomotive is aesthetically more pleasing than a diesel, even though it is less efficient. The aesthetic value seems to be not the efficiency alone but the capacity of the object to call attention to the fact that it was well made. Not the excellence alone but the *perceptibility* of that excellence—this must constitute the "intrinsic artistic value." The trouble with the diesel is that it conceals its finely tooled moving parts.

Yet even so qualified the idea of efficiency in this formula does not quite fit. What about the ornamentation on an old clock, for instance? Most obviously, it calls attention to the fact that the clock was made by somebody. But the most obviously "made" things may be the crude works of unpracticed hands; unmatched boards and bent nails testify to a carpenter who is deficient in skill. Ornamentation, on the other hand, signals artistic control, ease, the surplus of the artisan's energy; it expands the function of the artifact to include announcement of the maker's mastery.

Even in a practical object, then, the aesthetic value is independent of the practical. We may now define a work of fine art as one whose *primary* end is not to serve some purpose outside itself but simply to display how well it is made. Practical usefulness is now secondary.

The Idea of Form in Art

This ancient and familiar theory assumes less than do the other conceptions of art, for "making" is implied in all of them as well (except in the view of art as indefinable), with the addition in each case of some limiting end. Yet of all purposes we might attribute to artists, the least difficult to impute to all is that of making well. The consent of artists to this is not required, yet surely it would be a rare artist, even today, who would deny honestly that his or her work was meant to be admired or at least respected by someone—if not by others, at least by the maker. And what we in the audience always ask each other about a work of art is, "Did you like it?" which is a modest version of the key question, "Is it good?" Liking, or at least admiration, is always central. The work is made to be admired and is admired for the way it is made.

The theory has some problems. For example, we may admire a primitive artifact as art without knowing its "function" in the artist's eyes. We must eliminate the intention of the artist from the definition of art. Better to adapt Joseph Margolis's formula—"*A work of art is an artifact considered with respect to its design*"[3]—except that with "design" we have already made a leap we are not quite ready for, so that instead we might say here that the work of art is a made object *considered with respect to* the mastery visible in its making. "Considered with respect to" implies that if the mastery so considered is perceptible, the work will be judged good, and if not, it will be deemed bad. Such a definition keeps attention on what the critic is able to perceive— that is, on the aspect of the artifact that he chooses to "consider." The distinction between fine and useful is no longer an absolute distinction between art objects. The work of fine art is the work that, *in the critic's perception,* is so organized, so made, as to invite such consideration—this is its primary perceptible function.

There is also a problem in the connotations of our terms.

[3]Joseph Margolis, *The Language of Art and Art Criticism* (Detroit, 1965), p. 44. "By 'design' I have in mind only the artist's product considered as a set of materials organized in a certain way; to state how such materials are organized is to describe the design of some work." My modification of Margolis's excellent definition, which in itself is totally adequate and is defended by powerful arguments, is intended to retain the aspect of judgment or evaluation, implicit in my initial assumption.

"Skillful making," "excellent making," "mastery in making"—all these phrases sound like roundabout synonyms for the familiar expression "well made," which in turn suggests decorum and propriety, ideas inimical to many artists' aspirations for originality. Originality is one of the most universal artistic virtues,[4] whereas decorum and propriety have been virtues only in certain ages and schools of art. The term *well made* suggest perfection, not to be confused with *excellence*, which indicates the highest merit, the kind that surpasses. There is a difference between the possession of value and the absence of flaw.

Still another problem: How do we answer the admirers of a contemporary rock group who don't care about excellence, don't care about craft and skill, but care rather that the group's performance carries them away, stirs their guts, makes them forget who they are and everything, you know? To such enthusiastic but untrained listeners, artistic excellence is a special interest, esoteric, proper to critics, dilettantes, snobs, other artists, but no concern of theirs.

Obviously, other values (the sense of a communal group, for instance) may sometimes be responsible for our gut response. Still, our theory claims to account for the real power of art without referring to nonaesthetic factors. I suspect that there is a deep gap between the actual experience of powerful aesthetic values and the pallid critical attempt to explain them. I can't assert this yet, however—not without looking further into the theory.

THE VISIBLE FORM

The most obvious difficulty with the definition of art as making is its circularity: if artistic mastery is measured by the adaptation of means to the end, how can artistic mastery itself be the end? How can means be adapted to the end of showing how well they are adapted to that end?

Here *form* enters. The way out of the circle is to redefine the end of the self-contained work of art as the execution of a form unique, original, different for every work. *Its* function is

[4]See discussion of originality in chapter 4, "The Original Form."

simply—or at least essentially—to *appear,* thereby displaying the art of the maker. We may assume that *making* anything means putting parts together into a single whole (the artifact). But if the only function of this created whole is to display the mastery with which it was made, then this mastery will depend on the extent to which the parts are seen as constituting a whole. The perceptibility of wholeness would itself be the measure of artistic success.

This is a simple uncomplicated view, natural as well as broad and fruitful. The wholeness perceived is testimony that an artist has been at work; it is the means by which we judge the caliber of his art, whether tangible, intangible, spatial, or temporal. We require only that we—or someone—be able to perceive a whole of some kind. The theory requires, for the artist, the creation of a whole as his claim to artistry; for the audience, the perception of that whole as the essential artistic experience. To perceive a thing as a whole is to perceive a *form,* a principle of unity governing the parts making them seem pertinent to each other. Any perceptible entity has a form in this sense: the form, after all, is what enables us to distinguish the entity.

By this theory, then, art can be defined as *the process of making visible a created form.* The terms of this definition need to be qualified. It is important to recognize the quasi-subjective aspect of "form" here: it is a perception rather than an absolute property of things. You and I may perceive different entities, hence different forms. On the other hand, we must recognize the needful limits to such subjectivity. In my struggle to understand a work of art, I am trying to perceive a form that I do not yet see, though I am pretty sure it is there. My perception will improve: forms become visible that were not visible at first. The theory does not hold that no interpretation is more authoritative than any other; readers search out what they hope is there to be found; critics and teachers assist them in the search.[5]

I find it convenient, often, to think of a form as a principle of *predictability,* by virtue of which if I have one part I can foretell the locations of the others. If I know the form, I know its parts in relation to each other. My possession of the form of a tree ena-

---

[5] I discuss limits on the reader's perception of forms at the beginning of Part 2.

bles me to predict leaves and branches on the side I cannot see and protects me from having my eyes scratched out as I approach it. My knowledge of the form of women in general (a so-to-speak abstract, or general, form) enables me to predict, when I see a head and neck, that arms will follow, and my familiarity with the specific form of the Venus de Milo enables me to anticipate a lack of arms when I see her head. I have seen the statue and have learned its form. Predictability here is simply the sign of my possession of this knowledge.

Of course, predictability in this sense is not to be confused with my ability to anticipate events when I am reading a novel for the first time. The latter is not necessarily a virtue: if coming events are too easy to guess on the first reading we may regard this detectability as a flaw. But the predictability that constitutes the form is quite different; it is something I acquire only as I come to know the novel and to understand it thoroughly. It is my sense of sureness, of "rightness" ("appropriateness," "inevitability") about all the details, the events as well as the words, which expresses my understanding of the novel.

There is a difference between concrete and abstract forms. A concrete form is associated with *one* entity: this particular elm tree. It exists in a single embodiment only.[6] An abstract form on the other hand (the concept of elm tree) may have many embodiments; its parts are determined by their perceived common characteristics. The abstraction is a pattern of resemblance between a number of otherwise different concrete forms.

Concrete forms may differ in the degree to which they are arbitrary or determined. In an arbitrary form (some piece of driftwood, let us say) the parts can be predicted (justified, explained) only by direct observation. In a determined form, on the other hand (most things as perceived), we become aware of abstract forms informing the concrete to increase our sense of

---

[6]Some concrete forms may, however, be manifest in a number of "copies." These are embodiments whose distinctive feature is that we think of them solely with reference to an original entity, which is their source. A bound book, for example, could be regarded as a concrete embodiment of a novel, in which case the novel itself is an abstract form. For the reader, however, the bound book is merely an instrument that enables the reader to perceive the novel; in relation to the reader's experience the novel is a concrete form; it is unique no matter how many copies may exist to transmit it.

the inevitability of its parts. We know what to expect on the opposite side of this particular elm tree because we recognize the abstract form of "elm tree" in it. Similarly, abstract forms may vary in the degree to which they prescribe the particulars of their embodiments. The form "elm tree" predicts the general kinds of leaves and branches but not their specific distribution in a particular tree. It thus is less "determining" than is, say, the form "water," which permits no departure from the formula H_2O.

These distinctions help clarify an important difference between "artistic forms" in general and all others—what we may call "natural forms." The difference can be seen if we compare a simple perception of the art object with a comprehending perception of it. Anyone, even a child or a novice, can look at a painting or a statue, can hear the sounds of an orchestra or read the words on a page, and will perceive something, although not necessarily what the artist means him to. A painting is a flat surface with color on it. A statue is a solid object that I must not bump into. Music is a noise. So perceived, these objects are no different from natural forms—a tree, a piece of rock, the sounds of the city in the afternoon: mostly arbitrary concrete forms.

Place a carved statue—say Michelangelo's *Moses*—next to a jagged natural block of marble. Both are wholes. I see both well. But I recognize in the statue a form I do not find in the block— the form of an old man—a more "determined" form than that of the block of marble. It is in the difference between this determined form and the arbitrary form of the block of marble that I find the work of the artist. If when I looked at *Moses* I were to see only a block of marble, I would be seeing only the work of nature. If I am to see an object as a work of art, I must be made aware that an artist's mind has worked with the materials I am beholding. I regard the natural materials and the various manifestations of the artist's hand as signs pointing toward a form, which is not a simple collocation of the material parts but a conception of some kind originating in the artist's mind.

From the point of view of the perceiver, then, the real difference between the natural object (or even the man-made but not artistically considered object) and the work of art is that what are perceived merely as parts of the form in the first become

signs pointing to a form in the second. A sign signifies, calls attention to something beyond itself. It asks to be replaced in my mind by the thing it stands for. The marble represents flesh; we see it as such. On the other hand, though the sign asks to be replaced, it does not thereby disappear. Our minds as we observe retain a dual consciousness—we see the flesh *and* the marble.[7] If not, we would be terrified of the statue's size and pallor; we would be the yokels who attack the villain on the stage.

The theory does not limit the kinds of forms that may be indicated by signs. The example of *Moses* may suggest too simply a mimetic theory: the statue "imitates" a man. But the forms in music may be of a different order, and yet they too are not simply and directly perceivable but emerge, become visible to the perceiver who can recognize them, from the natural form of undiscriminated noise.

The visibility of a work of art may be sometimes more, sometimes less, successful. We may or may not see clearly the form the artist has created, standing out in its natural embodiment. It may shine forth,[8] with striking vividness, highly determined, in bold relief, or it may appear only murkily. You and I may differ: you may see it, I may not. Possibly neither of us will see what the artist intended us to, but perhaps a compatriot will. Perhaps no one will. Evidently the variability of the potential for visibility will be a criterion for artistic success or failure. Is there perhaps a proportion: the more vividly the visible artistic form stands out from its natural embodiment, the more impressive will be the artistic mastery that made this happen?

[7]Do we actually "see" the marble and flesh at the same instant? The argument of Wittgenstein's "duck-rabbit"—the diagram that represents, alternately, a duck and a rabbit, but never both at once—might suggest that we do not. I mean "seeing" here (as I do whenever I talk of seeing or perceiving a form) as including everything that enters into the organization of one's impressions into an entity. Surely in this sense the "perception" of a work of art includes our recognition of both the marble and the flesh, regardless of the momentary illusions or forgetting that may contribute to that recognition.

[8]See Susanne Langer, *Feeling and Form* (New York, 1953), chap. 4, for an extended discussion of the way the work of art stands out from the materials composing it. See also Seymour Chatman, "Towards a Theory of Narrative," *New Literary History* 6 (1975), p. 301, on Roman Ingarden's distinction between the "real object" and the "aesthetic object."

Maybe so, but the point is not clear enough as stated. Artistry is most impressive, I think, when the form it creates controls an abundance of complex and recalcitrant materials: the brightness of its visibility is a function of the form's control. An artist's materials may be difficult to work with (like marble). The medium of fiction is intrinsically recalcitrant in at least two ways. For one thing, though language often aims to stimulate the reader's imagination to sense perceptions (of people, places, events), it can do so only through words, signs whose sensory qualities are themselves quite different from the kind they are meant to signify.[9] And there is also recalcitrance in the extreme fluidity of language, the fact (as noted by I. A. Richards, for instance) that words do not have fixed meanings, that sentences to variable degrees will conjure up different images in the minds of different people. All novelists, like poets, have to struggle for vividness, but as we shall see in the next chapter, they regularly increase the recalcitrance of their materials by the arbitrary use of conventions to make their task still more difficult—and thereby to make the achievement of a visible form all the more striking.

Not simple visibility, then, but visibility emerging through the recalcitrance of the artistic materials seems to be the most general measure of specifically artistic mastery. This conclusion brings us to another difficulty and thereby to another important qualification of the idea of visibility. We usually derive our greatest pleasure in the process of reading (or listening) rather than in the cool perception of the whole thing after we have

[9]Such intrinsic recalcitrance varies according to the specific uses of the language. Thus Lessing in *Laocoon* argued that poetry was better suited to describing actions (less recalcitrant) than to describing objects. In fiction, the language in dialogue or directly quoted monologues is less recalcitrant in one respect than that in descriptive or narrative passages: its direct display of an aspect of the speaker's behavior (his actual words). Again, in some ways fictional language is intrinsically or potentially *less* recalcitrant (more direct, here) than any other medium whatever—notably in its ability to direct our analytical or intellectual understanding of fictional elements (e.g., the motivation or judgment of a character or the understanding of a complex sequence of causes), since it operates with the same means by which we formulate such understandings in our minds. Lessing's argument should remind us, by the way, that recalcitrance of materials is not a virtue unless the author can persuade us he has conquered it. His examples of ineffective descriptions illustrate the point vividly.

finished reading. Does this fact undermine our assumption that the aim of the artist is to make visible a form conceived as a principle of wholeness or completeness?

Actually the perusal of a work of art such as a novel is a fairly complicated process. We can distinguish between first reading and subsequent readings, including in the latter our reflections upon the novel after first reading, a kind of re-perusal. The first and subsequent readings differ, of course, in many ways, most notably in the loss of suspense and surprise in the later readings and the development of dramatic irony, based on the reader's foreknowledge, instead.[10] It won't do, however, to describe one of these readings as more significant than the others. The suspense of the first reading is often an important part of the novel's form. So is the later dramatic irony. The full visibility of the form cannot be discovered in one reading: it requires the subsequent readings or the equivalent. On these readings the effects peculiar to the first reading do not necessarily disappear. If they are truly a part of the form, I will observe them in my rereading in a kind of double view: I will perceive what the readers at first do not know, and I shall enjoy their ignorance, their suspense, against the context of my knowledge. When we reread a work we posit an implied first-time reader, who becomes part of our conception of the total form.

The process by which the form becomes visible is apparently, in the most admired works, never completed. These books most "reward" rereading: we not only rediscover what we have forgotten, we discover more. The form continues to reveal itself, to become more and more visible. And apparently I expect it to *continue to do so,* as I hope to read the book yet another time—which suggests that I do not believe I have even yet (after all of my readings) mastered the whole form. At the very least I expect, when I reread the most familiar of works (or listen again to the most familiar music), to *relive* the experience of discovering the form. A time may come when this process will pall; I know the work too well, and I will not want to return until I have begun to forget it.

---

[10]Wayne Booth demonstrates the difference in his analyses of mystery and dramatic irony in *Emma* and *The Brothers Karamazov. The Rhetoric of Fiction* (Chicago, 1961), pp. 255, 285.

The Idea of Form in Art

Thus it appears in a decisive way that it is not the ultimate and total visibility of the form that manifests the artistry of the work but the *process by which the form becomes visible*. We read with the expectation that a form will emerge, and we take our pleasure in the gradual process.[11] If a form does not appear, we will be disappointed, but we will be equally so if it manifests itself too quickly, too easily. It is not rapid comprehension that we value, not simplicity of perception or ready accessibility—not unless our artistic interest has been overshadowed by other interests, such as those proposed by Tolstoy's radical social theory of art. In general, for us, when the form of a work becomes wholly visible, we lose interest.

The fact—known to teachers—that intense study of almost any work seems to increase its visibility, if it has any complexity at all, suggests that full visibility is generally a hypothetical condition seldom perceived by any of us in our normal perusals of art. It is certainly not the condition of the works we love and admire, not while we are loving or admiring them.

Perhaps, then, we should modify our original definition of a work of art. *A work of art is an artifact* (composition, made object of any kind) *that displays a created form in the process of becoming visible.* Please forgive the shorthand "displays" that substitutes for "considered with respect to how it displays": it displays this form for whoever is considering it as a work of art. Most important, the artistic form is not visible but is always becoming so. The critic can analyze it as if it were so, describing the various principles that make it a determined form—but he must always be prepared for someone else (or himself later on) to correct and supersede his analysis.

[11]Thus Susanne Langer quotes Charles Morgan as saying, "In a play form is not valuable *in itself;* only the suspense of form has value. In a play, form is not and cannot be valuable in itself, because until the play is over form does not exist" (Langer, *Feeling and Form*, p. 309). Though she accepts this statement for drama, Langer does not abandon her idea that for art in general, "aesthetic intuition seizes the greatest form, and therefore the main import, at once," and argues that "in a work that requires an appreciable length of time for complete physical perception, such as a novel, . . . the author's first task is to imply, at the very outset, the scope and vital import of the whole" (p. 397). Scope, yes, vital import, maybe (depending on what that means)—but I find this view highly questionable if it is applied to form in the sense in which I use the term in this book.

[3]

Conventions

The means by which the artist makes the created form visible are all *conventions*. (We are still speaking not of the novel as such but of art in general.) A convention can be defined as an agreement between artist and audience as to the significance of features appearing in a work of art.[1] Dropping the curtain in a play is an example: it has a special meaning. The artist uses the device, the audience recognizes it and thereby learns how to understand, what to expect. If the form is a principle of predictability, conventions make prediction possible.

This does not mean that art should be "conventional" in the common understanding of the term (traditional, conservative). One need only show that works of art are not always immediately perceptible "by nature" to establish the need for conventions: they are the minimum required by any artist to control the audience's perceptions. The evidence for this assertion is everywhere. All arts using language, for example, are based on conventions: language itself is a system of them. In music, the conventional basis is indisputable; witness the time and growth needed for a child to learn to appreciate even the most elementary music. In traditional sculpture, true, we may need no convention to recognize the form of an old man in *Moses*. Yet even here our response is directed by agreed-upon custom: the human figure we see is not dead, not a petrified man, not a

---

[1]"The accepted postulate, the contract agreed on by the reader before he can start reading, is the same thing as a convention" (Northrop Frye, *Anatomy of Criticism* [New York, 1967], p. 76).

[40]

miracle struck into rock by lightning. Our appreciation is informed by knowledge based on the conventions which apply to this case. These constitute the only conceivable agency by which artistic form can be made to appear out of the accidental natural form of the object in which it occurs.

Structuralism and modern poetics, of course, have placed a heavy emphasis on the importance of conventions. Indeed, the heart of poetics could be defined as the study of them; they are, as Culler says, "not simply the property of readers but the basis of literary forms." Knowledge of conventions constitutes what he calls literary competence, and the study of poetics is the study of this expertise. It resembles the study of the linguistic system, in which we "concentrate . . . on the task of formulating the internalized competence which enables objects to have the properties they do for those who have mastered the system."[2]

The question before us here concerns how conventions function to establish the visible form of the work. Conventions carry "significance," which may be a "meaning" in the way in which a word has meaning but is most essentially an *expectation:* a note in a piece of music leads us to anticipate something else. In art, broadly speaking, that "something else" is a context into which one or another detail will fit—not necessarily a sequence, in the sense that one foresees links in a perceived chain of events in a story, though the former does include the latter. The least we ask of any artist is to establish through conventions a coherent set of formal expectations, a principle of predictability, a form.

THE ORIGINS OF CONVENTIONS

Conventions succeed because we recognize them: they are familiar to us. But if all conventions are *prior* agreements, where do they come from? How do they originate?

The words in a poem or a play, which originate outside the realm of art and are taken over by the artist for his use, can be called natural conventions. Other devices, such as the lowering

---

[2]Jonathan Culler, *Structuralist Poetics: Structuralism, Linguistics, and the Study of Literature* (Ithaca, 1975), pp. 117, 120.

of the curtain, exist only within works of art; they can be called artistic conventions. Since these practices have been invented by artists, at some point each such convention was used for the first time, not as a prior agreement, but as a new one that the artist asked the audience to accept. Similarly, each member of the audience must have had a first encounter with every convention he knows, at which time it was not "prior" but "new."

There is thus a distinction between "original" and "traditional" conventions. The former are invented by the artist in the work under consideration; the latter are adapted from other works. We become familiar with traditional conventions through experience and through teaching—that is, through the activities of teachers, critics, historians, all who have ever explained art in general or in specific cases. Yet most of what we learn about conventions in this way may also be traced back to someone's direct first experience with them. Ultimately all our understanding of traditional conventions derives from induction of their meaning through encounters in works of art.

I know no general principle by which artists make sure their original conventions will be understood. The gradual development of all arts suggests that if new conventions differ too radically from traditional ones, they will not be recognized. The obscurity in new and difficult works is an indication, usually, of our own unfamiliarity: eventually they become clear and we wonder why they seemed so hard. The new convention is a riddle whose presence we suspect because we can't find an adequate principle of necessity in what we are seeing. By continued perusal of the work, assisted by our understanding of works resembling it, we come finally to an understanding demonstrated by the stronger principle of predictability we have now gained.

Not until we have discovered such a principle do we believe we really "see" the work, but thereafter the convention assumes the status of a prior agreement. It is no mere quibble to insist that the agreement is "prior," even though it may often not be understood by the audience until after long familiarity with the work: it still precedes, and is necessary to, the perception of the form. A grasp of the convention is assumed by the artist as the condition necessary to a grasp of the form. If, as sometimes

happens, an effect of obscurity is positively sought by an artist, if slow or graduated comprehension of a work seems to be deliberately intended, then of course this sense of the irreconcilable or the impenetrable should itself be regarded as a convention contributing to a certain kind of form. In this way the nonpredictability of some element is made predictable.

Let us not restrict the scope of possible conventions. The tendency to elevate conventions into rules is a notorious critical error: the old assumption, for example, that all fiction, to be good, must be "realistic" is known by modern readers to be false. It is valid in the fiction of Howells, Dreiser, and Hemingway, but it is no rule—nor is the opposite convention ("realism is bad").

Nevertheless, the artist's invention cannot be wholly arbitrary, for conventions must work toward the formation of the whole or fail to be understood—as long, at any rate, as they remain "original." It is also easy to imagine an inept artist misusing traditional conventions so that they add little to the form of his work— another way in which an artist can go wrong. The justification of any convention is its contribution to predictability; without this contribution it will look meaningless, whether it is original or traditional: an excrescence, no real part of the whole, incomprehensible, hence disarmed even as a convention.

CONSTRUCTIVE AND RESTRICTIVE CONVENTIONS

Can we be more specific as to how conventions establish the visibility of the form?

Consider at random some familiar artistic phenomena: the agreement that the marble of the statue represents flesh—or fabric, or almost any substance other than marble; that ten syllables, mostly in iambic feet, can be anticipated in every line of a certain poem; that such regularity can be so varied as to be almost concealed; that the actors on the stage represent people other than themselves; that an aside is not heard by the other characters on the stage; that the teller of a story is no actual person in the world of the story he is telling; that that world has no actual, historical existence; that nothing will happen in it that is not in accord with what we regard as realistic probability; that a piece of music with Mozartean harmonies will not suddenly

develop Wagnerian chromaticism or shift into a rock-and-roll beat; that a so-called dissonance in a classical piece will ultimately be resolved into the tonic; that the same dissonance in a modern piece will not be resolved into the tonic; that the word "love" means love; that the word "love" does not mean love.

With such examples in mind, consider what conventions, according to the theory, must do. First, if the form is to be made visible, the things whose arrangement it predicts must themselves be visible. The parts must be made visible *as parts*. Since conventions convert the natural materials of an object into signs that arouse expectations, they identify the parts as such, and I shall call this the *identifying,* or *constructive,* function of conventions. A simple example: the identification of the actors on the stage as characters. Again: representation in marble of human flesh. The conventions involved, by themselves, will always go a long way toward justifying any detail in the given work. Without them, we see nothing; with them, the sense of necessity may become so strong that little else seems needed. In a play, for example, the characters and conditions established by the constructive conventions may lead to events seemingly so inevitable that we believe that we know all we need to. Once we have identified the marble as human flesh and the shape as a human shape, Moses becomes perceptible.

The power of such conventions explains the partial perception of a work—why it is possible to see and appreciate some aspects even when one cannot grasp the principle of the whole. But constructive conventions alone are never enough to make visible the total form of the completed work. What, for example, about the conventions of verse forms? Evidently some conventions have a *restrictive* power, which appears when I notice that the statue of Moses is not painted; that the actors on the stage do not actually kill each other; that the dramatist chooses not to represent *all* that is likely to happen, given such characters in such conditions, but only some of it; that methods of presentation do not change in the middle of the play—the actors are not sent home, for instance, after the second act, with the third act turned over to a narrator. Nor is this function merely the negative side of the constructive function of conventions. If it is argued that the statue is made only of marble because the artist has

no other medium available, we reply that such an economic accident has nothing to do with art: the lack of one material will not cause an artist to work with another except by choice. The controlling power of any form excludes as well as includes; the form of a play predicts that nothing shall be revealed except through the interaction of characters visibly moving and speaking with each other in the presence of the audience. The convention of realism in fiction is restrictive; so are most "rules," or principles, of narration; so are all verse forms. Restrictive conventions should be regarded neither as inexorable logic nor as necessary but limiting evils but rather as deliberately adopted devices to increase power or interest: consider how much grandeur Moses would lose if he were painted or what would happen if the words of a sonnet were rearranged.

Conventions function, then, either to identify or to restrict the materials that compose the work. All art employs conventions of both kinds, and together they establish the form.

To suggest the variety of constructive and restrictive conventions in a novel, let us consider briefly some examples in two works. In *A Farewell to Arms* the use of the first-person narrator depends on both kinds: "I" designates the character Frederick Henry (constructive), and the account is limited to what he is capable of reporting or knowing (restrictive). The narrative is further limited in its adherence to chronology (virtually no flashbacks, no flash-forwards) and to the reporting of events and settings with little explicit commentary, judgment, analysis, or statements of feeling. The language is likewise confined in famous ways to terms largely concrete and simple, both in vocabulary and in sentence structure. These restrictions cooperate with a constructive convention which attaches heavy emotional weight to the details in both the setting and the dialogue. All these are the familiar conventions of the celebrated Hemingway style.

But many other kinds of conventions are also at work here. As I have already suggested, the realism of the novel—its localism, its specificity of time and place—is itself a restriction, an aspect which it shares with many other novels. The conception of goodness which Frederick Henry manifests, as well as his im-

plicit scheme of values, is one convention, or a complex, by no means used only in this novel: it has come to be known, in fact, as the "Hemingway code." It operates constructively in directing us to judge Frederick as mainly a good man and restrictively in limiting the kinds of behavior he can exhibit and we can expect. The unhappy ending (and our anticipation of it) results from at least several conventions, of which I will mention only a few: that the world kills those who won't bend; that you can't escape the realities and horrors of the world; that death is everywhere (not just in war) and strikes arbitrarily. Somewhat differently, it is also established that expectations and a certain mood determined early will be followed through to the end—here a restrictive convention of coherence and consistency operates. This convention also demands that details (narrow hips, the ominous rain, Catherine's fears) will have forecasting significance.

The rain and other weather and landscape manifestations form an intricate constructive complex to set and fortify the emotional qualities of scenes—the rain as a sign of things going wrong, cold clear weather indicating emotional well-being. The idea that Catherine and Henry's love is good, an idyll, worth abandoning the world for, is also based on a constructive convention concerning the nature of love which many later readers have found rather hard to accept.

To show how thickly conventions pervade even a short and simple passage, consider the following relatively ordinary and unemphasized paragraph from Faulkner's *As I Lay Dying*.

> I light the kitchen lamp. The fish, cut into jagged pieces, bleeds quietly in the pan. I put it into the cupboard quick, listening into the hall, hearing. It took her ten days to die; maybe she dont know it is yet. Maybe she wont go until Cash. Or maybe until Jewel. I take the dish of greens from the cupboard and the bread pan from the cold stove, and I stop, watching the door.[3]

Here "I" stands for the character Dewey Dell, by the convention that each section is a first-person narrative belonging to the character whose name provides its title. The words depict a mo-

[3]William Faulkner, *As I Lay Dying* (New York, 1957), p. 57.

ment shortly after the death of Addie, as we know from the prevalent convention of the chronological coherence of the chapters. The present tense suggests action concurrent with the narrative, though this convention is not consistently maintained. The words are not spoken, however, and only some of them are Dewey Dell's. The first three sentences and the last translate into words her perception of her actions (we do not imagine her saying to herself as she picks up the dish, "I take the dish"); the others we read as her own thoughts. Our knowledge stems from the combining of two different kinds of first-person narrative conventions. In the sentence fragments the grammar expresses (constructively) her state of mind (just as do the linguistic features of the other narratives in this novel), in this case her impatient passivity, a quality which, though we see it also in other parts of the text, is here indicated only in this elliptical way (restrictively). We know from elsewhere how to fill in the ellipses: the word "her" means Addie, by the restrictive convention that prevents Dewey Dell from naming Addie, and there is an associated constructive convention that makes this verbal reticence a sign of the intensity of Dewey Dell's feeling. The idea that Addie is still alive, that she in some sense does not yet know she is dead and may not "go" until Cash finishes building the coffin or Jewel returns from his trip, becomes a figure of speech for Dewey Dell's difficulty (shared with others in the family) in adjusting to Addie's death: this we understand by the constructive convention forced upon us by the literal impossibility of the thought. The use of this figure of speech itself stems from an implicit restrictive convention that prohibits these characters from stating their problems in academic or intellectual language.

The most striking narrative convention in this novel is not necessary to our understanding of this passage, although it influences our perception of it. This convention permits "Darl" at several points to describe in detail scenes at which he was not present—notably Addie's death and the completion of her coffin. It also makes possible the narrative by the dead Addie. Normally first-person narratives (as in *A Farewell to Arms*) are restricted to what the "I" character could know or imagine. Yet the specificity of Darl's accounts invites us (again by a constructive convention) to accept them not as imaginings but as au-

thoritative. But though Darl is described as more intuitive than the other characters, he is not elsewhere given the amazing clairvoyance that such authority would imply. The natural conclusion is that Darl's narrative authority derives from another convention that insists on a distinction between the named narrator of each section and the character who bears that name. It specifies that the narrator and the character merely resemble each other and are not identical: Darl-the-narrator can describe Addie's death not because Darl-the-character is clairvoyant but because he (the character) has a more objective view of things in general than the others do. The choice of Darl for this purpose, with the suggestion of clairvoyance, which we quickly reject, tends to highlight by exaggeration (or by analogy between the two Darls) the intuitive quality in Darl-the-character. The convention has both constructive and restrictive aspects: constructive in that it makes the narrative authoritative; restrictive in that it arises from the author's refusal to resort to an overtly "omniscient" narrator; restrictive in another sense (which we shall consider again, later) in that it curbs the regularity of the other restrictions and adds another turn to the screw of recalcitrance. It functions vividly to call attention to the importance of convention itself in the work.

ARBITRARINESS OF RESTRICTIVE CONVENTIONS

The restrictive aspect of conventions enhances or increases the recalcitrance of the materials in a work. This function, when separate from that of identifying, is more or less arbitrary. Few critics nowadays will insist on a necessary correlation between a particular verse pattern and the "substance"—thoughts or even feelings—expressed by words arranged in that pattern. Nor is there any compelling reason, beyond the convention itself, why a playwright might not interrupt his play with a narrative or why a novelist might not include a painting of his hero to replace a description or why a statue of a man running might not be jointed at the knees with an electric motor to make the legs move. The large number of modern works defying tradition— the work that destroys itself, the composition played by kitchen

utensils, the conversion of "events" into works of art—is ample proof that restrictive conventions are in some sense arbitrary.

Restrictive conventions are arbitrary probably in *two* senses. They do not necessarily or logically depend on constructive conventions. Rather, they limit the latter by determining which of these may or may not be used. The artist is free to choose his restrictive conventions—he may compose a work from grains of sand if he wishes, a choice that will sharply confine, no doubt, the possible constructive conventions he may employ. Restrictive conventions, indeed, are much like the rules of a game, which the artist voluntarily accepts or invents for himself.

They are arbitrary also in the sense that they require no reference to any principle outside themselves (except that of consistency) in order to be perceived and accepted, provided the constructive conventions of the work have been recognized. The observer of course must assume consistency in the work before he can make predictions based on a restrictive convention (that is, before he can recognize the existence of the restrictive convention)—but of course he must have accepted this idea before he can make any predictions at all. He must also be able to perceive the constructive conventions—for obviously he cannot perceive restrictions if he cannot tell what is being restricted. One cannot recognize the absence of color on *Moses* until one has recognized Moses; one cannot recognize realism in fiction until one recognizes fiction; one cannot recognize the limitations upon expression imposed by rhyme and meter until one recognizes expression. In this sense, then, restrictive conventions are not prior but subsequent to identifying conventions. Once understanding of the latter is assumed, I see no necessary obstacle to the artist's freedom to restrict as he pleases.

Much modern criticism emphasizes the importance of *violation* of the rules of art. To Morse Peckham, for instance, violation is the cardinal principle, the distinguishing and motivating character of all art.[4] Art, says Peckham, depends above all on discontinuities. Verse patterns exist for the sake of disruption of

[4]Morse Peckham, *Man's Rage for Chaos: Biology, Behavior and the Arts* (New York, 1969).

their regularity, and rules in general (what I call restrictive conventions) exist to be broken. This is, to be sure, an overstatement: in fact many restrictive conventions do not exist to be violated. In realistic fiction, for example, the realistic convention is usually considered binding. In the performing arts, if the script or the score is regarded as a restrictive convention, then it, too, is usually binding. In most works the principle of discontinuity applies to only a few of the restrictive conventions, though admittedly (in Peckham's examples) they are prominent.

As we shall see later, discontinuity has indeed an important place in the formal theory of the novel. It, too, is a convention—restrictive and abstract, one which cooperates with some other restrictive convention to modify the regularity which the latter tries to impose.

DEPENDENCE OF CONSTRUCTIVE CONVENTIONS: IMITATION

Restrictive conventions, arbitrary though they are, can be identified by simple observation, possible only because their constructive counterparts have already been recognized. It remains to determine the source of the expectations which *original* constructive conventions presumably arouse. Do our expectations arise automatically from their mere presence? That is, are the constructive conventions also arbitrary, or must they derive persuasive power from somewhere else in order to be acknowledged?

It seems obvious to me that original constructive conventions (all of them when they were first used) cannot be merely arbitrary, for if they were, they would lack the means to call attention to anything other than themselves and would disappear, indistinguishable, in the "natural form" of the object. If the artist is free to decide what any sign may predict, no audience will ever discover that prediction without *something else* less arbitrary, in short, another convention, to clarify the intention.

The constructive convention must in some way be familiar before it can predict anything to us. Consider the convention that makes us, if we see the shape of a shoulder, expect an arm to be attached; the connection is hardly arbitrary. The convention is an agreement that some *already familiar* principle of predicta-

bility is to operate in this work. In the case of the shoulder, we agree that the sign (the shape at a certain point) shall signify something that it resembles, a resemblance that we recognize from the world outside the work. We agree to accept the sign as indicator of a *form* taken from the natural world, a referent with which it has something in common.

Any association, presumably, can become the basis of familiarity upon which a convention may depend. There are perhaps no limits, as long as the connection can be recognized, and conventions may often seem to be arbitrary in a loose sense. Words, for instance, are said to be arbitrary in the relation between their sound and meaning as in their origins, yet to people who use them words are indelibly, profoundly linked to particular ideas. A certain kind of orchestral coloring may, through more or less accidental circumstances, come to suggest to many minds some image of the American prairie, let us say (perhaps through the deliberate effort of some well-known composer); this association may well become the basis for future musical suggestions in compositions to come. An artist may decide, seemingly quite arbitrarily, that a series of X's will represent a certain state of inarticulate spiritual exaltation. No one will understand, perhaps, until the artist turns teacher and explains the meaning; thereafter, however, an association will have been created, in the minds of those who know, that may be sufficient to establish the convention for that particular audience.

Thus the principles of predictability utilized by constructive conventions come from outside the work. We recognize them through their familiarity, which may come from anywhere. They can be called forms. The constructive conventions identify the otherwise arbitrary elements of a work of art as forms taken from outside the work—forms "imposed," so to speak, upon those materials.

This is, however, the Aristotelian concept of imitation, which I tried to avoid as an initial assumption, but to which the logic of the theory has returned me. It can be accepted only most broadly, as meaning that art imposes a form upon matter not natural to it and that the visibility of the form is based on association or the familiarity of things outside the work itself. As we see from music, conventions may derive from other conventions

(for example, that the tonic will follow the dominant seventh) as well as from their direct resemblance to natural things. Such cases are instances of imitation nonetheless, since in relation to the work in question the conventions of other works constitute a world outside: they too are a world of "natural things."

We need such a conception of imitation in order to explain the effective power of conventions to enable us to recognize any form that an artist is trying to make visible. Narrower notions of imitation, associated with realism, or copying, are not relevant here. We recognize a form by its resemblance to forms already familiar to us—whether they are abstract or concrete, particular or universal, actual or imagined. I can imagine no other way.

ARTISTIC AND IMITATED FORM

Art imitates forms. Art creates forms. In formal theory these possibilities seem to be opposites. Yet both perhaps may be true. Although the idea of imitation to which my argument has brought me is perhaps easier to accept in criticism of the novel than in some other arts, it asserts no more than that the form made visible in the work, which we recognize, must have some common ground with things, ideas, images, or what you will, that exist somehow somewhere else, outside the work itself. The argument in no way denigrates so-called abstract, or nonrepresentational, art. It in no way supports or prefers the conventions of realism in any art.

If we turn to the question of the various kinds of forms that constitute the formal hierarchy of a work of art, we will see how art both imitates and creates form. In the statue, what does the artist make visible? I have already suggested that in order to see the work of art we must see not a mere block of marble, but the old man, Moses, carved in the marble. Is the man, then, the form that the artist makes visible? The difficulty with saying so is that although we do see the form of Moses, we do not exclude our perception of the materials of which the statue is composed: we are not deceived into thinking we see flesh and cloth; we see marble shaped to resemble them, just as in a play we do not mistake the characters for real people. A distinction must be made, therefore, between the *imitated form* and the *artistic form*.

The imitated form is that of the man which is taken from outside the work. The artistic form is the form of the statue as a whole, what we see when we perceive the work in its most visible state, most appreciatively and completely. The artistic form specifies not only where the shoulder will be but what it will be made of.

This artistic form combines the imitated form with the restrictive conventions that limit its embodiment. It is the Aristotelian "object of imitation" *as qualified by* the materials and techniques that the artist has chosen. This highly determined form—rather than the imitated form itself—is unquestionably what the artist wants to make visible by art. It is the true *created* form that, in our definition, a work of art "displays in the process of becoming visible." But notice this interesting subtlety: it becomes visible by making visible the imitated form. Its visibility depends on that of the latter.

In a novel the *imitated* form—the equivalent to seeing *Moses* as Moses—can only be the entire panoply of characters and action and world that the novel depicts: the complete fictional history. The *fictional world* consists in James's novel not merely of Isabel Archer herself, whoever she may be, nor of her history alone, but of all the people and events and places that together compose *The Portrait of a Lady*. The *artistic* form on the other hand—perception of both Moses and the marble—involves seeing this fictional world in the context of its artistry: Isabel not alone but as refracted through the narrator who describes her, the words in which she appears, the scenes that tell her story or, in brief, the restrictive conventions through which the image of her world is focused.

It is important to understand the sense in which the fictional world can be regarded as an imitation. For this form in all its complexity is unique, concrete. The fictional world of *The Portrait of a Lady* is to be found nowhere but in that particular novel. It is as truly individual as any real-life sequence of events. On the other hand, when we call it an imitation, we are saying that its form is taken from—abstracted from—nature. How can it be abstracted, imposed upon alien materials, if it exists only in this one embodiment?

The point, of course, is that the imitated form is entirely composed of abstract forms which, like all abstract forms given new

[53]

embodiments, are themselves imitated forms: conceptions of character, for instance, of place, of the way things happen. The presence of this abstract composite imparts to this imitated form, concrete though it is, much of its strong determined quality, its strong predictability. Isabel Archer is unique, but we see in her many concepts that are not: the American, the young woman, pride, intelligence, innocence, and many others. The same can also be said of the events and every other detail in the fictional world.

Thus we see that in a work of art, the imitated form, like the artistic, is also *created*. It is imitated because it is composed of imitations, a compound of abstract forms; it is created, original, unique, because it combines these abstractions into a concrete form. We see here the familiar tension, stressed by critics from Aristotle to James, between the typical in art and the unique: the object of imitation—the old man in the statue, the world and history of Isabel Archer—is unique, yet its individuality is weighted with the import of universality, not because Isabel Archer herself is a stereotype or an allegorical figure, but because she is composed of recognizable and typical traits. The abstract components constitute the knowledge we bring to the work, knowledge which consists essentially of recognitions of every kind of understood or imagined experience that the author may expect us to know, on the basis of which Isabel Archer and her story will take comprehensible shape before our eyes— visible.

A few examples can illustrate the difference between the artistic and imitated forms in a novel. If when asked why Isabel marries Osmond in *The Portrait of a Lady* we reply that it is because she is headstrong and proud, wants to decide things for herself, and is therefore heedless of her friends' advice, we are finding the necessity of that event in the *imitated* form: in certain conceptions or stereotypes about pride and heedlessness and marriage combined in Isabel's situation and character. If we reply, on the other hand, that she marries Osmond so that her character may be tested, so that she may be initiated into false-hood and evil, so that she may be given a particular opportunity for growth, we are finding necessity in the *artistic* form: in cer-

tain requirements of the plot. Again, if when asked why Henrietta Stackpole should be such a good friend of Isabel's, we reply by referring to her good nature and to Isabel's need for a strong-minded yet simple and devoted companion, we are explaining in terms of the imitated form: Isabel's needs, her habits, her desires. If, on the other hand, we reply that James needs a *ficelle* to help him dramatize his story and that he needs to make the ficelle as lively as possible, we are appealing to the artistic form: requirements of the narrative method he has chosen.

Yet the difference is not so simple, for even the explanations that refer chiefly to the imitated form are strongly influenced by the artistic form. If we attribute Isabel's marriage to her impetuous independence (imitated form), even this prediction depends on another explanation, namely that such a quality will have serious external consequences—a prediction from the artistic form. The noted "inevitability" of a tragedy is a consequence of particular conventions associated with the genre far more than of intrinsic qualities in its fictional world. The strong determination in most novels derives largely from the requirements of the artistic form as it controls and limits the imitated; without those strictures the imitated forms would appear, I think, quite arbitrary. This fact—I think it is one—confirms the idea that the artistic form, not the imitated one, is of most concern to both novelist and reader. This the art ultimately makes visible, and if the artistic form does not tend to become so, the imitated form itself will seem incoherent and obscure: the novel won't "make sense."

Let me illustrate with a modest example. The ending of *The Portrait of a Lady* has sometimes been rather naively criticized because it seems to leave in suspension the question of what later becomes of Isabel. James himself anticipated this charge. Certainly the imitated form in itself—the forces at work in the fictional world—gives us no reason to be satisfied with such an ending; the answer to the question "What happens next?" is much in doubt, for there are various possibilities. The end is satisfactory, appropriate, right, only because of the nature of the artistic form. Only our failure to understand the form on this point will lead us to claim that the ending doesn't make sense.

The Hierarchy of Form

How, then, can the artistic form be analyzed? This is the central question of all, for the artistic form is, as I have said, the true "form" of the novel as a whole, the principle whose presence we indicate by such terms as organic wholeness or formal unity. Here is the hierarchy we hope to probe.

[4]

Components of the Novel

To understand the artistic form of the novel we must define the genre. A genre is a "conventional form" (as distinct from the "original forms" of individual works), a collection of shared conventions. Knowledge of the conventional form contributes to the predictability of the parts and thus assists in making the individual form visible. (Such knowledge also helps us to recognize the artistry in individual works: insofar as the shared conventions are restrictive, they provide a standard for measuring artistic mastery, and insofar as they are shared, they provide a background for perceiving originality.) To define the novel we must isolate the shared conventions that compose the genre. This means that we can phrase our definition in terms of what we *expect* by virtue of knowing that a work is a novel, based on our experience of everything that we have been willing to call novels.

We see, then, that "novel" designates what Todorov would call a historical rather than a theoretical category. We can identify, in other words, no theoretical necessity for its existence or development; our definition is an induction from observed practice. If "theory of the novel" is a deduction, it is reached from a concept first arrived at inductively. Consequently our definition may have to change as the novel continues to develop: we cannot guarantee that our statement will cover all possible cases, nor will it necessarily be able to explain what theoretical necessity distinguishes the novel from other extended narratives—from narrative poems, for instance—beyond the obvious observable differences. Our definition seeks to describe a group of conven-

[57]

tions developing in time, finding in them rather than imposing on them some kind of comprehensible order.

The definition will be more or less specific according to the range of works we admit as novels. Let us start with the widest possible field: the novel is any "long work of prose fiction which makes some claim to be considered as a work of art." "Prose fiction" will have to be considered below; "considered as a work of art" refers to concepts already discussed, though we shall have to reexamine them as applied to the novel. As for "length," let us not be mathematical; the boundary is not definable by numbers. The novel and the short story overlap: what are *Maggie, Girl of the Streets, Heart of Darkness, The Old Man and the Sea?* Let us say that we expect a novel to be long enough to justify independent publication as a "book" without seeming exceptional or wasteful or coy.

A collection of short stories is not a novel (*The Collected Stories of William Faulkner*). Yet a strongly thematized or localized collection such as *Winesburg, Ohio* or *Dubliners* or *Go Down, Moses* is sometimes called one. Still, we usually put the burden of proof upon the critic who includes such works.[1] We expect something from a novel, in short, that a simple collection does not display: a principle of unity more stringent, less loose, than that which we find in collections.

Some critics narrow the field further. Sheldon Sacks, for example, excludes didactic works like *Gulliver's Travels* and *Rasselas.* He also disqualifies *Moll Flanders* (along with virtually everything before *Pamela*) on the ground of some inadequacy of unity: "The sense in which *Moll Flanders* is a single work is not dissimilar to the sense in which a collection of all the stories and novels in which a single detective hero appears may be viewed as a single work."[2] Northrop Frye further removes romances like *Wuthering Heights, Moby Dick,* and *The House of the Seven Gables.*[3]

---

[1] See discussion of collections, in chapter 5, "Looseness, Disunity, and Banality."

[2] Sheldon Sacks, *Fiction and the Shape of Belief* (Berkeley, 1967), p. 270.

[3] Northrop Frye, *The Anatomy of Criticism* (New York, 1967), pp. 304–6.

"The novel tends to be extroverted and personal; its chief interest is in human character as it manifests itself in society."[4]

Surely this last statement is too specific, too limiting to help us. We do not want a rigidly defined class of works, in any case, for we are trying to describe a collection of properties—what we *expect* to find, conventions we are prepared for—and if we find enough of them in a particular case, we will call it a novel. We can derive the characteristics from the general body of works that we consider to be novels without question, modifying them with caution by considering books that some people might regard as doubtful examples. Works that do not fully conform may be included if we choose, if we make allowance for the novelistic conventions they have ignored. In this way we can cope with the new and experimental as well as with fiction on the peripheries of the tradition. The novel (like any genre) is not a pigeonhole but an *ingredient,* an element, that enters into the art of novels and their relatives.

We can derive the convention from the central tradition: from the novels of Richardson and Fielding, Jane Austen and George Eliot, Dickens and Thackeray; also (yes) from Hawthorne and Melville and Emily Brontë; Tolstoy, Dostoevsky, and Turgenev; Flaubert and James and Conrad and Lawrence; Mann and Proust and Joyce; Hemingway and Fitzgerald and Faulkner; Hawkes and Pynchon and Barth; and all others who have contributed to our expectations in this richly developed art.

CONVENTIONS IN THE NOVEL: LANGUAGE

In the novel we expect, first of all a work revealed exclusively (usually) by a written text, composed largely or entirely of prose. The text presents (describes or otherwise reveals) events, along with whatever explanations, elaborations, causes, consequences, or significances the author deems relevant. This language, this

---

[4]Ibid., p. 308. Frye justifies such a distinction in part on the grounds that it protects the "peripheral novelist" from being unfairly judged by the wrong conventions: for example, "a great romancer should be examined in terms of the conventions he chose" (p. 305). True, although the introduction of more categories into which to place complete works may threaten to increase the difficulties of judging works by their individual merits.

prose, is related to the happenings much as the carved marble is related to the statue of Moses: it is the primary material, the medium, of which the novel is composed.

The medium is developed in an order controlled by the artist.[5] This order is an arrangement in *time;* the act of perusal, at least in the reading stage, is a temporal experience, in which the parts are in a sequence, although the actual time consumed is not controlled (we are free to stop, to go back, to read at any speed we wish). Such order contrasts with that found in music and drama, where the artist also controls the time elapsed, and also with painting and sculpture, where there is no necessary order of disclosure in time. This free movement through time is the "natural form" of the work, its form before we have differentiated it as art (its form as an undistinguished block of marble): a "reading experience," bounded by a beginning and end (temporal terms).

Are there further limitations on the medium, common to the novel in general? The broad category of prose seems to leave the door wide open, as if there were no more linguistic expectations specific to the novel as such. Individual novels or subgenres of novels may of course develop narrower conventions—especially in novels with notably mannered styles. The kinds of prose we expect in novels by Henry James or Hemingway or Faulkner will differ, with characteristics in each case that would have to be named in a definition of the subgenre: the Jamesian or Hemingwayesque or Faulknerian style. The openness of the medium in general, however, seems to imply that careful attention to language is not a necessary component in the art of the novel, whatever we may find in the art of individual specimens. Our expectations when we approach a novel, if we know nothing more than that it *is* one, do not relieve us of the possibility that we will encounter such sentences as the following from Dreiser:

> The effect of this adventure on Clyde was such as might have been expected in connection with one so new and strange to such a world as this. In spite of all that deep and urgent curiosity and

[5]"Loose-leaf novels" with movable pages exist but are departures from the novelistic convention—from what we expect in a novel. The same is true of "dossier" detective novels in which the reader puts the clues together.

desire that had eventually led him to that place and caused him to yield, still, because of the moral precepts with which he had so long been familiar, and also because of the nervous esthetic inhibitions which were characteristic of him, he could not but look back upon all this as decidedly degrading and sinful.[6]

Respectable novels with dull, flat, or awkward styles are perfectly possible, as the acceptance into the canon of Dreiser and James T. Farrell and James Fenimore Cooper shows.

Yet apparently the novelist's choice of prose does have artistic significance. We notice that if a novelist slips into verse in his fiction, he may be criticized for it—as Thomas Wolfe was for writing in concealed iambic pentameter (although a bold injection of verse, as in Nabokov's *Pale Fire* or novels by Thomas Pynchon, can be very effective). Consider also the difference in effect we expect to find between an unknown long verse narrative and a novel, and consider the preference we may often feel (depending on our mood?) for the novel. Evidently the exclusion of verse from the novel is not a convenience but a genuine restrictive convention. So is the exclusion (except for purposes of mimesis or parody) of jargon and of legal, medical, and scientific prose and the like.

But restrictive conventions bring artistic standards into play, and we may well ask what they are. The most general and simplest answer might be to identify the implied standard with that of "good prose" in general—language whose highest aims are to communicate a meaning, clearly, effectively, and precisely, with a maximum of efficiency, a minimum of obstruction or interference. Such language would call as little attention to itself as possible; it would approach the ideal of a "transparent" medium. For the novel in general the fictional world, action, characters, thought, would be of primary interest, with the language subservient. Such a conception would be a long way, of course, from the modern theory in which the novel shares with poetry the medium of opaque language. It would make the novel a kind of antithesis to the lyric poem.

The effectiveness of many great novels in translation seems to

---

[6]Theodore Dreiser, *An American Tragedy* (New York, 1964), p. 70.

confirm the ideal of transparent language. If from some distance we remember certain long novels—like *Middlemarch,* perhaps—more for events and characters and places than for quotable sentences, this fact, too, may support such a notion. The argument won't stand a closer view, however. The medium of the novel, like the marble in a statue, refuses, after all, to disappear: it does insist on being noticed, in its own distinctive way, and this aspect constitutes one (but not all) of the positive attractions of the art.

In the most detailed modern studies of the language of narrative (like those of Barthes and Genette) the self-focusing tendency is viewed as essential. How it is described depends on the terminologies of the particular critic. The constant is the power of such language to produce multiple meanings—as, for example, in the five codes of *S/Z* or the anomalies of Genette. Multiple meanings, or the extension of implications beyond any single denotation, bring the words sharply to our attention.

It is not necessary here to determine just what levels of meaning, or how many, or what sorts of anomalies or contradictions, are conventionally expected in the language of a novel. The most general and distinctively *novelistic* characteristic of such prose is probably a quality that can be illustrated vividly in another way in the following typical passage from Hemingway's *The Sun Also Rises:*

> In the morning it was bright, and they were sprinkling the streets of the town, and we all had breakfast in a café. Bayonne is a nice town. It is like a very clean Spanish town and it is on a big river. Already, so early in the morning, it was very hot on the bridge across the river. We walked out on the bridge and then took a walk through the town. . . . The car was to pick us up at the hotel in forty minutes, and we stopped at the café on the square where we had eaten breakfast, and had a beer. It was hot, but the town had a cool, fresh, early-morning smell and it was pleasant sitting in the café. A breeze started to blow, and you could feel that the air came from the sea. There were pigeons out in the square, and the houses were a yellow, sun-baked color, and I did not want to leave the café.[7]

[7]Ernest Hemingway, *The Sun Also Rises* (New York, 1954), pp. 90-91.

Though I have never been to Bayonne, I find these sentences very evocative, and the larger passage from which they come even more so. They call to mind images, detail, that cannot be found anywhere in the passage. (The fact that your images and mine are different and that both yours and mine are probably vague and shimmery and shifty is not important.) An effect of concentration is achieved, the words acquire richness well beyond their specifiable meanings.

The evocativeness in this particular case is sensual: it concerns a place and the particular mood of well-being, largely physical, of a man who is there at a certain time. The prose displays the very distinctive skill of Hemingway, the Hemingway style. Yet the passage simply develops in one strong direction an element we always expect in novelistic prose, no matter who the author: the concentration upon a moment of time. The evocation of place and feeling in place actually stirs us to awareness of a certain *moment* which is fixed or embodied in words, so that we can return to it at will.

I suspect that we expect all novelistic prose to capture time in this way. Not all is as evocative as our Hemingway example, to be sure. But even as abstract and analytical a sentence as this from *Pride and Prejudice*—"If gratitude and esteem are good foundations of affection, Elizabeth's change of sentiment will be neither improbable nor faulty."[8]—shares the essential quality when seen in its context. The prose evokes the temporal setting of what the passage describes: in this case the sentence reminds us of Elizabeth's laborious earlier discovery of her gratitude and esteem for Darcy, and it relates the present moment to the past—all of this meaning *beyond* what the words actually tell us.

How such effects are achieved is a question not of the nature of the prose but of what Aristotle would call the manner of imitation and what we will call narrative, to be discussed below. The result, however, is a prose that has a specially concentrated quality—prose in which the meanings of the words are always enriched by an unspoken reference to the passage of time. This "charged" quality distinguishes novelistic prose (along with the prose of the modern short story, not essentially different) from

---

[8]Jane Austen, *Pride and Prejudice* (Boston, 1956), p. 207.

good "ordinary prose."⁹ The words suggest much more than they say, so that the prose emerges from its invisibility and begins to call attention to itself, acquiring linguistic intensity.

The degree of linguistic intensity we expect in novelistic prose will vary, depending upon the subgenre of novel we are considering, but will probably never reach the level that we find in a lyric poem like, say, Wordsworth's "A Slumber Did My Spirit Seal." Generally speaking, we will find more highly developed linguistic intensity in some twentieth-century novels than in earlier ones. The charge also tends to be stronger in short fiction than in long: length overwhelms the claims of small units to attention. No sentence in the whole of *A Farewell to Arms* or *The Sun Also Rises* carries as much weight, word for word, in relation to the whole, as the wife's rebuke to her husband in Hemingway's story, "The Doctor and the Doctor's Wife": "Dear, I don't think, I really don't think that any one would really do a thing like that."¹⁰ The highest level of linguistic intensity achieved in fiction is surely in *Finnegans Wake*. That this work also presents the most notoriously difficult reading task in the history of the novel is due not merely to the erudition it requires but also no doubt to its length, in clear disregard of the principle just suggested.

Yet even in novels with high linguistic intensity, in Hemingway, in James, in Faulkner, Joyce, or Nabokov, the language is not verse but still prose. Is this just a question of degree—the language calls more attention to itself than in older styles, yet not as much as if it were verse? Why, if a novelist does not choose to make use of the transparency which is the advantage of good serviceable prose, does he or she not go all the way and write in verse? Possibly the material dealt with in the novel (the "imitated form," the "fictional world") is too massive and too complicated, even in a short novel (even in a short story, for that matter), to

⁹It should be noticed that not all narrative prose (i.e., prose describing a passage of time) is expected to possess the charged quality of novelistic prose. We do not look for this quality in reportage, for example. History books may or may not develop it. Insofar as the interest in history or biography is in determining, demonstrating, or analyzing events rather than in developing an "image" of them, we do not expect it.

¹⁰Ernest Hemingway, *The Short Stories of Ernest Hemingway* (New York, 1938), p. 200.

sustain the linguistic intensity of verse. We may imagine the effect of any novel we know cast into verse: a clear obstruction to our perception of the work. This reasoning implies, of course, a priority in the formal hierarchy of the novel, with lower position for the language than for the imitated form. Another possible answer derives from the origins of the novel as an imitation of true-life reporting. The language of journalism, history, and biography, is prose attempting to efface itself in the service of meanings. But in the language of the novel, which is not self-effacing, the rejection of verse is itself a significant convention: it says to us, this is language calling attention to the fact that it is prose, which has the power to serve all kinds and complexities of meanings *without* calling attention to itself. All the specialized styles have in common the pursuit of a linguistic intensity that in one way or another spotlights the capabilities of a language that would otherwise be self-effacing. Though it cannot achieve the intensity possible in verse, it pursues a similar kind while retaining at least an illusion of the advantages and interests of prose.

CONVENTIONS IN THE NOVEL: THE FICTIONAL WORLD.

The natural form of the novel, I have said, is a text, experienced in a controlled order (temporal) and presenting an account of events undistinguishable at first from any other, as in a history or a biography. In the convention of the novel, we expect the text to reveal a story, to present people involved in changing circumstances. But since it is a novel, we agree to understand the events in a special way, not as history or biography or autobiography but as *fiction*.

In the convention of fiction, people and events are presented without any claim to historical truth; if we read them as fiction we withhold the assumption of actuality and we refrain from judging them by it. The reverse does not necessarily follow: events in fiction may indeed copy actual events, like the battles and campaigns in *War and Peace* and the behavior of "Napoleon" and "Kutuzov." If we judge these events and characters for their historical accuracy or if the assumption of their actuality enters into our response to them—if, in other words, we actually do read these parts of *War and Peace* as history—to that extent we

are reading outside the conventions of fiction. Such is often the case in historical and autobiographical novels: *War and Peace* clearly claims that it should be read in part as history, and if we later encounter a historian who takes issue with the Tolstoyan view, we may have to adjust our total estimate of the book. If so, however, we are not judging the book as fiction. The use of historical names, and the names of real places, too, may or may not constitute a claim to be taken as history. "Harvard" in *The Sound and the Fury* is not Harvard and no one cares. Nor does anyone suppose that "Richard Nixon," the crazy narrator-protagonist of Robert Coover's *The Public Burning*, is a biographical representation of the former president. In every case, insofar as we regard such characters and events as fiction, they have *no necessary* connection to actual events; at most they will be enriched by the analogy to them.

We do not regard these described events as historically real, then, but as events in their own right, taking place in their own postulated world. This is the necessary minimum: we know, for instance, that Isabel Archer is real, since it is possible for me to discuss her—you know whom I mean—although she lives entirely within *The Portrait of a Lady*, existing only there. The characters and events of any fiction, then, occupy or compose a *fictional world*—they constitute what I have called the imitated form. And we expect every novel to display such a world. Though it may share ground with those of other novels—as Yoknapatawpha is shared by Faulkner's novels, for instance—ultimately each fictional world is distinct, peculiar to the novel in which it is displayed, unique (as the worlds of *Light in August* and *Sartoris* are distinct from each other—or as the world of *Swann's Way* is clearly delineated within the more comprehensive world of *Remembrance of Things Past*).

Still, it remains to determine how this fictional world relates to the real world, or to us. No doubt its primary general interest lies in the fact that we can recognize it as a fictional world. It is a form "made visible" by art. In this form we see resemblances to the real world composed into a unique new reality. The fictional world is hypothetical, a composite of at least conceivable possibilities. It is concrete, consisting of imitated forms *abstracted* from the real world. Aristotle's ancient description is simpler

and clearer, provided it is understood broadly rather than narrowly: tragedy, he says (or the novel, say I), imitates not what has happened but what *might* happen. It thus creates an abstraction from that which we can imagine, events in dreams if not in reality. There is always a connection of some kind between the concrete fictional world and the life we have actually or imaginatively known. This connection both enables us to recognize the existence of a fictional world and arouses our interest in it.

As I have noted, such a connection does not necessarily imply "realism" in fiction. A fictional world may be extravagantly "distorted" and may still be accepted if the writer can make us see it as a fictional world in some sense (almost any). We will find it believable if a writer makes it appear coherent by utilizing resemblances from any aspect of our experience whatever, including the lives of dream and hallucination, myth, and literary tradition. "Believable" means recognizable as world, as person, as event.

It is important to realize how much the recognition of a fictional world depends upon conventions. From the moment we recognize the presence of fiction and its basic convention (namely: the "I" in the text is not necessarily the author, and the events and people are not necessarily historical), we leap to the conventions that follow. Their nature depends upon the author and the tradition in which he writes. Having acknowledged that the events and people are not "real," we agree to regard them as if they were, and by other conventions we determine what kind of reality they have. By convention we expect lovers to quarrel, a man with a gun to use it, a rich old man to die, a dead man to stay dead. Also, by other conventions, we expect the opposite to occur in stories of other kinds. What Aristotelian critics call *probabilities and necessities,* what structuralists call *verisimilitude,* the forces that drive an action to its conclusion, are all recognizable by convention. So, too, we recognize the resemblances to the real world—abstractions, as I have noted—which make the fictional world cohere.

Just as abstracting in general signals essentials by stripping away nonessentials, so abstractions embodied concretely in a fictional world command attention as the powers that make that world operate and hold together. No doubt this attention is the

primary source of the vividness, clarity, and intensity of the fictional picture—its very visibility. It is also the basis for whatever personal involvement or identification we may feel. No doubt, too, this attention explains why almost any well-presented fictional world is more vivid than the world conveyed in a historical account and why historical accounts themselves are more vivid when conventions of fiction are employed.

We usually expect the center of the fictional world to be an "action" of some kind—human beings involved in conditions or circumstances that change. All studies of a novel's "subject matter," themes, society, depicted problems, or characters considered as people are studies of its fictional world—which is no doubt the aspect of the novel that has always been most studied.

Probably the best-known attempt to distinguish formally among fictional worlds is Frye's classification of "fictional modes."[11] Frye's modes divide according to two criteria: (1) the kind and degree of power of action possessed by protagonists in relation to ourselves, and (2) the kind and degree of power of action possessed by them in relation to their environments. The five modes descend in both categories from the level of the first mode, myth—where the characters are gods superior in both degree and kind of power to ourselves and to their environment—to irony, where the characters are inferior to both ourselves and their environment. Frye's system has been incisively criticized by several,[12] and alternative schemes have been provided.

I believe that a more fundamental basis for distinguishing fictional worlds lies not in the characters' power to act but in the *source* of activity in the fictional world: its origin and the field of the energy it expresses. If so, the primary distinction would be between fictional worlds in which events are generated ostensibly entirely from within and those in which they are to a significant degree determined from without—that is, by the authorial process itself. The difference is, to be sure, conventional, appar-

---

[11]Frye, *Anatomy of Criticism*, pp. 33ff.

[12]E.g., Tzvetan Todorov, *The Fantastic: A Structural Approach to a Literary Genre*, trans. Richard Howard (Ithaca, 1975), pp. 8–21.

ent in the postulates we agree to—for of course, in actuality all events are controlled by their inventor, the author.

The postulates, however, create a kind of spectrum. At one extreme, self-generated worlds reach a point where they cease to be fictional and become historical or biographical, with actions and characters that claim to represent actual (or supposedly actual) particulars of the real world. They are "controlled," ostensibly, by the actualities of history; the author takes them—the whole historical world that he presents to us—as given. It was from a point close to this that the novel itself is traditionally said to have developed.[13] From this point history can move into fiction by dropping the claim to actuality. The historical world becomes fictional. But the author can still pretend to be merely reporting, not inventing. Events—in any so-called traditional novel, from *Moll Flanders* or *Pamela* or *Tom Jones* through *Light in August* and *Mr. Sammler's Planet*—are caused by the interactions of characters and milieu and chance, changing conditions conventionally understood to lie entirely within the fictional world, unaffected by the author's presence.

From the imaginary border line with history (straddled by *War and Peace* and other historical novels) we move into fiction through progessive degrees of abstraction. I think of the fictional possibilities as fanning out rather than moving through a linear set of modes: a variety of possibilities by which the contingencies of actuality are removed from the picture. As they move, different questions provide different distinctions; they cut across each other, and the fanning out results from their separate thrusts. One question concerns the degree of actuality claimed for the characters, events, times, and places: a range of possibility between the near and locally familiar (a novel about midtown Manhattan in 1927) to the faraway, the remote, the strange (*The Castle*). Another will ask about the kind and degree of stature, importance, weight, magnitude, attached to events and characters, good or bad: encompassing such depths as those of *The Stranger* or *The Tin Drum,* Jamesian high society, and the heroes and villains of romance and the gods and demons of

[13]See Ian Watt's account in *The Rise of the Novel* (Berkeley, 1967).

myths, though the last are seldom found in novels. Still another inquires about causality—whether blind force and mechanism (*Sister Carrie, An American Tragedy, Studs Lonigan*), or the free will of responsible characters (*Emma,* perhaps), or perhaps supernatural magic or the modern magic, rationalized as mechanism, of science fiction. A related question addresses the faculties of the characters and the extent to which they influence the action—with a scale starting from worlds full of stupidity or blundering and ending with worlds full of wisdom and power. Yet another question will focus on archetypal patterns. All such differences contribute to differences in mode, but they are most useful to designate not a small number of distinct modal categories but a large number of complex and highly differentiated possibilities.

At the other end of the spectrum are what I call *narrator-controlled* worlds. This concept will have to be explained at some length. Here the ostensible autonomy of the fictional world is denied, and the events appear to be manipulated by the narrative process itself. This trait became prominent after the decline of realism and naturalism, and its emergence in the novel has been accompanied by a vigorous critical assault upon the assumptions of the more familiar modes. The term *narrator controlled* is of course figurative. I shall discuss the convention of the narrator in the next section; the relevant point here is the pretended distinction in traditional fiction between the author's inventive and narrative functions: as I have already observed, the traditional narrator, whether first or third person, within the fictional world or outside, restricted or omniscient, pretends to be reporting events that exist independently of his telling, and the events claim to be caused entirely by forces—characters, motives, change, circumstance, fate—within the fictional world. In narrator-controlled fiction, on the other hand, the postulated forces in the fictional world are inadequate to account for the sequence or to make it coherent; whatever coherence there is cannot be understood or explained without reference to the intervention of the author as inventor. This destruction of the autonomy of the fictional world breaks down the inventive/narrative distinction: in effect, the inventor's manipulations

have become the teller's, implicitly seeming to reflect the latter's creative, expressive, or rhetorical needs.[14]

This last statement is true not only of the radically constructed worlds of much new fiction but also of such traditional kinds as allegory and various didactic forms. The sign of the narrator-controlled fictional world is that it is not "integrated" internally, it is not self-contained, its parts do not cohere in its own terms. We see this characteristic most obviously when characters tend to lose their identities, to "merge into each other," as Eliot says in one of his notes to *The Waste Land*. Indeed, if *The Waste Land* is a fiction, as it no doubt is, it will be a striking example—with its characters all melting into each other and joining finally in Tiresias—of such a dis-integrated fictional world. In the novels of Robbe-Grillet, if it is true that a chronology cannot be reconstructed,[15] we have another example, time rather than character having been dis-integrated in this case.

If the characters lose their separate identities and merge, if the external chronology is actually contradictory (rather than merely seeming so in the blurred or hallucinatory vision of some character), if the causation of events violates the level of reality established for the work, we become aware of the hand of the author intervening in his fictional world to make it do what he wants. Merging characters have only a momentary identity; like characters in a dream we understand them as symbolic, expressions of the mind that projects them. Incoherent time is

[14]The narrative/inventive distinction is premised upon the ostensible autonomy of the fictional world and collapses when that autonomy breaks down. The concept of the narrator-controlled world is likely to be misunderstood, however, without one important qualification. In practice the seeming narrator of the story may stand in the same relation to events as do traditional narrators—reporting action that seems to have an autonomous existence, as far as he or she can see. (It is we, the readers, who perceive the breakdown of autonomy.) The source of the manipulations of the fictional world is at a deeper level, as we see, for instance, in Hawkes's *Second Skin*. We have to speak in such a case of the ostensible narrator, Skipper, as a "projection" of the latent manipulating narrator (see chapter 12, n. 16).

[15]In *For a New Novel: Essays on Fiction*, trans. Richard Howard (New York, 1965), Alain Robbe-Grillet says that the narrative in *Jealousy* was "made in such a way that any attempt to reconstruct an external chronology would lead, sooner or later, to a series of contradictions, hence to an impasse" (p. 154).

similarly expressive, as are also breaches of traditional probability: all direct our attention to the storyteller as manipulator rather than reporter or observer and to his fictional world as an arena of expression (or of rhetoric) rather than of ostensible observation.

Narrator-controlled worlds are clearly visible in such novels as Faulkner's *Absalom, Absalom!,* Flann O'Brien's *At Swim-Two-Birds,* and Robert Coover's *The Universal Baseball Association,* in each of which a character whose own fictional status seems secure "invents" a fictional world which takes on a reality of its own, thereby upsetting the conventional logical distinction between real and unreal. Another kind of narrator-controlled fictional world appears in John Hawkes's *Second Skin,* in which events in one part of the action fulfill all Skipper's worst fears, and in another part all his wishes—both in a seemingly realistic setting and without a suggestion of supernatural doings or "mind over matter." Still another sort appears in John Fowles's *The French Lieutenant's Woman,* with its double ending. Narrator control emerges sometimes even in traditional novels: in *Vanity Fair,* for instance, Thackeray speaks of his characters as puppets, which he can put back into their box. Though the fictional world here is roughly self-contained and the action follows realistic conventions, the puppet references put the whole fictional world into a different relation to the narrator, if only for a moment.

Such narrator-controlled worlds may be called *expressive* in the broadest sense of the term: our perception of the fictional world requires a perception of its invention as well, with an awareness, usually, that this fictional world is tied to some authorial purpose other than itself—which may be to "express" (in a more specific sense) by projecting an image or may be to exemplify a point or idea for a more deliberately communicative or rhetorical end. The distinction between self-generated (integrated) and narrator-controlled (expressive) fictional worlds is probably more fundamental than the simple one between realistic and mythic modes. It separates the farthest extremes that novelists have so far reached in composing fictional worlds. This distinction should not be confused with others. We must keep clear the difference between narrative distortions, or manipulations in the telling, and narrative *control* of the fictional world. Many

"surrealistic effects" in modern fiction are still resolvable into naturalistic conventions: fantasies and other mental phenomena of characters who nevertheless have solid ontological status in their fictional worlds (the deathbed fantasies in Conrad Aiken's "Mr. Arcturus," Katherine Anne Porter's "The Jilting of Granny Weatherall," Hemingway's "The Snows of Kilimanjaro," for instance). When past and present merge in the Benjy section of *The Sound and the Fury* (or when Darl becomes clairvoyant in *As I Lay Dying,* as we saw in chapter 3), the surreal component is explainable as a special convention at work to show state of mind or situation within an understood naturalistic context. Still another kind of pseudosurreal effect is seen in the depictions of a character's changing view of reality, in which the reality itself is assumed to exist—as in Ford's *The Good Soldier* or my own novel *Camden's Eyes.*

The distinction should also not be confused by the argument that *all* fictional worlds are narrator controlled and expressive. Of course they are: even the most naturalistic novel by Dreiser or the most realistic novel in the Jamesian sense is controlled by the author to serve authorial ends. The distinction is a difference in conventions, in suppositions. An integrated world poses a hypothesis that the reader by convention accepts: "Let us suppose," it says, "that these people, these events, have an existence independent of me, the teller." In an expressive fictional world, on the other hand, this hypothesis is more or less conspicuously denied: "Do *not* suppose that these events have an existence independent of me, the teller." Thus Robbe-Grillet: "[The book] was not a narrative mingled with a simple anecdote external to itself, but again the very unfolding of a story which had no other reality than that of the narrative, an occurrence which functioned nowhere else except in the mind of the invisible narrator, in other words of the writer, and of the reader."[16] Or the denial may be veiled, inferable through the prominence of some specific purpose that requires it, whether didactic, allegorical, or something else.

Narrator intervention should also not be confused with the operation of various "formal conventions" such as will be dis-

[16]Ibid.

cussed below. As noted earlier, we anticipate tragic events in a tragedy in part because we have recognized the work as a tragedy. In comedy the activity of formal conventions is even more evident: "comic safety" is a prominent feature. We know the man teetering on the cliff will not fall off, or if he does he will not be hurt. How does this intervention differ from that of a narrator in an expressive fictional world?

The distinction may at times be hard to draw, because the narrator-controlled world is itself a kind of formal convention. In integrated fictional worlds, however, the formal convention (the tragic, the comic, or whatever) expresses itself as the operation of "chance" or "fortune" or "fate"—"comic fortune," "comic safety," "tragic fate"—which moves within normal coordinates (a chronology and distinguishable agents) based on consistent ontological premises. In an expressive world, on the other hand, the inconsistency of such premises, whether in the merging of characters and destruction of time or simply in the demand that we read things as simultaneously imaginary and real, as in *Absalom, Absalom!*, prevents us from interpreting events in such ways. We are forced instead to see them as projections, emblems, symbolic or exemplary, in some overlooking and shaping mind.

Characters in a tragedy may be read allegorically, certainly, but we need not read them in this way to understand and appreciate them. An event in an allegory, however, cannot be accounted for without reference to what the characters symbolize. Every fictional world can be interpreted expressively if one wishes to do so; an expressive fictional world cannot be interpreted in any other way. (For a detailed discussion of an example of a narrator-controlled world, see below, chapter 12, on *Pale Fire*.)

Notice should be taken here of those contemporary critics who appear to deny the existence in fiction of any such thing as a fictional world. They hold that characters and events in fiction are phantoms, that our real interest is the language in which they flit, that they have no existence outside that language, that any tendency we may have to think of them as "real" is naive and childish and has nothing to do with the true seriousness of the

art. I find this proposition difficult to accept, since it seems to deny obvious and inescapable phenomena. Or have these critics merely overstated an important and necessary point? Certainly it must be conceded that the fictional world has no existence outside the work of art in which it is shown.[17] In this sense it does not exist outside the language which reveals it. And it must also be conceded—as William Gass so effectively argues—that to concentrate simply upon the "people" in fiction, as if they were real, friends or enemies, to describe fiction as a kind of stimulus for our fantasies of human relations, is to reduce the art to something more simpleminded than it actually is or is capable of being. But should we therefore conclude that the fictional world, its events, its characters, do not exist? More to the point, should we decide that the art of fiction can be discussed without reference to them? It seems obvious to me that our ability to discuss them shows that they exist, nor can I conceive of talking long about fiction without referring to them: even Barthes, while insisting that Sarrasine is only a proper noun with some adjectives attached, speaks of him in *S/Z* as if he were real in the course of hundreds of comments.[18]

The attack on the reality of the fictional world is closely related to the concept of opaque language. Is it claimed that we don't see a fictional world because our attention has been fixed on the language in the foreground? We don't see a fictional world; we only think we do? But of course, no fiction ever claimed more than that. If a critic tells me I don't see what I think I see, I am inclined to prefer my own interpretation of my experience. I suspect that the real source of the problem is the

[17]Seymour Chatman qualifies this point with respect to characters in *Story and Discourse: Narrative structure in Fiction and Film* (Ithaca, 1978), pp. 117-19.

[18]William H. Gass, *Fiction and the Figures of Life* (Boston, 1971), pp. 34-54, and Roland Barthes, *S/Z*, trans. Richard Miller (New York, 1974). Gass also argues that the novelist's business is not to "render the world" but to "make one" (p. 24). This is a prescriptive rather than a descriptive statement, since he presents it as something which novelists have been learning ("the novelist now better understands his medium"). I find this particular distinction hard to understand (unless "rendering" means simply a realistic treatment), for as I argue in chapter 3, it is difficult to conceive of any created form that is not in some sense an imitation (a rendering) of something.

confrontation between the concept of the fictional world and that of multiple meanings. If, as Barthes and his colleagues argue, any good sentence in fiction is charged with a plural of meanings flashing off in many directions, I would contend not that the fictional world disappears but that those meanings, multiple though they are, become part of it, part, that is, of our view of it: they enter into its description. The fictional world exists only as seen through the language, and the multiplicity of meanings simply complicates that vision: makes it ambiguous, perhaps, makes it glitter as with mirrors, resonate with the possibility of contradiction. As we have seen, often, especially in modern fiction, that multiplicity may shatter its seeming coherence, jar it, break it into fragments. Still the fictional world does exist; a fragmented world is a world, for all that. It simply makes no claim to being self-generated or internally coherent; the evidence by which we perceive it as a form comes from without.

CONVENTIONS IN THE NOVEL: NARRATIVE

Our expectations in the novel always include a range of possibilities as to how the story will be told—how the words of the text will be used to reveal the image of the fictional world. This aspect Aristotle called the manner of imitation, and the possible limits remain, as far as I can see, the same as those he described: the dramatic method at one extreme and the narrative at the other, these being the two radically opposite relationships possible between a word and the image it conveys. In the dramatic method the words, themselves part of what is represented, lie within the action, so to speak, speech that the characters themselves utter as they act. In the narrative method the words are spoken by someone—a narrator—who stands outside the action he or she is speaking about. Rather than manifesting the action, the words describe it. Readers or listeners learn of the action through the mediation of the narrator, whereas in the dramatic method they see it directly.

All questions of point of view and narrative technique, so thoroughly studied in modern criticism, are developments of problems arising from the primary need to choose between these two ways of using words. It is not necessary to recapitulate

the possibilities here beyond making a few general points.[19] First, in novels we usually expect a dominantly narrative rather than dramatic presentation, though the narrator's relationship to author and characters may vary greatly. There are three possible functions: the author, the narrator (or narrators), and the characters. Narrators may be linked, on the one hand, with the (implied) author,[20] standing outside the fictional world; they may be identified, on the other hand, with one of the characters, in which case they are within the fictional world, and the narrative assumes a quasi-dramatic quality. Or they may fall between these two possibilities—not characters and yet not connected with the author as that author is presented in the book. All three possibilities exist in novels, along with variations, and no general convention dictates one rather than another.

We also expect, though less consistently, that the narrator at times will turn to a dramatic presentation: he or she will speak with words of the characters, as in dramatic scenes. But again, as the conventions of different traditions differ, so there is no general rule. Each of the two extremes has different advantages. Generally speaking, the dramatic method is potentially more vivid, direct, and immediate in its presentation of the fictional world; the narrative method, on the other hand, can cover a larger range of material (in both time and space) with brevity and can more securely direct and make explicit the reader's desired interpretations of events and characters. The narrative method is less limited also in the kinds of materials that it can present conveniently, and it has the potential for an additional source of attraction (apart from the depicted action) in the mind and person of the narrator.[21]

It is said that the history of the novel shows steady develop-

---

[19]For possibilities, see Wayne Booth, *The Rhetoric of Fiction* (Chicago, 1961). See also my book, *The American Short Story in the Twenties* (Chicago, 1961), part 3.

[20]"Implied author"—Wayne Booth's term (*The Rhetoric of Fiction*) for whatever of the author can be inferred from the work itself.

[21]I discuss advantages of both methods at greater length in *The American Short Story in the Twenties*. The first major discussion of the comparative advantages of the two methods was of course that in Percy Lubbock, *The Craft of Fiction* (New York, 1957, originally published in 1926). On the question of the narrator as an independent attraction, see Booth's *Rhetoric of Fiction*, especially his analysis of *Emma*.

ment toward narratives that incorporate dramatic advantages. In classic nineteenth-century novels the most emphatic moments tend to be presented in dramatic scenes, with narrative segments in between. In the twentieth century the narrative possibilities are exploited, and qualities of drama are also obtained without such heavy reliance on scenes. Attributes of drama that increase vividness—such as its effect of temporal immediacy (present tense), its temporal coherence, its particularity (always representing unique events), its avoidance of an interpreting commentator, and its reliance on the audience's powers of drawing inferences—all can be adapted by a narrator without becoming explicitly dramatic. The result has been called dramatic narrative, a way—that is, a great variety of ways—to maintain both the vividness and immediacy of drama and the sweep, range, concision, and personal vision of narrative.

Perhaps the only general expectation concerning narration that we bring to all novels is that *art* will be displayed in its use—art appropriate to the particular work's place in the history of the genre. By "art" here I mean that restrictive conventions of some stringency will be observed, aiming at economy and efficiency. I have been tempted to make this statement more specific by suggesting that we normally expect "consistency" in the use of narrative (consistency in point of view), and it is evident that many critics as well as students do judge writers by this standard. It is also clear, however, that narrative consistency is frequently disrupted by the very best writers (for example, the abandonment of the first-person narrator in *Madame Bovary*), and these exceptions in classic literature tend not to be noticed until some critic digs them up. In contemporary literature they sometimes become conspicuous and positive virtues. I can only conclude that a consistent point of view is not as important as it has sometimes been thought to be, and as with other restrictive conventions violations of it may often be a source of interest and power.

CONVENTIONS IN THE NOVEL: FORM

There remains to consider the question of the conventional basis for the unity or organic wholeness of the novel. Is there a category of "formal conventions," pertaining to our perception of

the work as a whole, as a single artistic form? And if so, what limits do such conventions impose upon the novel?

In eliminating collections and loosely joined groups of episodes from the original field of "novels," I have no doubt made sure that my definition will include a convention of unity. Such a convention evidently exists, since we do distinguish novels from collections. A few commonplace observations sufficiently demonstrate its importance beyond question. First, when we read a novel, we begin at the beginning and expect to read through to the end. We do not pick out chapters here and there as we may stories in a collection—or if we do, we do so apologetically, for we know that we are not supposed to read the book this way. Further, if we are fully absorbed, we do not expect, do not even like, to be told what is ahead until we get there under our own power—otherwise we may object that the novel was "spoiled for us" because someone "gave away the ending." Further, we expect—or at least we hope—that the novel will sustain our interest as we read; each part will arouse our curiosity or our desire to go on and read the next. If the novel is very successful, we may find ourselves saying, "I couldn't put it down." If the novel does not sustain our interest, we regard this as someone's failure—either the novelist's or our own—a significant observation, since there are many books (again, for example, collections) in which we do not expect to maintain a sustained interest. Usually with a novel, however, we expect our impetus to increase as we proceed, and in addition we expect to achieve at the end a sense of completeness, a sense of conclusion, a termination of the desire to keep going. We do not necessarily expect that perfect disposition of all characters and tying of loose ends so popular in the nineteenth century. At times, too, we naturally feel that we would "like to go on reading"; I must acknowledge too the continuing activity that many a modern novel provokes after the end, as we try to make sense of what we have just read. Nor am I forgetting E. M. Forster's complaints about the unsatisfactory conclusions of most novels. The desire to keep reading is, however, usually simply a sign of regret that an enjoyable artistic experience has finished; the activity that follows our reading of some modern novels may be stimulated deliberately by the convention of the rounded-off ending—it is such an outcome,

perhaps, that we continue to look for after reaching the end. Similarly, when a work terminates in instability, as many modern novels do, this same convention of completeness makes us regard that very instability as a settled condition—just as the same convention may lead us when the form truly baffles us, to call the work a *fragment*, a term that itself implies a standard of wholeness. As for Forster's complaint, the very objection is testimony to the universality of the convention, which Forster himself realizes cannot simply be abandoned.

And so we see the great importance of a strong formal convention in the definition of the novel—an expectation of some principle of wholeness and unity more than the sum of its parts, stronger also than principles that may give unity to the parts in themselves. (Such strength is what mainly distinguishes this principle from the formal principle of a work like *Dubliners* or *Winesburg*.) The order of these parts is temporal—the sequence in which they appear as we read. We expect the formal principle to make this order coherent, so that the arranged parts will seem to depend for their being upon their connections to the rest. We expect to find the formal principle contributing to the attraction or power of every part; the primary interest of the novel ("I couldn't put it down") might well be described as an interest in the whole. More perhaps than we may realize, the vitality, vividness, intensity of individual parts, scenes, episodes, and the sense of movement and pace, of vitally functioning words, are drawn (while we read) from the expectation of a context and of a whole which is being built and (in retrospect) from the fulfillment of that expectation.

This view of the importance of unity in the literary work (if not specifically in the novel) has been held by critics as various as Aristotle, Coleridge, James, Croce, Langer, the New Critics, and the neo-Aristotelians. It has nevertheless been seriously attacked by some contemporary critics, as we have seen, and we should therefore be precise about our claims. It is not contended that the reader's "interest in the whole" overrides the interest in the reading process; quite the contrary—I have argued that our interest in reading a novel in its proper sequence is an expression of our interest in the whole. Nor is it asserted that this interest in totality excludes an independent interest in the parts;

such a notion would be vain and is refuted, for starters, by the popularity of public readings of extracts from novels, which often please audiences even though the whole remains unknown. Nor is it argued that "every reader" must share this same interest in the whole; who knows what every reader might enjoy or why every reader reads? One might read *War and Peace* to learn about Napoleon or *An American Tragedy* for its detailed account of life in upstate New York. What I have called the primary interest is conventional: the primary expectation that a reader with "literary competence" (to use Culler's term) brings to the work when he is reading it *as a novel*. Let us not insist on "primary" in a literal sense, either, for the term becomes ambiguous. I mean by it only that I am unable to discover any other equally specific convention which contributes so much to the interest of *every* novel.

The student who fails to grasp the form of a story pays tribute to the convention with the question "What's the point?" The knowing reader will find it everywhere in the works he or she calls novels, shaping the interest even of those details that seem at casual glance to be most independent, autonomous. Is it an evocative descriptive passage? I have already remarked how the Bayonne scene quoted earlier from *The Sun Also Rises* depends for its effect upon its context of time—which is only a way of saying its place in a development: the contrast to what lies behind it (Jake in Paris), the preparation for what lies ahead, what Jake hopes for (restorative rituals of fishing and bullfighting with a few chosen friends) qualified retrospectively by what actually does lie ahead. Is it rather a thematic statement of the kind critics like to isolate for clues to the author's general beliefs—like the speeches by Schlossberg in Bellow's *The Victim* ("I'll tell you. It's bad to be less than human and it's bad to be more than human.... Have dignity, you understand me? Choose dignity"[22])? But we expect such passages to be incorporated into the specific development of the novel (as Schlossberg's speeches are integrated in the cafeteria scene, which in turn is subsumed into Leventhal's development at a particular point); otherwise we tend to consider them blemishes, problems—a response that also

[22]Saul Bellow, *The Victim* (New York, 1956), pp. 133-34.

reflects the importance of the formal convention. Is it a larger episode, capable of standing by itself, like the trolley strike in *Sister Carrie,* which certainly could be extracted from the novel and read as a coherent, well-shaped episode in its own right? This is surely not a blemish or an excrescence; on the contrary, it is in fact one of the most memorable episodes in the book. One soon realizes, however, that its full power is by no means accounted for by its independent "intrinsic interest." Its interest in the work as a whole depends not merely upon Hurstwood's step-by-step discovery of what it is like to become a scab in a trolley strike but also—mightily—upon our long-developed sense of how terribly he has fallen, how desperate is his need, and how bitterly unfortunate is the way he has chosen to pull himself out of his apathy. The intrinsic interest of the episode, it seems to me, is wholly absorbed in this context, to such an extent that I can scarcely imagine the episode without this knowledge of Hurstwood's whole story. But if the episode did indeed refuse to be integrated, then again we would find the force of the formal convention asserting itself in the judgment we would pass upon it.[23]

Though the specific formal principle of any novel is not in itself a convention, the expectation of such a principle is one. It specifies that the novel will have a principle of unity stronger than that of any of the parts when considered in themselves. In novels of particular kinds, such as detective stories or mysteries

[23]It is an interesting question whether in a novel in which the formal convention is strongly established, a truly independent episode could establish itself even as a blemish. The force of the formal convention would tend to absorb the episode, no matter how hard that segment might be to "explain." A good example might be the Bulkington episode in *Moby-Dick.* On its face this moment is pretty well cut out from the development of the rest—by virtue at least of the character who is apotheosized and thereafter "forgotten," though the chapter does, it is true, fit into the chronology. The activity of the critics in justifying this episode testifies to the power of the convention, which forces us to find connections between the episode and the rest. The passage provides a good example of the way the convention can oblige us to find richness in the work, by turning the episode into a metaphor. I do not mean that there can be no blemishes or excrescences or violations of unity in a work. See chapter 5. The speeches of Gavin Stevens in Faulkner's *Intruder in the Dust,* which seem addressed to us rather than to Chick Mallison, are not saved (in my view, at any rate) by the formal convention in that book.

or gothic romances, the formal convention will be more narrowly specified, often even defining the kind of hero, action, and milieu in some particular interaction. The question remains as to whether the formal convention for the novel "in general" also needs to be more precisely defined.

Because of the initial specification of length, we are able to distinguish the novel from the short story—although it should be noticed that in every other respect, including that of the formal convention, the definition of the short story appears to be identical. We have also seen that our definition excludes collections, including those with a loose thematic organization. But what about other long fictions that are single in some sense but still are seldom or uncertainly regarded as novels: *Gulliver's Travels, Rasselas, Morte d'Arthur, Arcadia* or, for that matter, *Moll Flanders*? I have taken pains to avoid some of the seemingly too narrow criteria often used to identify novels: I would not confine the genre to a focus on the individual in society, for instance, nor to realism. Have I, in so doing, simply opened the door to all long and minimally organized fictions in prose?

Sacks excludes *Gulliver's Travels* from novels because it is a satire, and *Rasselas* because it is an apologue. I would prefer to do otherwise because his criteria would force me to exclude *1984*, which is a novel as satire, and *Darkness at Noon*, a novel as apologue. If we still want to exclude the two earlier works (as it seems appropriate to do), it must be not because they are satires and apologues but because they differ in some other quality from the two twentieth-century works. This quality, quite obviously, pertains to the formal convention. The two earlier works are episodic in some sense—that is, they fall short of some standard of strictly *fictional* "concentration" which the twentieth-century works meet.[24] They do not lack unity or organization but the fictional elements (the components of their worlds) are not developed by principles drawn from those worlds (fictional cause-effect, character, and the like). This point is shown clearly

---

[24]Both Mary Doyle Springer, in *Forms of the Modern Novella* (Chicago, 1975), and David Richter, in *Fable's End: Completeness and Closure in Rhetorical Fiction* (Chicago, 1974), note the extent to which modern didactic fiction has gone beyond earlier didactic forms in the use of purely fictional techniques and materials.

by Sacks in his effort to demonstrate the incompatibility between satire and novel, apologue and novel.[25] The mark of such fictional "concentration" is the interrelatedness of fictional details, especially the constant subordination of some to others. A pure, spare linear account in an anecdote, for instance, would display a relatively low degree of concentration, even though it might be quite coherent; a description of a physical setting that reflects a character's state of mind as he makes a decision would display a relatively high degree. An episodic plot, episodes connected by little except a common character, say, might be concentrated in the separate episodes but unconcentrated as a whole because of the lack of fictional concentration in the connections.

Without a certain standard of fictional concentration, evidently, we shall raise questions as to whether the work should be called a novel. It is a question of degree rather than kind and cannot be stated precisely. Our definition of the formal convention in general can say only that in the novel *we expect a principle of wholeness sufficiently strong to control the parts, of a kind to invest those parts with a "certain" (fairly high) degree of specifically fictional concentration.* As we have seen, this requirement need not exclude a didactic or satirical organizing principle for the whole nor a radically dis-integrated or narrator-controlled fictional world (*Absalom, Absalom!* or *The Universal Baseball Association*), for a work can have concentrated fictional materials without necessarily having a fully integrated fictional world.

Even readers who accept this definition will differ as to the degree of concentration that makes a novel. Most will probably agree that *Gulliver's Travels* is not a novel, but *1984* is; everyone will include *War and Peace,* and most will probably exclude *Morte d'Arthur;* perhaps we will continue to differ on *Go Down, Moses.* Such differences do not really matter—not, certainly, if we remember that the novel is a cluster of conventions rather than a rigidly bounded class of works. Like all genres, it is, as I have noted, an ingredient, and we can expect to find it, partially or fully, in any work we call a novel.

---

[25]Sacks, *Fiction and the Shape of Belief,* pp. 1–20.

Components of the Novel

If the novel is a conventional form, the artistic form of any individual novel is, as I have said, an original form. The distinction is obvious. There is in fact no such thing (except in the useful and performing arts) as an unoriginal work of art. The conventions on which a novel depends, constituting its conventional form, make its originality manifest; some of them also appear as measures by which or against which its originality can be displayed.

Not all novels are equally original, however; there are many opportunities which a novelist may or may not take. Originality manifests itself in two ways. It appears in the conventions invented for the work. Novels may differ greatly in their use of such conventions; when they are prominent, the novel has a quality we call avant-garde or experimental or innovative. But originality manifests itself most significantly in the uniqueness of the formal principle. This kind of originality is absolute; every novel has it, and it gives to each a unique artistic identity. It lies in the novelist's combination of all the elements. Still, although this uniqueness is absolute, the ground broken may seem to vary in its extent from work to work as a result of differences in the specificity of the formal convention in each novel. Since, we have seen, formal conventions are more specifically defined for some types of novel than for the novel in general, the scope for originality in some works is narrower than in others. Todorov has observed how in "popular" genres (the detective story, for instance), the examples best admired and enjoyed are those which adhere most closely to their generic specifications; such genres are conventional forms which (in the language of my book) have strongly limiting formal conventions.[26] I do not mean, of course, that there is no originality in such works. No doubt the reader's enjoyment depends in part on the familiarity of the conventional form itself, exactly as one takes pleasure in *rereading* something well known. But most readers are looking, after all, for a new

---

[26]Tzvetan Todorov, *The Poetics of Prose*, trans. Richard Howard (Ithaca, 1977), p. 43.

variant. The kind of originality aimed for (freshness in the familiar, so to speak) is very precisely defined in such cases, its scope well marked out; any reader accustomed to the genre can judge it easily. The criteria of the art are clearly established, and maybe that is why it is "popular." Not so with the so-called serious work, which, according to Todorov, aims at just the opposite, seeking an escape from genre and constituting a new genre in itself. Of course we know that escape from genre is impossible. The formal convention is merely less specific, as we have seen, and the writer is free to explore a larger field of possibilities to be original.

The crucial question that I wish to consider now faces us. Granted the theoretical necessity for a formal principle in a work of art and granted also the conventional expectation of finding it in the novel, can a real critic actually discuss it? Can an analysis of it, hierarchical or otherwise, actually be made? Where should we look for this principle? How can we expect to describe it in a study of real novels?

[5]

The Formal Principle

As we saw in chapter 1, the metaphor of the organic whole suggests the great difficulty of trying to describe the formal principle of a novel. After all, in a truly organic body—a human one, say—everything influences everything else. One might conclude that no abstractions can be made or (at any rate) no ruling or governing principle. The first supposition is of course false (one can draw a picture of a human body or map the circulation of the blood). The second, however, is not so easily denied.

The problem is that if the work is a unique whole, any principle capable of encompassing every detail could be fully expressed only through those details. If we attempt to analyze the hierarchical form by postulating a principle that integrates it, we will find that the integrative principle is not separable from that form. There is a difference of a kind, to be sure: the integrative principle is the form seen with regard to its wholeness, coherence, predictability: it would be, so to speak, the "form of the form."[1] It is related to everything else in the compound hierarchy as form is to matter. The matter embodies the form (brings it into being), and the form shapes or controls the matter. But a full description of the form would also be a description of its matter; it cannot therefore be abstracted. (The converse is not true. It is possible to describe the matter without regard to how it

---

[1] So R. S. Crane in a somewhat similar way spoke of the "power" or "effect" as the "form of the plot" ("The Concept of Plot and the Plot of *Tom Jones*," in *Critics and Criticism*, ed. Crane [Chicago, 1952], p. 622), and he also at various times would speak of plot in Aristotle's analysis as form for the matter of character, of character as form for the matter of thought, of thought as form for diction.

is shaped or organized.) Yet the form can be approached—as I suggested in chapter 1 with the figure of the differential unit in calculus. Using a combination of reductive and aggregative methods, perhaps we can construct a useful abstracted hierarchical principle, remembering that we seek not the perfect and final analysis but the one that distorts least.

THE STRUCTURE OF THE FORMAL PRINCIPLE

Let us define the *formal principle* as this imperfect but approachable conception: namely, as whatever *abstractable* principle most adequately expresses the integrative power of the artistic form, the power that gives to its parts their appearance of necessity, of predictability. It should be the simplest means of accounting (most powerfully) for the location of those parts: "simplest," although any principle capable of doing such work must be highly complicated; "most powerfully," since different hypotheses may imply different degrees of inevitability in a form; "location," since the text is first of all an arrangement in sequence. If it can be analyzed at all—I also assume—this principle will be analyzable as a compound hierarchy.

Can we build a model of the general structure of such a hierarchy? Can we identify its components and determine any relationship among them? Let us consider first how we show that a part is integral in a whole, for example, the character Gilbert Osmond in James's *Portrait of a Lady*. We would have to demonstrate that Osmond's presence is required by something else, presumably more important, which is also integral. Since this other thing is integral, it will also depend on something still more important, and so it goes: the end of the chain of dependencies can only be the whole itself, which itself is most important. The process reflects the hierarchy but still gives us no way to analyze it.

Perhaps we can find a clue, however, in James's own account of how he built up *The Portrait of a Lady* from an original "germ," namely, the conception of a character, Isabel Archer, "affronting her destiny."[2] Asking himself, "What will she do?" he deter-

---

[2] Henry James, "Preface to 'The Portrait of a Lady,'" *The Art of the Novel* (New York, 1947), pp. 40-58.

mined that she would go to Europe, and from this idea he developed her story, adding brick on brick, in the course of which all the other characters, such as Lord Warburton, Ralph Touchett, Madame Merle, and Gilbert Osmond, came into existence as necessary parts. It is clear that for James in the Preface this germ is not only the starting point but also the center: the novel builds it up, fleshes it out. In some sense it is "the most important thing" in the novel—which implies that, in some sense, it must be the same as the whole itself, although it remains only the germ.

Let us defer for the moment the question of the precise nature of this germ and ask only how the character Gilbert Osmond depends on it. How, in other words, does fleshing out the germ lead specifically to the creation of a Gilbert Osmond? James's discussion of the ficelle Henrietta Stackpole indicates one possible kind of development. James describes her as belonging not to the *subject* but to the *treatment,* a character who runs "beside the coach" rather than riding in it. She is sharply distinguished from those (such as Osmond) who are true "parts of the subject." Her presence is determined by the requirements of the narrative manner—chiefly by the author's desire to "dramatize" Isabel's story, a requirement that in his view calls for the introduction of a confidante. She is accounted for (determined, "predicted") by the application of certain restrictive conventions (dramatization) to the germinal idea.

It is easy, of course, to object to the oversimplification that excludes Henrietta from the coach: no character of any prominence in an integrated novel can ever belong simply to the treatment but not to the subject.[3] Our problem, however, concerns Osmond: how, since he is surely not implicit in the concept of Isabel Archer, did he get *into* the coach? What principles must have been applied to the germinal idea to create him?

To answer such a question, we would find ourself reconstructing a great many specific artistic and compositional decisions the author must have made. Insofar as these decisions do not appear

---

[3]See Wayne Booth's discussion of the Jamesian ficelle and the problem of distinguishing "where, in the process of growth of James's subjects, the essential 'matter' leaves off and the rhetorical 'manner' begins" (*The Rhetoric of Fiction* [Chicago, 1961], pp. 101–6).

to be arbitrary, each will express implicitly some determining principle: we would find ourselves postulating a variety of such principles, separate and distinct from each other, combining to make the development of the germ seem inevitable, predictable. These might include, for example, in the case of Osmond, such ideas as that Isabel's destiny should be manifested in suffering, that the suffering (of Isabel, the free spirit) should ironically be manifested in a trap, that the trap (in her world) should be marital, that Isabel should have fallen into it by failing to see the evil behind the appearance of what she had thought was the highest good, that this false appearance should involve the confusion of aesthetic and moral value. These principles and an almost unlimited number of others combine to make Gilbert's creation seem inevitable. In the sense that the germ itself is equivalent to the whole (and the statement of this germ is simply an extreme abstraction from the whole)—all these principles are implicit in the germ, as is Osmond himself. But if the germ is simply an abstraction equivalent to the statement that describes it, then all these principles are *independent* of it, as they are also, in many cases, of each other.

The *formal principle* is the composite formed by the interaction of all these various compositional principles. Its components are the decisions (or their manifestations) to which these principles give rise; its hierarchy is the hierarchy of dependencies of these decisions; and its power as an integrating principle depends on the abundance and strength of these principles.

To construct a model that will show the hierarchy in general, then, we need first to find some specifiable principle equivalent to James's germ, some formulable idea beyond which the dependencies of the parts cannot go. Let us strip from this notion its genetic implications for James and define it for the moment simply as "whatever is to be found at the top of the hierarchy."

Second, we need to find some organization that reduces as much as possible the independence of the various principles by which the germ is developed (materialized). For this task the classification of conventions in the novel, given in chapter 4, provides a natural starting point. Among principles developing the germ it is easy to distinguish between those that contribute to the creation of the *fictional world* and those that work toward the

composition of the *narrative*. The first category would include, for example, the notion that Isabel's suffering should be manifest in an upper-class international society and focused in marriage. I call this a principle of *invention*. The second group would include the kinds of ideas that I mentioned above as contributing to the creation of Henrietta Stackpole—the notion that certain lights on Isabel should be presented dramatically through the use of a confidante. I would call these principles of *presentation* (concerned with narration and dramatization, with how the words are adapted to the fiction, with Aristotle's "manner of imitation"), and I would add to them, for the completion of the narrative, principles of *style* (relating to the kind of language used). We should also notice principles according to which Isabel is seen as good or bad, attractive or otherwise. I would call these principles of *evaluation* (concerned with what have often been called the ethical norms of the work, which Sacks call the beliefs and which we extend to cover every kind of appraisal, ethical and emotional). We can also derive from the previous chapter a fifth category, principles of *construction*, bearing directly on the constituting and organizing of the *form* as developed from the germ. If principles of invention and evaluation compose the concepts of Isabel, her naivete, her maturity, and the like, for example, principles of construction build the idea of her growth into a richly developed action. The last include such matters as the economy of means, the aptness of fate, development through antithesis or juxtaposition, climax or denouement, reversal, contrast, and any number of more specific decisions ("growth is to be displayed through a sequence of choices in dilemmas"). Of the five types of principle, the fifth comes first in the novelist's art, and supervises those of invention, evaluation, presentation, and style.

Six components altogether, then: the germ, defined as whatever is at the top of the hypothetical hierarchy, and the five sorts of principles which develop it. For purposes of arranging these components tentatively, let us suppose an imaginary *Portrait of a Lady*, resembling the real one but perfectly unified and also simplified for the sake of exposition. Let us also formulate a somewhat more manageable germ: "Isabel's growth from naivete into full moral maturity." We can then determine without great

difficulty certain primary commitments that limit the principles used in most of the five categories.

The principles of *invention* are bound by a primary commitment to a self-generating fictional world, low mimetic, realistic, contemporary, international, upper-class, and so on. Primary among the principles of *evaluation* is the conception of morality which Isabel learns, which organizes a complex and subtle scheme of values. Among the principles of *presentation,* the first commitment is to narrative itself, then to a narrator outside the fictional world, one with an independent personality, a point of view with broad privilege, close to Isabel but not always so, with dramatizing restrictions, an attitude of mild irony and sympathy, and so on. Among the principles of *style,* the primary commitment is to Jamesian language, with all that statement implies.

In each of these categories, the principles are organized in a hierarchy. As here described, the hierarchies are simple, not compound: the higher principle does not prescribe but simply limits the lower principles, which are otherwise independent, or given. The decision to have a self-generating fictional world analytically precedes the decision to have a low mimetic one; the decision to have a narrator is prior to any decision as to kind.

Seen in this way (and disregarding for the moment the principles of construction), the four other sets of principles appear to be quite independent of each other and *almost* independent of the germ—which seems to exert only the broadest kinds of limits on them. Yet if we try to imagine for the germ that kind of central significance James thought it had, we find these sets beginning to constitute themselves into an implicit hierarchy, too. For although the principles of presentation are not in any way determined by the fictional world, yet the narrative here exists in order to display that world, and therefore decisions concerning narrative are limited by the requirements of that display. Similarly, though the Jamesian style considered in general is independent of any particular novel, yet its actual exercise in this novel is only made possible by the analytically prior decision to use narrative and is limited throughout by the requirements of that narrative. The fictional world itself, despite its richness and complexity, is also sharply limited by the require-

ments of the germ; if the germ is really as central as it is supposed to be, there will be nothing (in this perfectly unified work)
in the fictional world that does not bear on it in some sense.

Such a hierarchy is pyramidical in structure (the decision to
make Lord Warburton the flower of English manhood and Caspar Goodwood the flower of American both depend on the decision to people Isabel's world with the best possible male repre-
sentatives of various cultures, but neither decision is subordinate
to the other). As in all simple hierarchies, the higher principles
are broader and less specifying than the lower. If developed in a
practical analysis, such a hierarchy can give us, no doubt, a
rough idea of a novel's formal structure. It can show how the
germ is developed in such and such a fictional world by such and
such principles of presentation. This is the manner of the usual
kind of plot analysis. But it cannot give any very powerful sense
of the novel's integration, since it retains so many independents
or givens in its constitution. It is still essentially an aggregative
analysis which has been given a modest appearance of order by
the abstracted germ.

To devise a more effective model for the formal principle we
shall need to know more about the germ. In the hierarchy I have
just considered it lacks definition and seems arbitrary in two
ways. In the first place, what is to keep us, in the hierarchy as so
far analyzed and defined, from identifying Osmond himself as
germ, or Henrietta? Centrality, we reply, but does this still save
us from making Ralph Touchett the germ? Couldn't we describe
the novel as the vindication of Ralph Touchett and find that
description pretty nearly as determining as the germ we have
used? Or couldn't we for a change postulate a germ of a totally
different kind: An Exercise in Jamesian Language?

Well, the concept of centrality, vague though it is, probably
does prevent us from making Ralph the germ, since the idea
does intuitively seem outrageous, despite the case that could be
made for it. The Exercise in Jamesian Language reminds us,
perhaps, of possible objections to our whole procedure, questions to which I will return, but at this point the linguistic notion
can be safely dismissed for setting even more vague limits than
our sentence about Isabel. *Every* novel by James is an Exercise in

Jamesian Language. Only *some* are about one's growth to full moral maturity. Only *one* is about Isabel.[4]

Then, too, how specific, how detailed should our statement of the germ be? And how much does it imply that is not expressed? How much of a character may we assume from that germinal statement itself? Actually, if the germ is simply the "central idea" of the novel, we have no reason not to make it much more specific: "The novel shows (in such a way, and so forth) how Isabel, the intelligent and proud would-be free spirit, seeking to preserve and exercise her freedom, is drawn into a trap, whereby she learns and grows. This is accomplished in an action divided into two parts, in the first of which . . ." and so on, to include a specification of her three suitors, the role of the Touchetts, and those of Madame Merle and Gilbert Osmond. By this time the germ may seem pretty cumbersome, and its unifying force may well be concealed beneath its complications. On the other hand, what is to prevent us—and here is the second kind of arbitrariness—from moving in the other direction, making the germ still more abstract than we have so far, until it is the most irreducible principle of order that can be found? But at what point does a reducible principle become irreducible? Why not abstract "the growth of a girl as she pursues her destiny" to "the growth of a girl" or simply to "growth" or even to "an interesting change in character"?

The germ, like the form of the whole, is itself a compound of seemingly independent principles that have somehow been integrated. And just as each increase in the specification of the germ tends to blur its force as a unifying principle, so each push back into abstraction takes it further away from the novel and also

---

[4]To this argument one reader, highly sophisticated in critical matters, objects: "It is facile to dismiss the 'Jamesian language' as germinal principle on the grounds that it joins James's *Portrait* to all his other works, while there is only one Isabel Archer. For the 'Jamesian heroine,' the 'Jamesian myth,' link Isabel to his other novels, while each sentence in the *Portrait* is just as unique as Isabel, appearing in no other of James's works." I reply that Isabel is by no means identical with or even hard to distinguish from Fleda Vetch or Milly Theale or any other Jamesian heroine, despite the obvious family resemblances. As for sentences, I would be hard put to find any one of those unique sentences in the *Portrait* which dominates the others as Isabel does.

weakens the description of unity of the whole, since it leaves more in the category of the given or arbitrary. Since I want my description of a formal principle to specify both my sense of the wholeness and my sense of the individuality and complexity of the work, and especially my awareness of the effectual functioning of the parts, it should be both as abstract and as specific as possible.

We must therefore consider more narrowly how the germ must be composed. We know that close to the top of the formal hierarchy there must be, as I have just suggested, some principle of singleness, of unity, because we perceive the work as single. This abstract principle must be embodied, initially, in some fundamental principle of construction by which oneness is made manifest. This could be the display of a coherent action or an unfolding character or a parallelism of actions or a meditation or an argument or almost anything words are capable of. Made single and adapted to fiction, such a principle becomes something like "the depiction of a loss of fortune" or a "forming of character"; it could be "the display of a process of disillusionment" or the "resolution of a dilemma." Or it could be "a completed set of illustrations of a theme" or (to go outside the novel) simply a "collection of stories about a woman." There are probably no limits to the possibilities. Such a principle does indeed stand at the top of the hierarchy, for it ultimately limits everything in the work.

I call this primary conception the *design principle* of the work. If the next stage of embodiment is simply some further specification of each of its terms, our formulation will resemble what we were calling the germ, along with the primary commitments in the areas of the fictional world, evaluation, presentation, and style. "Depiction of" yields to "narrative" and "Jamesian style," the "forming of character" becomes "Isabel's growth from naivete to full moral maturity," and the whole is qualified by "in a self-generating fictional world." The result is: "the narrative in a Jamesian style of Isabel's growth from naivete to full moral maturity in a self-generating fictional world." This phrase specifies the *germinal principle,* a concept broader in scope than our earlier "germ."

The germinal principle seems to be the simplest (most abstract)

[95]

definition that can be given to the specific individualized material that is made single by the design principle. It imposes broad limits on the principles of invention, evaluation, representation, and style, as we have seen, and by combining with them it contributes to the necessity of every part of the work; it *enters into* the prediction of every part. The germinal principle will thus have to be cited at some point in a satisfactory justification of any part. Why, for instance, does Countess Gemini's revelation come so late in the novel? Our answer will refer to the state of Isabel's growth at that point—and thus to the germinal principle.

As we have seen, the germinal principle consists of terms indicating the primary commitments made in language, fictional world, evaluation, and presentation (the major aspects into which we have divided fiction), plus the central phrase, "Isabel's growth from naivete to maturity." This phrase seems to occupy a privileged position in the hierarchy. The other parts of the germinal principle either serve it ("narrative," "Jamesian style") or modify it ("in a self-generating fictional world"). I will therefore call this privileged phrase the *subject*, defined simply as that part of the germinal principle, constituting a unity, to which the other parts are subordinated. (And let us add, if this subordination cannot be shown convincingly in a particular case, to that extent identification of the subject will remain, as it must, a tentative matter.)

Subjects might be supposed to share some general features. In our example, the stated subject can be analyzed into three aspects that dominate its development in the novel: an *action* whose limits are specified (change from "naivete to maturity"), an *agent* (Isabel), and a *judgment* (implied in "growth," a term signifying approval). For novels in general, however, these terms are probably too restrictive. What if the privileged item in the germinal principle seems to be not a character in action but the development of an argument? Or—why not?—the development of an extended metaphor or some allegorical relationship? The terms must be expanded. If not all subjects have an *action*, we can expect at any rate that every subject meeting my definition will specify a *process* of some sort, since the novel is organized as a sequence in time. As there is a process, so there should be something that is processed: if it is not an *agent*, it might, most gener-

ally, be called a *topic*. As for *judgment*, attaching to the process, let me replace this term with *interest*: the implied (or hypothetical) significance or importance, judgmental or emotional, which the subject is designed to have for its implied reader. Topic, process, and interest: these will be the major divisions, presumably, in the composition of any subject.

The formal principle (defined as our best approach to what unifies and organizes the work as a whole) could be described as equivalent to the germinal principle as developed—into a fictional world (by the principles of invention and evaluation), in a narrative embodying that fictional world (developed by the principles of presentation), in a text materializing that narrative (developed by the principles of style). (The developing principles in this description have all been limited but not defined by the primary terms of the germinal principle.) We have not yet explained how these elements are organized, however. The determinant is that part of the germinal principle which I have called the subject—most narrowly, in its aspect of "process." The *organization* (of the formal principle, as of the work itself) is, specifically, a development of the subject.

The principles of construction, organizing the other contributing principles, develop the subject into the fictional world and hence the narrative. As the subject orders world and narrative, so in a sense it is prior to them and, in combination with the contributing principles, creates them. By "development of the subject" I mean, of course, the high specification of each of its components in the work.

Thus the word "Isabel" becomes the complex character. The "naivete" and "full maturity" become complexly specified conditions. The most important term of all is "growth," which as expanded becomes the whole action of the novel, with its divisions into stages and episodes, primary parts and contributory parts, and so on. The interest, which is the implied approval in the term "growth," becomes the enormously complex attitude, judgment, or effect which the novel seems to show toward the action.

Since the fully developed subject itself resembles what some critics have called *plot*, let me so designate it here: the plot is the

fully developed subject. It displays the organizing or integrative power of the subject in all the details of the work. How does this plot relate to the other major givens—the fictional world, the narrative? Simply stated, the narrative depicts the plot, makes it visible by narrative principles initially independent of the plot. The fictional world provides the surroundings, the circumstances, the conditions within which the plot develops. So we say, but soon we discover that if the novel is indeed the integrated thing we are supposing, the fictional world will disappear and become thoroughly absorbed by the plot. Of course, it is often convenient to speak of the fictional word as if it were an independent and given body of principles—and so, in relation to the abstracted germ, it actually is—but as soon as we have seen how the plot is developed, we cease to find the fictional world independent. Its coherence is explained by that of the plot, its problems are those of the plot, and its population contains nothing that is not specified or required by the plot. The fictional world is, essentially, a specification of the agent and action in the subject.

In a similar way, the narrative, too, is "absorbed" into the plot. The narrative proper—the text—is determined by the plot in combination with the given principles of narration *and* style. In relation to the abstracted germ, these, too, are independent; nothing in the subject, for instance, requires that dramatic scenes be used for moments of high confrontation. If such a use of scenes becomes a principle, however, it follows that certain moments in the plot will be so presented. The interaction between narrative and plot principles can be observed in many ways: the use of a ficelle is, as we saw earlier, a dramatizing, hence representational, device: it produces Henrietta, who then takes a fairly substantial position in the plot. The great fireside vigil that James himself considered "the best thing in the book" is certainly a significant episode in discovery for Isabel, a major point in the plot; yet its nature has been determined to a considerable degree by James's discovery of a method of inner dramatizing.[5] In matters like these, one might say that the development of the plot from the subject is influenced by principles of narrative, but it

[5] James, "Preface to 'The Portrait,'" p. 57.

seems more accurate to absorb those principles themselves into the constructional principles of the plot, which is to say that the presentation itself has become part of the subject, part of the plot. In the same way, to the extent that the narrator's personality itself becomes an "independent attraction" outside the fictional world,[6] an adequate accounting of the plot should include that independent attraction—not by trying to force it to function in the given plot but by revising the conception of the plot so as to find its place in it.[7] (On the other hand, the modern idea that the narrative generates the plot entire is, as far as I can understand it, a theory about how texts are brought into being, not about what integrates them. How it works I do not know.)

Let us now recapitulate the chief formal entities that I have been considering:

The *artistic form* is the visible form of the work itself as a whole. It is the unanalyzable organic wholeness of the work.

The *formal principle* is the imaginable but enormously complex best abstraction that can be made to describe the artistic form. I called it, above, "the simplest such form capable of accounting (most powerfully) for the location of the parts of the text."

The *germinal principle* is whatever we place at the top of the hierarchy of the formal principle. It is the simplest (most abstract) definition that can be given to the specific, individualized material that is unified in the work. It specifies not only a subject but also the primary commitments governing the composition and evaluation of the fictional world, the narrative, and the language.

The *subject* is that part of the germinal principle, constituting a unity, to which the other parts are subordinate. It is divisible into topic, process, and interest.

Notice that each of the above entities is an abstraction from the one before. Now, when they are developed in the novel, they give rise to the following aspects of the formal principle, which are also formal entities:

The *plot* is the full development of the subject by the applica-

---

[6]See Booth's treatment of the narrator of *Emma* in *The Rhetoric of Fiction*.
[7]Most likely by incorporating some phrase like "as seen by" in the germinal formulation of the subject.

tion of principles of construction, invention, and evaluation to it. It expresses the integrative power of the formal principle by manifesting (in the work) whatever is dominant in the hierarchy.

The *narrative* is the embodiment of the plot in words. It is formed by the application of the principles of presentation and style to the plot.

The *fictional world* is the material of the plot considered without regard to how it is organized by the plot. In relation to the germinal subject it may be considered as independent, as setting for that subject, but in relation to the fully developed plot it disappears and has no separate existence.

Finally, contributing to the development of these various formal entities are the compositional principles. The principles of *style* govern the use of language in vocabulary and sentences, and the adaptation of this to whoever is conceived as speaker or narrator. The principles of *presentation* govern the "manner of imitation"—how the words, of speaker or narrator, relate to the fiction. The principles of *invention* provide the materials of which the fictional world is built; they govern the references in the text: all appropriations by the text of ostensibly "nonliterary" types outside the text (whether these are regarded as coming from some "reality" or as stereotypes and conventional ideas). The principles of *evaluation* provide the standards, of whatever kind, by which the materials of the fictional world are judged, ethically and emotionally. The principles of *construction* govern the organization of the contributions and other operations of the other compositional principles, so as to create a form.

We may note several corollaries. The narration is of course the text itself. The artistic form is that text seen as an emerging visible form. The formal principle is an abstraction of the visibility of that text, formed by combining the plot with the principles of presentation and style.

Certain features of the foregoing analysis need to be clarified. It should be noted, first, that my model of formal relationships is itself an abstract, fictional construction, simply a provisional set of standards against which to measure the questions we ask when analyzing unity. The model appears to be based upon the traditional novel—the kind of novel, mimetic, in which language

is used to represent characters and action in a coherent fictional world, the kind of novel with a "plot." Yet the description I have given suggests the model's flexibility. There is no requirement, for instance, that the plot be of the traditional sort, that it have a protagonist or show an action in a fictional world. Nor does my model insist that the fictional world be coherent or that materials from it be the dominant element in the subject. The fiction is not even prohibited from shaping itself to look like a fragment of some sort—for as we have seen, an imitation of a fragment can be a whole as readily as any other, once we have recognized it for that.

We may similarly regard multiplicity of meanings in the text. Every good reader delights, even revels, in multiplicity—resonance, echo, reflection, suggestion, depth, ambiguity, sparkle, wit. Such effects are in no way antagonistic to the abstract unity pictured in my model. Multiple meanings in a novel will be either fragmentary (flashes of ambiguity in many directions as the text proceeds) or sustained (multiple levels of coherent meaning continued throughout). A full account of the form must take stock of these multiplicities, for they are part of that form. The model challenges us to find a context of unity for them, as a qualification either of the details, if fragmentary (ambiguities of substance or of interest), or, if sustained prominently enough, of the subject itself. The simplest kind of multiplicity is doubleness which, sustained, will give us an allegory or other developed metaphor. Our analysis of subject and plot should indicate this sort of multiplicity or any other.

It is true that the model ignores the process by which we approach awareness of the form—the process which, as I have stressed, is more important to our pleasure than the fully visible form itself. The model describes only the perception that we are trying to achieve. In practice our model will always be, as I have noted, hypothetical and incomplete but nevertheless indispensable, since the process itself can only be understood in terms of its destination.

Finally, it may be objected that the formal principle is a circular concept: the germinal principle is derived from our perception of the plot, and the plot is developed from the germinal principle. Perhaps to break into such a chain we may use a kind

of oscillating, or dialectical, process. No doubt the process of grasping the formal principle is comparable to the act of contemplating a picture; to see both the basic design and the detail, the viewer must stand both as far back as possible, squinting, and as close as possible. Our perception of the formal principle also requires both vantage points; hence the proper way to abstract it will be to test it hierarchically by dialectic, that is, to move back from the picture—while moving toward it.

LOOSENESS, DISUNITY, AND BANALITY

Our model, intended to describe unity, therefore assumes a perfectly unified and integrated novel. But what if the work is not as tightly integrated as my working example, *The Portrait of a Lady?* As I hope this discussion will make clear, most of the works we are likely to encounter are better unified than they may seem at first, for the formal convention is strong, and apparent lack of unity is often merely a failure on our parts to recognize some unfamiliar possibility.[8]

We must consider, however, the question of degrees of unity. Unity would appear to be a concept not subject to comparison: a thing is one or it is not. Most people would agree, however, that *The Portrait of a Lady* is a strongly unified work, more so than, say, a picaresque novel. The very expression "strongly unified" admits the possibility of "weakly unified." Common experience confirms this—not simply the observable differences between novels compact and novels loose but the everyday practice of novelists as they revise to "tighten up" their work. Some works are indeed more tightly unified than others—in the sense not of "being one" but of being "bound together into one," or "integrated."

The formal principle of a tight work differs from that of a loose one essentially in having a determined rather than an arbi-

---

[8]William H. Gass takes a somewhat different view of this matter: "Since no work can exhibit a conformity to principle so complete each word is, in its place and time, inevitable and predictable, all fictional worlds contain at least an element of chance, and some, of course, a very high degree of it. It is merely a critical prejudice that requires from fiction a rigidly determined order" (*Fiction and the Figures of Life* [Boston, 1971], p.22).

trary form. An arbitrary abstract form allows variation in the disposition of parts in its embodiments: for example, the exact arrangement of branches in a particular elm tree is arbitrary within the limits of the general form "elm tree"; so, too, the concept "a sequence of adventures" does not specify what those adventures shall be. Of two works, the tighter exerts a more specific control over all the parts. It determines—within narrower limits—not what the details may be but what they *must* be.[9]

In a collection of stories showing a general thematic or emotional progression (*Winesburg, Dubliners, In Our Time*), unity is provided by the society, or by certain recurring characters and problems, but the tight sequential unity of the novel is not present. Each of the individual stories in *Winesburg* is a tightly unified whole, but though we find a rich common ground between them as a group, and though we also detect a rough progression or change between beginning and end, I doubt that a detailed justification of the order in which the stories are arranged is possible. It is still less likely that the internal construction of the stories could be referred to any principle in the book as a whole more specific than the rule that the stories should be complete and developed in themselves. If someone proves me wrong, then I have insufficiently seen *Winesburg,* but my mistake does not weaken the theoretical point that looseness is the presence of prominent arbitrary elements (which themselves may be strongly developed, strongly determined internally) under the cover of a relatively unspecifying "formal principle."

I would not limit "looseness" to any particular level in the formal hierarchy. Any element of the formal principle, at any level of abstraction, may prescribe its parts with greater or less control. The test of tightness is the perception that a part is superior in its place to any conceivable alternative. In tight

---

[9]More fully stated in the terms I have defined: the inevitability (predictability) of the artistic form, which is itself a concrete form, comes from the various abstract forms that compose it—as I have been showing throughout this chapter. To the extent that these abstract forms are arbitrary in the sense defined here and in chapter 2, the artistic form is also arbitrary or "loose." As with any arbitrary concrete form, its parts, insofar as they are arbitrary, can be recognized only by observation. They do appear, however, to be parts of the artistic form—not true in the case of disunity.

forms, the integration of parts is greater because of the greater number of strong abstract forms that gather to predict them; we can offer more reasons for the presence and location of the parts. In the loose work we are more aware of the possibilities that have not been selected by the artist. By this definition, tightness of form and economy of the whole are identical qualities.

My pleasure in reading *Dubliners, In Our Time,* or *Winesburg* from beginning to end proves that looseness is not a serious fault, if it is a fault at all. It does not follow, however, that formal unity is not an important value. In these short story collections, although the controlling principle of the whole is loose, the individual stories are well-crafted, tightly unified works. Though disregarding tightness overall, the authors have produced it within the stories themselves. Still, not all the stories are equally compelling. In *Winesburg,* the story "Tandy," for instance, strikes me as inferior to the others: "vague," "fuzzy," straining for an unrealized effect. The feeling expressed by the characters and implied by the narrator is not validated by concrete conditions; I call it sentimental. Or I could call it a failure to make a form progress toward visibility—progress as I would like or as I am accustomed to expect or as I think this story, in its context, invites me to expect. This seeming nonprogression is a failure of form and, in the case of "Tandy," obviously, damaging.

So a distinction can be drawn between two kinds of formal weakness: between *looseness* on the one hand and *disunity* on the other. I will define looseness as the presence of arbitrary particulars within limits predicted by the formal principle: the particulars themselves may be internally highly determined and visible. Virtually all works of any magnitude and complexity must be loose to some extent, and looseness may be easily compensated for, justified, even necessitated by other powers in the work. The term is relative, useful for making comparisons, and by no means necessarily pejorative. *Disunity* is the presence of parts that cannot be accounted for, that are not justified by any perceptible formal principle. Their connection to the germinal principle is not made clear (this is the case in "Tandy") or, if the disunity is considerable, a single germinal principle may not be discoverable.

Sometimes it may be difficult to distinguish looseness from disunity. In a work that is merely loose, the looseness will not obscure the visibility of the parts. Disunity, on the other hand, will seem to do so. When the obscurity or opacity in a work of art refuses to be penetrated (by the qualified reader),[10] that is a sign of disunity. So, too, when a discrepancy or disharmony between parts refuses to be resolved. And when parts seem to ask to be embodied in some other more developed form—in other words, works that seem genuinely fragmentary—that, too, is a sign of disunity. For disunity is simply the failure of the artistic form to become visible or to promise to do so. If the aim and measure of art is to make forms visible, then disunity is the primary artistic failure.

This brings us, to be sure, into apparent conflict with those for whom disunity is, on the contrary, the most desirable artistic or poetic virtue. Here is the attack on the very concept of wholeness which I noted at the outset. There is Barthes in *S/Z* with his "writerly text," Robbe-Grillet with the irreconcilable contradictions placed in his novels, Culler with the "strangeness" of the text (valued for resisting naturalization or recuperation for as long as possible); there are the deconstructionists, denying stable meaning of any kind. Our difference with the latter depends on a different order of assumptions, not to be addressed here, but our difference with the others is to some extent a question only of the meaning of our terms. It is well to remember that Barthes's "writerly text" with its postulated "unlimited plural" is "not a thing, we would have a hard time finding it in a bookstore." It does not exist except in the head of the writer who is actually at work. The text we read, the "readerly"—which is to say any—text has its "parsimonious plural," and as soon as this parsimoniousness is conceded, our common ground appears. So, too, the

---

[10]Some readers can resolve any disunity into unity—just as some contemporaries can find disunity in anything. Again we see how the form of a work depends on what the reader sees there and how it is subject to constant revision in our eyes. Whether I accept some critic's overingenious account of a work's unity depends on whether he can persuade me to see the same work he does. Whence the hypothetical nature of every analysis of form. The "qualified reader" in this statement is the reader who has what Jonathan Culler calls "literary competence": a proper knowledge of the conventions of the work in question and of the work's own implied audience.

"strangeness" of the text resists the naturalizing tendency in a losing battle, and contradiction in Robbe-Grillet encounters the most powerful efforts of the reader to resolve it. In all these cases, the so-called desirable disunity struggles to maintain itself against the overpowering force of the convention of unity, nor can it even be perceived except under the glass of that convention.

The so-called disunity, or discontinuity, which these writers value is thus the equivalent not of the artistic failure which I have here called disunity but of that *delay* in the progress toward the perception of a form which I too have called essential to the artistic effect. Our pleasure is in the progress toward visibility; we seldom do perceive the fully visible form in an interesting work. In a work of genuine interest, the obscurity, the opacity, the disharmony, the fragmentation that looks like disunity, are a reflection more likely of the incompleteness of our own perception before we have progressed far toward the form than they are of genuine disunity. We do not judge it as disunity as long as we are making progress—in fact, the contrary is the case. Even the deliberately constructed contradictions may yield ultimately to a unity of contradictions (consider, for example, Robert Coover's short story "The Baby Sitter," constructed of contradictions). The sign of disunity (in the sense in which I use the word here) is the frustration and loss of interest we feel when such progress ceases, when parts continue to refuse to "make sense" by any discoverable principle. If this happens, the fault may of course be our own—we don't recognize the conventions—but it may be a real obstacle in the work. The wise critic may never be certain, but experience and knowledge should be a pretty good guide most of the time.

The most obvious place to expect real disunity (least likely, anyway, to provoke an argument) is in the works of amateurs and novices—also in first drafts by writers who revise a lot. Published works that have attracted some audience (in any art) are less likely to display flagrant disunity, since even a small acceptance implies that some sort of form has been made visible. Often, though, we meet subtler kinds of disunity, which we describe as "dullness," "monotony," "slickness" (that is to say, lack of depth, which is lack of development), or "sentimentality" (lack

of emotional validation, which is lack of development, as in "Tandy").

Disunity is the prime formal fault, but there is a related fault of form, to which the same terms are often applied, when full visibility is achieved too easily and quickly: further progress stops because there is nothing more to be seen. This *banality of form* (the form has been exhausted) is likely to irritate us as triteness and clichés do—in fact, clichés are banal verbal forms. Like all formal qualities, banality depends for its perception upon the reader's experience. Banality is a secondary formal fault that, like a disease, may eventually overtake all but the greatest works. Neither disunity nor banality should be confused with looseness, which is innocuous.

[6]

The Plot

The key to the study of the formal principle is the study of the *plot*, if we understand this term as I have defined it. So understood, it is the nearest thing to a ruling principle in the formal hierarchy, a "form of the form." The other elements (the narration and style) are subordinated—given principles whose specific application is determined (in theory) by the demands of the plot. We must consider how, in the theoretical construction I have been developing, it may be composed and expected to function. Plot: "the *subject* as developed by the principles of construction" —but our definition needs to be made more specific.

MODELS FOR PLOT

It will be useful to note at the outset, briefly, the two familiar ways in which "plot" may be understood by critics. First are conceptions of plot as an abstraction shared by numbers of works, seen whenever we hear someone say that two works "have the same plot" or that one work treats a certain plot comically, whereas another treats *that same plot* tragically, or that a motion picture takes its plot from a novel. Plot is usually so regarded by modern structuralists. In Propp's celebrated study of Russian fairy tales, for instance, which seeks the common elements of their common plot, it is so conceived. Similarly, Northrop Frye reduces his "mythoi" into four great archetypal patterns. The case is the same with the plots dealt with in most attempts to define plot types (as distinct from categories for the various

components of which plots may be composed, which is another matter). Seymour Chatman (for whom "plot, story-as-discoursed, exists at a more general level than any particular objectification, any given movie, novel, or whatever") sums up the difficulties of trying to compose such typologies in his attempt to analyze fiction by structuralist principles:

> [T]he characterization of plot into macrostructures and typologies depends upon an understanding of cultural codes and their interplay with literary and artistic codes and codes of ordinary life.... It is clear that the categorization of plot-types is the most problematic area of narrative studies and may well have to wait until we have a number of in-depth analyses like *S/Z* and access to a general semiotics of culture.[1]

As I noted in chapter 1, plot so conceived would be an element in a simple, as opposed to compound, hierarchy. It is not likely to tell us much about the formal principle of a work, nor does it in any way resemble what I called plot in the previous chapter.

The second category includes all conceptions in which plot is considered as unique to each particular work. A familiar and simple example is E. M. Forster's idea that plot is the sequence of events in a novel conceived as causally connected. "The king died and then the queen died" is not a plot, but "the king died and then the queen died of grief" is one.[2] In this view, however, though plot is individualized, it is but one ingredient among many—a contributor to the unity of the work, perhaps, but not by any means necessarily the dominant one. So it, too, falls short of what I have called the plot in my model of the formal principle.

The closest approach to plot in this model is the concept offered by the neo-Aristotelian critics, most notably and explicitly by Crane, Olson, and Norman Friedman, but also implicitly by Sheldon Sacks, Wayne Booth, and David Richter—not to speak of Aristotle himself. These critics are distinctive in claiming that either plot is itself the forming principle of the work (novel,

---

[1]Seymour Chatman, *Story and Discourse: Narrative Structure in Fiction and Film* (Ithaca, 1978), pp. 43, 95.

[2]E. M. Forster, *Aspects of the Novel* (New York, 1927), p. 130.

play) or it dominates the forming principles (form of the form). It thus has a status in the formal hierarchy similar to that which I have given it in the previous chapter.

To be sure, these critics differ from each other in many particulars. The ground they share is more significant than their differences, however, and a composite description can be reconstructed. This composite, though it differs in some ways from my idea of plot, provides a useful opening into it. The main points are the following:

1. As conceived by the neo-Aristotelian critics, plot is the "organizing," "synthesizing," or "controlling" principle in a work of fiction, providing only that the work is not "didactic" (an exclusion made by some but not all these critics) and is (since it is not clear what all these writers might say about short fictions, poems, and the like) a work of some length and complexity.

2. The plot is a pattern, shape, arrangement, or ordering of materials in the fictional world, that is, of action, character, and thought: a "synthesis . . . of action, character, and thought,"[3] "change . . . in fortune, character, or thought,"[4] "system of actions,"[5] "unstable relationships . . . complicated . . . until the complication is finally resolved."[6] It is thus distinguished from the "representation," which may reorganize its materials for exhibitional purposes, but the plot itself finds its organization in the fictional world rather than in the text or the presentation.[7]

3. The most important property of a plot is its specific "effect," its "working or power," its "power to affect us." This point is emphasized by all those critics. The effect is attributed in all cases to certain qualities in the action and characters which it is the duty of the representation to bring out: they are "morally

---

[3]R. S. Crane, "The Concept of Plot and the Plot of *Tom Jones*," in *Critics and Criticism*, ed. Crane (Chicago, 1952), p. 620.

[4]Norman Friedman, *Form and Meaning in Fiction* (Athens, Ga., 1975), p. 82.

[5]Elder Olson, *Tragedy and the Theory of Drama* (Detroit, 1961), p. 37.

[6]Sheldon Sacks, *Fiction and the Shape of Belief* (Berkeley, 1967), p. 26.

[7]For example, a plot may be described as a sequence of events moving from A to Z. The placing in the text of certain events prior to A chronologically and necessary to our understanding of A will be a matter of "representation" rather than of "plot construction" (whether to present such events in the beginning or later in a flashback).

determinate,"[8] the action involves characters "about whose fates
we are made to care."[9] Here is the most obvious difference between this conception of plot and less integrated ones: the moral
and emotional aspect of the events is itself a part, a qualifier or
modifier in the definition of a specific plot. The events in a
tragedy are not merely a loss of fortune for the protagonist but a
"pitiful and terrible" loss of fortune.

The critics I have named also make a fundamental distinction
between "mimetic" and "didactic" works of fiction. A didactic
work subordinates the fictional component (characters, action)
to a thesis or argument. In a mimetic work the fiction is dominant: the work "imitates" character, action, or thought. The distinction appears to be exhaustive; the neo-Aristotelian critic
usually equates what I have been calling "self-contained" art with
"mimetic" art. For some of these critics, only mimetic novels
have plots; in didactic novels—functional, persuasive, instruc-
tive, satirical—a different kind of formal principle will control.
Others allow for both didactic and mimetic plots. Beyond this
first distinction, these critics offer a variety of ways of distinguishing among kinds of plots.[10]

The question now concerns the degree to which this composite Aristotelian conception of plot corresponds to the model I
have described. First, though my model retains the Aristotelian
distinction between representation and plot, the Aristotelian
specification that plot finds its organization in the materials of
the fictional world is not necessarily implied in the model, much

[8]Olson, *Tragedy and the Theory of Drama*, p. 38.
[9]Sacks, *Fiction and the Shape of Belief*, p. 26.
[10]Thus Crane divides plots into those of action, character, and thought ("The
Concept of Plot," p. 620). Olson divides them in several ways, according to
magnitude into closed situations, scenes, episodes, and grand plots; according to
unifying principle into the consequential plot, the descriptive plot, the pattern
plot, and the didactic plot ("An Outline of Poetic Theory," in *Critics and Criticism*,
ed. R. S. Crane [Chicago, 1952], p. 560, and *Tragedy*, p. 47). Sacks, dealing with
fiction, besides distinguishing the novel from two kinds of didactic organizations
divides novel plots into three kinds—the tragic, the comic, and the serious (*Fiction and the Shape of Belief*, pp. 21–26). Friedman, also dealing with fiction, adds
the static plot to Crane's three kinds and develops the latter into the most elaborate classification of all (*Form and Meaning in Fiction*, pp. 79–101).

less that these materials are divided necessarily into the categories of action, character, and thought. These specifications may very well apply to what we have been calling the traditional novel, but there is nothing in my development of the formal principle and plot in the formal principle that requires that they always be such.

Second, the model by no means requires that there be a basic and exhaustive two-part distinction between mimetic plots and didactic forms—whether the latter are called plots also or something else. Such a distinction can usefully be drawn between many kinds of traditional novels, but as will be seen below, it far from covers the field of possibilities in the model.

Third, the model does not immediately or obviously, at any rate, confirm the Aristotelian emphasis on the importance of the specific "effect," the "working or power," as the necessary first principle of plot. To be sure, I took some care not to overlook the element of "value" in my reconstruction of the germinal subject—but that this necessarily leads to a concept of effect comparable to Aristotle's "catharsis of pity and fear," with its seemingly kinetic conception of art, does not seem to follow from my inquiry.[11]

Apart from such limitations as these, however, the neo-Aristotelian composite does seem to be a helpful guide into the structure of the principles we are now trying to define.

---

[11]A fourth problem I have omitted from my summary of the Aristotelian composite. This is the occasional appearance, particularly in the early writings, of the concept of "ornamentation," which is anathema to most critics who care about formal unity because it implies less than full integration. The implication is that parts pleasing but trivial can be detached and removed with no great loss of essential aesthetic interest—whereas "organic unity" means that nothing can be displaced without damaging the whole. I am convinced, to be sure, that when Crane and Olson speak of ornamentation, they ordinarily do not intend the word's unfortunate implications: the infelicity arises merely from the great difficulties we confront in describing the relationships in a compound hierarchy. Yet sometimes in practical criticism the ornamental conception also appears, as when Crane remarks in his analysis of the plot of *Tom Jones:* "[T]here are many strokes in the representation of Partridge, for instance, which no one would wish away, yet which are bound to seem gratuitous when considered merely in the light of his somewhat minor role in the evolution of the comic action" ("The Concept of Plot," p. 645).

The Plot

As the central element in the formal principle, which the other elements exist to materialize, the plot enables the formal principle to justify the parts in their location in the whole. Plot's ability to do so may be tested if we break down its function into separable aspects. A given plot is the primary principle of unity, of exclusion, of organization, of coherence, and of emphasis in a work. For any novel that is not disunified, a proposed plot hypothesis is adequate if it is able, in combination with the principles of presentation and style, implicitly or explicitly, to account for all these aspects.

As a crude illustration, consider a possible hypothesis for the plot of Conrad's *Heart of Darkness*—a novella rather than a novel, which I have chosen for the sake of simplicity and which I have no doubt simplified still more. Let us suppose the plot to be the *process* by which Marlow the protagonist discovers, with horror (or dread), the "precariousness" of civilization.[12] This discovery develops through concrete manifestations, Marlow's observations and feelings during his journey into the heart of Africa, and it culminates in his encounter with Kurtz, the revelation of the latter's perversions, the terrible emptiness behind his great talents, his high regard, and his great power over people. Such a hypothesis *unifies* the story: the early events, for instance, appear as part of the process preparing Marlow emotionally and intellectually for his discovery; the last European scenes, including the one with the Intended, give it its final focus; the frame narrative at the beginning, by associating the early Britons with the African savages, enlarges our understanding of what the experience means to Marlow. Again, the hypothesis *excludes* what is not in the story: it provides the reason why, for instance, there is no further development of Kurtz's relationship with his Intended, nor of his childhood, nor his parents: because Marlow, not Kurtz, is protagonist, and Kurtz counts only for his very particular meaning to Marlow. Again, the hypothesis *organizes*

---

[12]This phrase was applied to Marlow's discovery by R. S. Crane in an informal discussion, many years ago.

the story. It arranges the chronology of Marlow's discovery to correspond to the steps of his journey, moving gradually toward Kurtz, his death, and the final display (after Marlow's return) of the Europeans' failure to recognize what Marlow has seen through Kurtz. The hypothesis, in combination with the "principles of presentation" (narrative, leaving much to inference), also accounts for the departures from chronology, both that of the frame narrative, whose function I have already suggested, and those in Marlow's own narrative—which serve to draw out, intensify, and further define Marlow's shock in his discovery of Kurtz. The hypothesis also accounts for the story's *coherence:* the process of discovery, the chronology of the journey, the expectations of portentousness and elusive significance ("to [Marlow] the meaning of an episode was not inside like a kernel but outside, enveloping the tale which brought it out only as a glow brings out a haze"[13]) established early to prepare the effect of the later parts. And of course, the hypothesis explains the *emphasis* in the story: why Kurtz receives more attention, for instance, than does the accountant or the Russian adventurer or the Intended, all of whom are foils, contrasts, victims, or illuminators in other ways of that perversion of power and rejection of civilized constraint which Marlow finds so disturbing in Kurtz.

KINDS OF PLOT SUBJECTS

Certain important distinctions between plots will help us, not to establish "types," but to clarify the conception itself.

The first distinction relates to kinds of plot subjects. In our working example in chapter 5 the germinal subject was "Isabel's growth from naivete to maturity." This subject was a development of the abstract design principle, "a change of character," which in turn was an application of the idea of singleness to the concepts of change and of character. The latter concept ("character") implies a potential fictional world as its source and setting; thus the germ postulates the idea of a *fictional world;* the subject is "based on" such an idea.

---

[13]Joseph Conrad, *Heart of Darkness* (New York, 1971), p. 5.

The Plot

The primary function of traditional fiction is normally to depict characters and action. Still, there is no requirement that this be true in all novels. We know from our definition that the germinal principle of a novel must include some provision for fictional materials. It must also, as we have seen, provide for the development of narrative and style (since the novel always exists in language), and it must include some indication of value or significance. The theory requires that the germinal principle of a novel include these elements but not that the subject be "based" in this sense on the fictional materials. The Aristotelian discrimination of didactic fiction implies a different kind of subject, and the experiments of contemporary novelists suggest still other possibilities. Why can't any of the primary elements in the germinal principle be the basis for a subject of some kind?

We can imagine at least five radically different kinds of subjects according broadly to different kinds of possible design principles. These would give rise to five different kinds of plots (although all five have not necessarily been used for actual novels).

1. *Mimetic* plots. The subject is based on an "ordinary" abstract imitated form—that is, fictional materials implying a fictional world, describable by reference to action, character, thought, or other comparable terms. This is the usual kind of plot in traditional novels, and to it the term *plot* itself, even in the Aristotelian critics, is usually limited.

2. *Rhetorical* plots. The early neo-Aristotelian critics used the term *didactic*. Sheldon Sacks abandoned that term and replaced it with two, mutually exclusive: *apologue* and *satire*. Later, David Richter substituted the general term *rhetorical novel*,[14] which I shall use here because it is a little more graceful and lacks the negative connotations that seem to cluster around "didactic." Rhetorical plots could be described in either of two ways. Simply, the subject and hence the whole are adapted to some definite end outside the work itself: the art is functional or kinetic, like propaganda. Most good rhetorical novels, however, are appreciated not for their usefulness but for their art. Artistically

---

[14]Sacks, *Fiction and the Shape of Belief.* David H. Richter, *Fable's End: Completeness and Closure in Rhetorical Fiction* (Chicago, 1974).

speaking, a rhetorical plot is one whose subject is "based on" the element of "interest" or "evaluation"—that is to say, a primary development of the principles of evaluation as such. The fiction itself is subordinated to some more general or external value—which it not simply possesses, as in mimetic fiction, but by which it is controlled. The plot therefore is most economically analyzed as a process of either persuasion (argument) or ridicule.

The three remaining possibilities are less obvious and demand greater explanation.

3. *Creative* plots. I call a plot creative when the subject is based upon principles of construction that call attention to themselves. The fictional world, which in mimetic fiction is brought into being by the principles of construction, is here instead subordinated to those principles. Usually (but not necessarily) something is made to interfere with our apprehension of the fictional world as a fully functioning coherent whole, and in this way our attention is directed to the construction itself. The result is emphasis on the *creation* of fiction: the subject could be described in general *as* that creation, seen, however, not as taking place within an already created fictional world (this would simply be another kind of mimetic plot, for example, one about a novelist) but as creating whatever fictional world the novel may have. With such an emphasis, the motivation of this creation is likely to acquire more significance than it would otherwise and the whole process will tend to acquire symbolic significance—symbolic in a way and to a degree unusual in other fiction.

Creative plots ordinarily make use of what I have called expressive or narrator-controlled fictional worlds. (See chapter 4 as well as the discussion of *Pale Fire* in part 2.) There are many varieties. Besides such plots as those of *Absalom, Absalom!*, *At Swim-Two-Birds*, *The Universal Baseball Association*, and *Second Skin*, already mentioned, in which a character's acts of imagination create or alter his fictional world, there is, for example, a plot like that of Kafka's *The Trial*, developed according to a constant pattern that irrationally frustrates supposedly rational expectations. *The Metamorphosis*, on the other hand, develops a metaphor into a fiction. *La Jalousie* (by the author's own account) and "The Baby Sitter" base their plots upon the development of contradiction in their fictional worlds. Creative plots are increas-

ingly common in the present-day novel, but they are by no means new. There are prominent precursors, especially outside the novel in stories shaped (for instance) by their symbolic interconnections, such as "The Fall of the House of Usher." I believe, further, that many, perhaps most, allegories have creative plots, since their art can be better described by an analysis that focuses attention upon the correspondence of their two lines of action (a principle of construction) than by an attempt to explain them as didactic arguments. For similar reasons, a work organized as a parody would have a creative plot; *The Sot-Weed Factor* is a large-scale example. At this point, incidentally, we see the clear link between creative plots and the formal principles of many old and familiar short works, such as the kind of lyric poem whose organization is determined by the development of a metaphor or other conceit.

4. *Narrational* plots. I use this clumsy term to signify plots in which the subject is based upon principles of presentation or narration. The forming principle is the problem of "executing" a form—when this process is distinguished from the problem of "constructing" a form—which of course appears to be a contradiction in terms: a preexisting form when executed becomes a different form.

The composition of such a plot can be suggested by comparison of the novel with other arts. Technique, presentation, and execution constitute the formal principle preeminently in the so-called performing arts. Here what we perceive (the performance) is a collaboration between two artists, but from the performer's point of view the form created is a parasite upon another form (the score) already given: it is thus a form of execution.

Analogous in fiction would be a work in which the normal interest in a fictional world (characters, action) is so suppressed that primary attention is diverted to the manner in which that world is presented or seen. In the extreme case the fictional world (or story) would be offered as given, uninvented, predetermined, so as to throw all attention on the artistry by which it is displayed. Though this shift in focus is normal in particular tellings of folktales, for instance, it would seem to be virtually impossible in a work with the size and scope of a novel. Novels

that "retell" given stories which the reader is expected to recall invariably make new stories out of them (*The Once and Future King, Grendel*), and historical and autobiographical novels are always understood as fiction to just the extent that they are understood as *not* being history or autobiography. The contemporary phenomenon, the "nonfiction novel," does seem to express an impulse toward the extreme possibility of an uninvented fictional world: by calling it nonfiction the author renounces his claim to invention, and by describing it as a novel he renounces the claim of history to be judged as fact. The events and people are assumed to be given; the author's contribution is to "bring out" what is given by the skillful manipulation of narration. To be sure, for many readers the very topic chosen for such treatment—for example, Gary Gilmore—attracts such powerful attention to itself that the reader may neglect the narration as such, and the plot is likely to seem historical or rhetorical or truly mimetic, after all. Yet if the reader is able to apply the convention of the "nonfiction novel" to the act of reading—as the implied reader presumably does—the formal principle will be a narrational plot.

But though such plots are rare, two other kinds, although they do not dispense with an invented fictional world, do appear to subordinate it in some ruthless fashion to the special interests of the presentation and might also be called narrational plots. In one sort—much the more common and popular—everything is subordinated to the problem of penetrating to the fictional world through a severe restriction on the narrative point of view. The epitome of this type is the mystery or the detective story. The problem is concentrated in a puzzle which is created by a limitation on the narrator's point of view, and it is developed by the process of solving that puzzle—typically through the activity of the detective. It is "narrational" rather than mimetic because everything in the fictional world is subordinated to the mystery (murder, for instance, is denied seriousness), which itself would be quickly unraveled by a shift in the point of view (from that of the detective, for instance, to that of the murderer). The interest in such a plot tends to be circumstantial and intellectual: curiosity about the story that is concealed and its eventual satisfac-

tion.[15] Most variations on the old formula of the "pure" detective story will remove it from the category of the narrational plot. If the emphasis shifts from mystery to adventure, for instance, or if the problem itself is complicated psychologically, so that it ceases to depend merely on point of view, or if the puzzle or its solution is loaded with emotional or philosophical freight, or if the character of the detective becomes more important than the mystery, or if the detective's methods do—any of these developments will quickly return a potentially narrational plot to the realm of the mimetic.

The other prominent kind of narrational plot subordinates the fictional world and story to problems in the articulation of the narrative. The interest here lies not in restriction of the point of view but in the difficulty of finding words adequate to encompass all the narrator's presumed knowledge. In such a plot the personality of the narrator is likely to be important and again may threaten to turn the narrational plot into a mimetic (or

---

[15]Consider, among thousands of possibilities, Erle Stanley Gardner's *The Case of the Substitute Face* (1938). Perry Mason is hired to help a woman in a predicament caused by an embezzlement seemingly committed by her husband. The action begins on board ship; soon the husband is murdered and thrown overboard—or so it seems. Mason does not know (nor do we) who actually committed the embezzlement nor the murder; he does not even know that the initial murder itself was faked but was later followed by a real murder. His learning of these circumstances (and *our* learning after him) constitutes the plot—a process by which we overcome the limitations of the point of view. To keep our attention on this problem, the characters are all made simple, stereotypes. Thought and feeling, other than what is involved in detection, are minimal. Except for Mason himself and his loyal assistants, none of the characters is sympathetic enough to be ruled out as a possible suspect: if we desire during part of the story that Mrs. Moar (who hired Mason) be cleared, we do so not for her sake but because we do not want to be disappointed by a premature solution. The risks that Mason runs are slight, and the convention tells us not to worry about them. There is an interest in points of law (Mason is a lawyer and part of the unravelment takes place through courtroom procedure), but this concern remains secondary to the detective process. As a character Mason embodies the essential restriction on the point of view and acts as reader's guide. Toward the end, however, his calculations outstrip the reader's, and he learns things we don't know. Our subsequent knowledge comes through dialogue, as he produces information in the courtroom scene. The reader's point of view is then even more restricted than Mason's; it is limited to what Mason reveals in dialogue. The plot is the process of penetrating to the events which this restricted point of view has screened from us.

perhaps a creative) one. Such a plot is much rarer than the other
kind, but Sterne's *Tristram Shandy* is possibly one great example:
the interest relates to the constant interference in the narration
caused by the narrative self-consciousness. To be sure, this work
could be analyzed as having a mimetic disclosure plot of "character" (disclosure of the character of Tristram through his problems
in narration, or perhaps of a compound protagonist, his father and
his uncle Toby). But the extension of the process of obstruction,
delay, and digression, continuing to absorb our attention long
after our perception of character and situation has been completed (not to speak of the open-ended construction, the author's plan to keep adding volumes as long as he lived), seems to
make the narrational plot a stronger hypothesis.

  5. *Linguistic* plots. This possibility is no doubt most rare of all,
though it has been adumbrated effectively by William Gass.[16] In
a plot of this sort, not only the construction of a fictional world
but also the narrative interests are suppressed in order to focus
attention simply on the imperatives or pleasures of verbal utter-
ance. The language is "foregrounded," or "opaque"—in a stricter sense than that in which I have discussed the concept
above.[17] I mean not that the words are signs that refuse to disappear in the fictional world they depict (this much is true, I
have insisted, of all fiction) but that no fictional world at all can
appear through the screen of words. (Fictional materials do
exist, or we could not call the work fiction, but they function only
to make the words possible.) Flaubert imagined such a possibility
more than a hundred years ago: "a book about nothing, a book
dependent on nothing external, which would be held together
by the strength of its style . . . a book which would have almost no
subject, or at least in which the subject would be almost invisible,
if such a thing is possible."[18]

  The epitome, the easily understood type of a purely verbal
"form," might be a pun—word play, word game. The recognizable verbal forms are all small, at the level of the most minute

---

[16]William H. Gass, *Fiction and the Figures of Life* (Boston, 1971). Gass cites some
of the novels of Gertrude Stein as examples of the ideal he has in mind.

[17]See chapters 2 and 4.

[18]*The Selected Letters of Gustave Flaubert*, ed. and trans. Francis Steegmuller
(New York, 1953), pp. 127-28.

units that may constitute a novel: riddles, jokes, figures of speech. But what kind of verbal form can be expanded to the size of a novel's plot? I have spoken above of a plot which develops a metaphor—but this is a plot of construction, a creative plot. It is difficult to see how a verbal form can be expanded to the size of a plot and still remain a verbal form: in the very expansion other elements take over and dominate.

Yet here, too, one great possible case suggests itself: Joyce's *Finnegans Wake*. I name it hesitantly because my understanding of it is so limited. If it is interpreted as essentially a mimesis of a dream, or, for that matter, "a mighty allegory of the fall and resurrection of mankind . . . , compress[ing] all periods of history, all phases of individual and racial development, into a circular design, of which every part is beginning, middle, and end,"[19] its plot will not of course be linguistic. If, however (as my reading suggests), the ruling principle is in that aspect which forces us to stop at virtually every word, to explore the words and phrases for the sake of the display of verbal possibilities— the play of meanings, of verbal associations brought up—then the plot can properly be so described. Everything in the text seems to support this purpose—the devices of its linguistic convention (the combinings of words, the alterations of spellings, the use of rhythms, of familiar language forms, of literary echoes, of nursery rhymes, songs, proverbs, and many others) and the marked resistance of the fictional world to ordering according to conventional expectations. Unlike the traditional novel in which the words embody the fictional development or pattern, here the fiction, such as it is, makes possible the purely verbal patterns. That is, the "story" or "stories" one can dimly perceive through the book are merely a frame, an outer manifestation, a context whose purpose is to provide new and changing opportunities for display of verbal power, verbal invention, verbal reminiscence. Is this actually possible in a work the size and scope of *Finnegans Wake*? No doubt its linguistic convention (which is here the subject) includes a principle of extension, of renewal of cases without repeating. The linguistic plot is kept

---

[19]Joseph Campbell and Henry Morton Robinson, *A Skeleton Key to "Finnegans Wake"* (New York, 1961), p. 3.

from becoming mimetic or creative by the constant subversion of mimetic elements and the constant attention to the smallest detail of the language. The dominant effect arises from this constant attention.[20] A formal analysis would focus primarily on the principles governing the linguistic display; a description of sequential organization would only come after and would attempt, if possible, to relate the "story" aspects to the changing kinds of linguistic opportunities that they provide.

Apart from *Finnegans Wake,* the clearest examples of linguistic plot I can think of occur in very short forms—for example, the short series of parallel speeches each in the rhythm of the Lord's Prayer, which constitute the story "Glossolalia" in John Barth's *Lost in the Funhouse* or a story such as "Sentence" by Donald Barthelme, composed entirely of a long unfinished sentence developing through strings of subordination—a process in which interest in the extension of the sentence exceeds interest in anything the sentence might be "about."

The question arises: can these different kinds of plots be combined? Do they grade into each other, or are they mutually exclusive kinds? It should be clearly understood in the first place that each of my five categories is derived from an element that is present in the germinal principles of all novels. Hence every "mimetic" novel will have its rhetorical, creative, narrational, and linguistic dimensions, just as every novel in one of the other categories will have the other dimensions, too. My categories define only the central aspect, what comes first.

Certainly some prominent modern novels seem clearly intended—whether or not they succeed—to combine some of these functions equally: *The Grapes of Wrath, Darkness at Noon, 1984.* These works all develop character and action richly, like mimetic novels, while at the same time making a distinct political

---

[20]Does this attention to detail violate our original definition of the novel as a work with a formal principle of large magnitude, the whole greater than the sum of the parts—and thereby render the linguistic plot and the novel mutually incompatible? No, for a distinction is possible between a work which focuses great attention upon the parts, though the whole is tightly integrated, and a work in which the parts have a greater integrity than the whole, as when the plot is episodic. A poem, for example, gives great attention to the details without in any way undermining the integrity of the whole.

or social point, like rhetorical novels. In the face of such works the question "Is it rhetorical *or* mimetic *or* creative?" sounds like semantic monkey business, pedantry. We might conclude that we should join Frye and the structuralists in saying that all works combine these elements, either as coequal aspects or in some scheme of "levels."

Yet we must not do so. Not in theory, not if we are concerned with discovering the nature of the distinctive integrating principle. In theory the kinds of subjects indicated in my five categories are incompatible, for each insists on the subordination of the components that the others would make primary. A mimetic plot is distinguishable from a rhetorical one because its element of mimetic development is clearer, more coherent, than its organization as an argument: the latter is, relatively speaking, diffuse; it provides a poorer, weaker explanation of the inclusion, exclusion, organization, coherence of elements. In a rhetorical plot the reverse is true: the mimetic elements may "hang together," but the story they form lacks the compelling explanatory force it would acquire when seen as the exemplum of a thesis or as the embodiment of an argument or a dialectic. So, too, a creative plot depends on the negation of the coherence of both the mimetic and rhetorical elements relative to the coherence of the constructional element. The same is true, in their own terms, of the narrational and linguistic plots.

If a work does indeed achieve a truly equal mimetic and rhetorical development—harmoniously, in a unity—and joins both elements together for our attention, then the central artistic achievement will be in that uniting itself: an allegory, itself a distinguishable kind of plot, essentially creative. An equal uniting of any of the other kinds seems to me impossible to conceive, since they all by definition depend on the underdevelopment of the other components.

THE ANALYSIS OF SUBJECT

The most important questions in the analysis of a specific plot concern its "subject." In my original definition I divided the germinal subject into three parts: the topic, the process, and the interest (to the implied reader). Let us consider briefly, then,

how these elements, the key to a plot analysis, might be developed in each of the five categories.

Kinds of Topics. In the case of mimetic plots, we speak of the "topic" (the "agent") as the *protagonist,* for us, simply the center of attention in the fictional world, whatever that may be. The protagonist is whatever the process of the plot concerns—often considered as an entity subject to change but not as the change itself. The protagonist is surrounded by a *milieu,* which consists of everything in the fictional world that is not the protagonist.

We usually think of the protagonist as a person, a character: Isabel Archer, Emma Bovary, Raskolnikov, Jake Barnes. The other characters make up the milieu and exist subordinately, contributory parts of the protagonist's story: Gilbert Osmond, Charles Bovary, Sonia, Brett Ashley. There is no law that the protagonist must be a single character, however, and indeed many novels have what I call a *compound,* or composite, protagonist. In such novels the center of attention is a group of some kind that is more important than any individual; the process involves the group, and in the analysis of the plot's unity the group constitutes a unit. There may, of course, be great differences between the "members" of such a protagonist as well as in what happens to them. Their membership in a compound protagonist does mean, however, that the common ground between them (consisting of contrast as well as similarity) is ultimately of more essential interest than their separate individual cases.

There are many kinds of compound protagonists, bound in many different types of relationships. (Generally speaking, the binding *relationship* may be regarded as the true protagonist.) The possibilities include a pair, a trio, a group of four, five, six, or more, a family, a village, a whole city, a society. The protagonist may be directly concerned with its own identity as a group or as a relationship (for example, a pair of lovers); the tie may be a common venture (the Bundren family) or the effects of some particular revision of the laws of nature (some science fiction). It may be a group leading diverse lives but sharing a certain kind of experience (the five members of the protagonist grow old in *War and Peace*), or a collection of lives that contrast

in some essential way (Amelia and Becky). Ahab and Ishmael.Daniel Deronda and Gwendolyn Harleth. The Recon Patrol. Hester and Dimmesdale (and possibly Chillingworth). Nick Carroway and Jay Gatsby. Anna and Levin. The compound protagonist is almost as common among the great novels of the world as the single one.

In a rhetorical plot, the germinal subject is an argument which may advance some general idea ("religious feeling cannot be suppressed") or else may either attack or support some entity, general or individual ("military attitudes," "American small towns," "Okies," "the Republican party") existing outside the fictional world. The effect depends largely on specially constructed fictional materials. Accordingly, the "topic" of a rhetorical plot—equivalent to the mimetic protagonist—has two parts, the proposition which the argument supports and the center of whatever fictional organization makes that argument. In modern rhetorical fiction this center is likely to be a figure resembling the protagonist of a mimetic novel (Rubashov in *Darkness at Noon* or the society in *1984*),[21] and there is no harm in using the term, provided one remembers that the primacy of a truly mimetic protagonist is lacking. Accordingly, any expansion of the topic must first describe not the protagonist's character but its rhetorical function.

In a creative plot the scope of possible topics seems still harder to limit to clear and extreme alternatives than it is in either mimetic or rhetorical plots. The reason may be that in most such plots the true center, the origin of the process, lies out of our sight—being what I call a "latent protagonist." If, as I have said above, the general subject of a creative plot is the creation of fiction, the latent protagonist is the postulable creator of that fiction—the imaginable figure whose expression the plot constitutes, the source of the symbolic significance it possesses. Such a figure is not identical to the "implied author" but is not separate either. The latent protagonist is that aspect or face of the implied author which is expressed by the so-called intervention in the fictional world, by the destruction of the ostensible au-

[21]The rhetorical protagonist of *1984* is clearly not Winston Smith but the peculiar society in which he lives and which his experience enables us to perceive.

tonomy of that world. Some properties, "traits," may or may not make this figure into a fictional "character." In *The Universal Baseball Association* he is neither "Robert Coover," implied author possessed of so many skills, conventions, and attitudes, nor J. Henry Waugh, fictional creator of his imaginary baseball world, but rather that aspect of "Robert Coover" which is expressed by his endowing Waugh's imaginary world with the same reality as Waugh's external world and his building a plot upon that base.

The fictional world is a "projection" by the latent protagonist's creative or expressive imagination. There is no limit, perhaps, to the possible kinds of projections—they are as various as the posibilities of dream, no doubt. An overt protagonist may be projected in relation to a self-reflecting world that expresses certain states of feeling, as in *Second Skin* or *The Crying of Lot 49*, or there may be a double protagonist whose relationship expresses a complex perception and feelings about history or myth, as in *Absalom, Absalom!* (the latent protagonist here is not Quentin but the unseen creator projecting into the double overt protagonist which is Quentin-and-Sutpen). Or the manifest topic may be not a protagonist (fictional figure) at all but instead, as I suggested above, a figure of speech, a turn of thought: the two-part correspondence between a fiction and an idea that forms the base for an allegory or the development of some other kind of metaphor. It may be a fictional situation capable of giving rise to different and contradictory fictional developments, like the baby-sitting and elevator situations in Coover's short stories. It may be the pattern of contradiction itself which makes it impossible to reconstruct a chronology in the fictional world of one of Robbe-Grillet's stories. The possibilities seem endless and their limits unknown, yet to be discovered by writers.

Narrational and linguistic plots can also be regarded as projections of the interests of a "latent protagonist," who can, here, too, be conceived as the plot's creator—although the designation may seem an unnecessary analytical complication for a work as simple as a mystery story. In narrational plots in general the center of the projection will be whatever centralizes the narrative problem on which the plot is based. In mystery plots this element may be the detective or (often) his companion or observer (his Watson): generally speaking, the figure who serves to restrict the

reader's view of the action. If no single character is used for this purpose, then the centralizing force can only be described as the operation of that restriction itself. In plots of narrative articulation (like that in *Tristram Shandy*), the projection will be onto the narrator. In linguistic plots, I would expect the center of the projection to be not a character or speaker or narrator at all, but some verbal pattern, habit, practice, or category, capable of being extended through variations or in some kind of chain.

Kinds of Process. Mimetic plots show essentially two kinds of processes: actions (changes in the fictional world, which may be either external, circumstantial, or inner, taking place within the characters) and processes of disclosure (the reader, through the narrative, becomes aware of aspects of the fictional world that may not change). Accordingly, in mimetic plots we must distinguish between *dynamic* plots (the germinal process is an action—a completed change of some kind) and *disclosure* plots (the germinal process is the revelation to the reader of unchanging things in the fictional world). Of course, disclosure plots will almost always have action, too, but it is subordinate to the revelation of what does not change—that is, we find the primary interest located in that revelation. Such plots are still fairly rare in novels though common in modern short stories. Perhaps the most notable distinction is between those in which disclosure of that which does not change is made by means of a coherent episode, in itself complete, that calls attention to the constant element and those in which the unchanging situation is revealed through narrative manipulation of its various aspects, often in nonchronological order. The first possibility is illustrated most simply by short stories such as "Hills Like White Elephants," the second by stories such as "A Rose for Emily." Among novels the most striking example I know is *The Sound and the Fury*, to be discussed below in part 2. *The Portrait of a Lady*, on the other hand, dealing with change of several kinds, has a dynamic plot.

The germinal change or disclosure belongs to the protagonist, of course, whether the latter is compound or single. Both dynamic and disclosure plots can be distinguished according to what changes or is disclosed. Crane has drawn some basic lines: change or disclosure in the protagonist's situation, or in his na-

ture, or in his knowledge or suppositions, or in his feelings. Combinations are possible.[22] So many critics have studied further distinctions, also possible, that I shall make no attempt to repeat them here. I must note, however, the importance of subordinate or multiple actions in many plots. Subordinate actions may advance the main action, or exemplify some stage in it, or clarify something, or comment on it by contrast or by analogy or in some other way. Many novels have subplots—extended development of subordinate actions—and in many, especially those with compound protagonists, a number of strands of action or subplots may in combination form the "main action" of the plot. An adequate statement of the plot process must account for the subplots. If the subordination of a subplot cannot be adequately explained, it may better be analyzed as part of a multiple action with a compound protagonist. And if the narrator should become a powerful enough presence in his own right, he, too, should perhaps be viewed as part of a compound protagonist and our analysis of the plot changed accordingly.

The actions in plots with compound protagonists demand a larger vocabulary of possible plot processes than those we are accustomed to find in plots with single protagonists. What, for instance, is the essential action of *Moby-Dick* if the protagonist is, as I think, neither Ahab nor Ishmael but the composite of the two? The destruction of Ahab and the survival of Ishmael each form only a part. Is the action not, rather, the story of the interaction and profound contrast between them? And if so, what can the outcome of such a story be said to be?

Turning to another point, I must take issue with the common view that the plot process is necessarily—as Olson puts it—"time bound," that is, chronological.[23] In the traditional view, all inversions of chronology in the text (flashbacks, for instance) are manipulations of the "representation," doing its business of presenting the plot to us in the most effective manner. Such an explanation will not do for disclosure plots, however, and I doubt that it will do for dynamic plots, either. The assumption is that plot is strictly the ordering principle of events *within* the

[22]See above, n. 10.
[23]Olson, *Tragedy*, p. 35.

fictional world. In my analysis, however, plot is not so confined, nor can it be if we want it to perform the ordering functions I claim for it. In a disclosure plot the process of disclosure is by no means necessarily chronological. Dynamic plots when developed also often contain parts that are in themselves organized according to principles of disclosure, and yet these, too, are "parts of the plot." Plot as I understand it informs every decision about order that the author must make; it does so in combination with the presentation—so that to explain the location of some detail I have to refer both to the plot and to the principles of presentation.

We must also notice in a mimetic plot the kind and degree of connectedness between the events, which reflect the distinction in the previous chapter between tight unity and loose unity. The episodes in a plot can be part of a tightly connected movement of events or loosely strung together—"episodic." The same distinction can also be made between a main line of action and subplots—they can be integrated quite tightly or may appear to have only loose connections. Such differences should appear in an expanded statement of the germinal action: "the events are tightly bound in a cause-effect sequence," "the events develop this change gradually through a series of reiterative or parallel episodes," "the change occurs only after a series of quasi-independent parallel episodes have demonstrated the initial situation," and so on.

In a rhetorical plot, the essential plot process will develop the relationship between the fictional element and the argument it is intended to make. Generally speaking, the analysis of such a process must pay attention to the progression of both the fiction and the argument. If the fiction is an action exemplifying the truth of a proposition, it may develop a single typifying or epitomizing case or a series of cases in a dialectical progression. The exemplification may be by exaggeration for ridicule, as in satire. It may proceed by parallel instances, multiplying the point until the demonstration has been exhausted. In such cases the fiction is symbolic: it relates by synecdoche or analogy to the external case with which the argument is concerned. Or the fiction may deal directly with the rhetorical argument; the characters themselves may discuss or discover the truth of the

proposition. Thus in *Catch-22* the characters and action manifest the absurdity that is being ridiculed; in *Darkness at Noon*, Rubashov learns and his lesson becomes ours; and in *The Grapes of Wrath* the Joads both exemplify the injustice of the Okie's misfortune and learn (Ma and Tom) the lesson that we also learn.

The essential process of a creative plot is likely to be (if my diagnosis above is correct) a creative imaginative process with symbolic (expressive) significance. I cannot predict, however, what possible shapes such processes might take nor what terms will best describe any given case. No doubt the primary distinctions in processes will follow from the primary distinctions in topics: plots whose topic is a latent projection onto a fictional figure, for example (onto a "manifest protagonist" such as Skipper or Sutpen-Quentin), will tend to have processes that resemble the mimetic possibilities (with a difference) more than do plots whose topic is an abstraction, an allegorical correspondence, a figure of speech, a fictional situation.

The plot process in narrational plots is simply the unfolding of the narrative problem, whatever it may be, until it is either resolved (as in a mystery) or exhausted. The activity of the detective will develop the mystery and finally solve it. The activity of the narrator trying to develop his narrative through the difficulties of articulation will continue until those difficulties have been fully played out. Similarly, in a linguistic plot, the process will be the extension of the variations or chain or other potentiality in the verbal pattern which is the center, until it is exhausted.

Kinds of Interest. This term refers to the significance, relevance, or value that the reader (strictly: the hypothetical implied reader) is expected to find in the plot subject. In mimetic plots, this is the familiar "Aristotelian effect": the "pity and fear" that describes a tragic plot, for instance. For plot processes in general, however, I prefer a broader term, which is not so likely to be interpreted as a response to the fictional world solely. The term *interest*, adapted from Booth,[24] covers the whole range of

[24]See Wayne Booth, *The Rhetoric of Fiction* (Chicago, 1961).

possible connections which a subject can claim between itself and its readers.

The most obvious problem with the conception of interest is the question, interest for whom? Who experiences the "effect" of a novel? For of course the actual effect of a work of art upon audiences is not measurable, and even if it were it would never be constant. My emotions in response to a given work are always changing, not only between one reading and another but also between different moments of reflection in the same reading. Furthermore, they are controlled at least as much by private and personal circumstances as by anything belonging to the work. All critics concerned with interest or effect must make this important distinction between the emotions of actual audiences and those which the work may be calculated to produce in some specific audience.

The concept of an implied reader is therefore most useful for the concept of interest and effect.[25] *The implied reader* is a collective term to embrace knowledge of the conventions (knowledge, attitudes, values) operative in the work, assumed to be in it, necessary to its comprehension—whether or not they have actually been grasped. These conventions are assumed to be recoverable by experience and by historical scholarship; the implied reader is the imaginable figure who possesses them. If the figure can be conceived and described, then the interest of the work can be attached to this person: it will be the interest which the work is calculated to have for such a reader. It can thus be distinguished from the interests and emotions of actual readers, and it can be discussed and argued about on some firmer grounds than mere impressionism.

This fiction of the implied reader will perhaps reconcile the idea of "effect" and the objections of aestheticians and philosophers to the "arousal" of emotions by art. It expresses the

[25]For example, Booth speaks of the "mock reader" (*The Rhetoric of Fiction*, p. 138) and the "postulated reader" (p. 177). Tzvetan Todorov refers to an "implicit reader" throughout his discussion in *The Fantastic: A Structural Approach to a Literary Genre*, trans. Richard Howard (Ithaca, 1975). I am using the term *implied reader* for somewhat different purposes from those of Wolfgang Iser (*The Implied Reader* [Baltimore, 1974]).

same fact that Susanne Langer describes when she says that art does not evoke emotions, it presents *knowledge* of them: "What art expresses is *not* actual feeling, but ideas of feeling; as language does not express actual things and events but ideas of them.... [The artist] is an artist not so much because of his own feelings, as by virtue of his intuitive recognition of forms symbolic of feeling, and his tendency to project emotive knowledge into such objective forms."[26]

The effect is really the "implied effect." Not that real emotions in real readers are not legitimate—nevertheless, they are not the effect but only clues to it, and critics must learn to what extent they can depend on such clues. The implied effect is the concept that enables real readers to bridge the gap between their own responses and those of others, not by the lowest common denominator but by just the opposite: for the implied audience may well be more perceptive, more responsive, more capable of attention, than any individual member is likely to be.

A second, related point concerns the distinction between the interest of the plot and the interests of the work as a whole. Discussions traditionally treat effect as if it were the final end of the whole artistic process.[27] My analysis of the formal principle shows clearly, however, that the interest, the effect, is not by any means the artistic *end* of the work but is itself a part of the *object of imitation*, a part of the imitated form which the work represents to us. We behold not a fall that arouses tragic emotions in the beholder but a fall that possesses a tragic quality. "Tragic pleasure" may or may not exist; the pleasure we take in the emergence of the form includes but is not confined to the perception of the tragic quality in the plot—a quality that our own vicarious grief may help us to discover and our fiction of an implied reader moved to pity and fear may help us to explain.

The *interest* of a mimetic plot—the "effect"—consists, then, of

---

[26]Langer, *Feeling and Form* (New York, 1953), pp. 59, 390.

[27]Thus the implication of the phrase "working or power" or Crane's description of the effect as "the final end which everything in the work ... must be made ... to serve" ("The Concept of Plot," p. 622). So, too, the idea of a proper tragic pleasure or comic pleasure to which a work is supposed to give rise. Such suggestions of a kinetic theory of art obscure somewhat the subtlety of the Aristotelian critics' conception of form.

judgment and emotion implied in the implied reader, directed to the components of the fictional world, and is a part of the perception of that world. Not emotion in the sense of "affect" (as Edgar Allan Poe, no Aristotelian, so notoriously insisted), and certainly not sensation; Sacks's phrase "characters about whose fates we are made to care"[28] better implies its nature, but even the "we" in this statement must be taken as somewhat hypothetical. Since all kinds of plots will partake of this kind of interest insofar as they incorporate fictional materials, I shall consider mimetic effects at greater length in the following chapter.

The interest of a rhetorical plot is, most generally, the persuasiveness of its argument. In detail, it would be the process of persuasive appeals, emotional and intellectual, as they develop. No doubt these appeals will be based in most cases to a high degree on mimetic effects, since the arguments are based on fictional means, but these effects will be given general application of one sort or another by the arguments.

And what kinds of interest will we find in creative, narrational, and linguistic plots? Insofar as they involve fictional worlds, however fragmented, here, too, I would expect to find at least the rudiments of mimetic effects. But since the fictional elements are subordinated to the creative, narrational, or linguistic process, I would expect these mimetic effects to be likewise subordinated or transformed. No doubt the interest of such plots will always involve some close sympathetic identification with the concerns of the latent protagonist, a bond which will primarily involve, for all three kinds of plots, an appreciation of the specialized virtuosity to which such plots call attention. In creative plots the common ground of such virtuosity would be the disruption of conventional mimetic coherence, replacing it with some other kind. The reader would appreciate this skill in the reorientation that follows disorientation in his view of the fictional world. In narrational plots of the mystery kind, the virtuosity would be appreciated through the raising and satisfy-

---

[28]Sacks, *Fiction and the Shape of Belief*, p. 15. Note how Sacks qualifies this statement in a footnote: "It would undoubtedly be more accurate to say something like 'characters who are evaluated by devices of disclosure in a manner consonant with the artistic end to which all elements of the work contribute' .... But it would be terribly inconvenient to do so."

ing of curiosity; in plots similar to that of *Tristram Shandy*, through the raising and frustrating of narrative expectations (and by making us expect and even desire this frustration). In linguistic plots, the feat is in the verbal power that is displayed, of whatever kind it may be.[29]

Besides this interest in virtuosity, there will also be, in some of these plots, an appreciation of whatever vision (with whatever attitudes or emotions) is expressed by the plot symbolically. A symbolic reading becomes necessary whenever the fictional world is denied its autonomy, its coherence is broken, or it is fragmented—in other words, in every creative plot. In a different sense, *every* plot is symbolic. In *Crime and Punishment*, a mimetic plot, we may read Raskolnikov as symbolic of a certain kind of intellectual revolutionary, because he *is* a certain kind of intellectual revolutionary. But in *The Trial*, a creative plot, when we perceive that everything in Joseph K.'s world is governed by a pattern of irrationality, of violation of rational or normal expectation, his story begins to acquire symbolic significance of another kind. Searching, as we must in such a case, for the cause, the ground, for the breach in the mimetic convention, we discover the implied creator of this breach. As soon as we inquire into this latent protagonist's motives beyond the purely artistic or virtuosic, we are led to an expressive, symbolic interpretation. (In *Crime and Punishment*, on the other hand, such a question of motive is not forced upon us, as we are fully absorbed in the artistic completion of the mimesis.) In Joseph K.'s case, we may find that his story, projecting the latent protagonist's vision, symbolizes everything it resembles—we can't pin it down to allegory. In *Absalom, Absalom!* we would find perhaps in Quentin-Shreve's reconstruction of the Sutpen story a symbolic expression of a latent protagonist's profound attitudes and feelings about the past and the South.

Narrational plots seem to be less likely to force symbolic readings, doubtless because it is not in their interest to disrupt

---

[29]As is implied by the theory throughout this book, appreciation of the novelist's virtuosity is an important part of the total effect of every good novel. The virtuosity I speak of here, however, is specialized, and enjoyment of it (through our identification with the latent protagonist) is incorporated into and becomes a visible part of the created form.

the fictional world—hence we tend not to read detective stories symbolically. On the other hand, a linguistic plot like that of *Finnegans Wake* (if it is indeed a linguistic plot) certainly does call for symbolic reading—a constant play of symbols—as part of its exploitation of the multiple powers of language.

THE LIMITS OF ANALYSIS

As I have noted, a plot statement is a reduction from the formal principle, itself a reduction from the full integration of the novel as a whole. As a result any plot analysis, even the best, cannot fully account for the work; at best it remains a hypothesis expected to stand only until a more persuasive one, more capable of predicting, comes along. We should also bear in mind that since the visibility of any living work is an incompleted process, every plot analysis is temporary, not final, not definitive—marking only what is seen at a certain stage in the process. The most valuable quality of a good plot analysis, then, is not its finality but its willingness to accept contradiction and grow with it.

The good plot analysis should of course include if possible some accounting of the process by which a form gains visibility. Still, the critic can ordinarily describe only the part of the process that is under the control of the artist. The individual psychology by which your insight leaps more rapidly than mine to a perception in the work (or by a different path) is usually beyond my reach: as a critic I can only describe the obstacles to that insight—and not even these until I have overcome them myself. I can of course observe all the distant obscurities that are penetrated on second reading or upon mature reflection, and I can try to recognize what still seems uncertain at the time of analysis. But such consideration of the process of visibility will only partially disclose that process, for I as critic am of course still within it, and it is still unfinished.

Finally, we must consider what a plot study can or should do about differences in perception brought about by the passage of time? Does the form alter as a work ages? We have discovered many unconscious assumptions in the conventions and forms of works of the past: archetypes, image patterns, Freudian rela-

tionships, for instance. "Contemporary parallels" in past works—Antigone and modern challengers of oppression, Hamlet and modern heroes of alienation, Jim in *Huck Finn* and the modern stereotype of Uncle Tom, Uncle Tom himself and the modern stereotype of Uncle Tom—alter our vision of such works. Sometimes it becomes impossible to see certain characters in the same light in which they were seen by their implied audiences. Conventions change and die, and the forms on which they are built likewise change. In such cases, clearly, the critic's task is neither to reject the modern consciousness nor to incorporate it uncritically in an analysis of the form. The task merges with that of the historical scholar, and the most important caution is that the plot analysis should *specify* the status of the plot being analyzed: whether it has been restored to its historical purity (an uncertain possibility, ambiguous in view of the principle of progressive visibility) or has been altered by the passage of time. The critic should say. Sometimes the passage of time makes a work brighter and clearer than when it first appeared. More usually, of course, the form becomes banal, obscure, or both; the brightness fades, and the work disappears from view.

[7]

The Mimetic Effect

If it is true, as Aristotelians assume, that the most important part of a plot is its effect, then no plot analysis is adequate that does not specify that effect. To be sure, the Aristotelian assumption needs to be qualified. For plots in general I have replaced the term *effect* with the term *interest,* restricting the former to mimetic plots: effect is the interest of mimetic plots. As we have seen, it is not the "end" of a plot essentially kinetic, nor a phenomenon in the reader, but a part of what the plot displays; it is a property of the imitated form. Its importance among the artistic qualities of the whole is the same as (no more nor less than) that of the *imitated form* itself.

Despite its importance, interest is the least studied of all parts of the plot, no doubt because it seems so tenuous, elusive—the least susceptible to formulaic treatment. My own discussion here will be limited—suggestive and speculative—restricted to the mimetic effect, not just because of the historical importance of mimetic plots but because the interest of other kinds of plots will always include a component of mimetic—that is, fictional—interest. It is central to the question of interest in the novel generally. Rhetorical, creative, and other kinds of interest, however, lack this central pertinence; their further exploration, independent of their mimetic components, must be left for other occasions.

It is important to understand that the interest of any given work is unique. The "tragic effect," for instance, is a category, a ground of resemblance between the effects of works called tragedies; as Olson has put it, "fear" is not one but a family of

emotions.[1] Specific feelings are defined by the specific circumstances that produce them: my reluctance to get up this morning is similar to but not the same as my reluctance to get up yesterday.

To discuss the interest of plots, therefore, I can only discuss the particulars it is based on; to discuss effects, I can only discuss the sources of effect. The mimetic effect of a novel is the given interest of the concrete imitated form—the fiction, the fictional world—as this is made manifest by the plot. It can be divided into four aspects, each contributed by a different source, a different germinal component of the formal principle, in each case in combination with principles of evaluation.

Interest is generated in the fiction by (1) the principles governing style and the use of language (the *linguistic effect*); (2) the principles governing presentation, the creation of the narration (the *presentational effect*); (3) the principles of invention, when these are considered as given, independent of, or prior to their specific organization by the plot (the *modal effect*); and (4) the principles of construction which, as qualified by the principles of evaluation, form the intrinsic interest of the subject itself, equivalent to the "Aristotelian effect" (I call this the *specific fictional effect*).

All four effects, and not just the fourth, are aspects of the interest of the mimetic plot. The question now is how to systematize their possibilities.

LINGUISTIC EFFECTS

Interests generated in the fiction by the principles of style appear to have at least two aspects. There is the coloration given to the fiction by the associations of the particular language used, that is, its vocabulary and diction, or more precisely, its "codes"—associations brought to our perception of the fictional world by virtue of its linguistic connections to what is outside itself. And there are the interests generated by the efficacy of the language in revealing the fiction to us—the clarity or obscurity, intensity or simplicity of the linguistic process. In both cases the

[1]Elder Olson, *Tragedy and the Theory of Drama* (Detroit, 1961), p. 135.

linguistic effect is, strictly speaking, an interest in the meanings (which constitute the fiction) as produced in a certain way, rather than an interest in those meanings in themselves. For illustration, consider the moment in *Absalom, Absalom!* when Mr. Compson says to Quentin: "Have you noticed how so often when we try to reconstruct the causes which lead up to the actions of men and women, how with a sort of astonishment we find ourselves now and then reduced to the belief, the only possible belief, that they stemmed from some of the old virtues? . . . love . . . pity . . . true pride."[2] The passage tells us something about Mr. Compson; it also helps define the fictional world as one in which such virtues exist. But we may also find that world colored by our recognition of a code that takes us outside the work—a peculiarly Faulknerian code of big abstractions, on its way perhaps to becoming his Nobel Prize speech—and imports back into the fiction whatever emotions or interests we have attached to it. This is the linguistic effect in its first aspect.

The second aspect could be illustrated by some effects in the first two pages of the same book. The complex play of meanings there is a feature of the fictional world itself; the attitude implied in the narrative that presents them belongs to the narrative effect (to be considered below); but the excitement generated by the combinations that actually bring these meanings together so intensely (indicated by my italics) is part of the linguistic effect:

> Out of *quiet thunderclap* he would *abrupt* (man-horse-demon) upon a scene *peaceful and decorous* as a schoolprize water color, *faint sulphur-reek* still in hair clothes and beard, with grouped behind him his band of wild niggers like beasts half tamed to walk upright like men, in attitudes *wild and reposed.* . . . Then in the long *unamaze* Quentin seemed to watch them overrun suddenly the hundred square miles of *tranquil and astonished* earth and drag house and formal gardens *violently out of the soundless Nothing* and clap them down like cards upon a table beneath the up-palm immobile and pontific, creating the Sutpen's Hundred, the *Be Sutpen's Hundred* like the oldentime *Be Light.* [Pp. 8–9; italics in all but the last two phrases are added.]

[2]William Faulkner, *Absalom, Absalom!* (New York, 1972), p. 121. Page numbers in the text refer to this edition.

In a comparable way, this aspect of the linguistic effect in a late Jamesian style may be seen in the delay in the perception of the fictional world caused by the intellectual complexity of the Jamesian language (which at the same time complicates that perception); it is seen in the Hemingway style in its production of a sharp, vivid, concretely evocative image of a fictional world that is itself, in consequence, sharp and vivid and concrete. Our perception of the style as obstacle and access, and the excitement or impatience, or impatience relieved, which this creates, constitute this aspect of the linguistic effect.

The analysis of the linguistic effect in the first aspect would doubtless entail a complicated analysis of codes, on the order of Barthes's *S/Z*. In the second aspect it would also entail an atomizing investigation, sentence (or lexia) by sentence (or lexia). Perhaps at this point the seemingly incompatible methods of formal plot analysis and deconstructive analysis would meet, if a meeting became possible.Linguistic effects are, of course, a significant part of the effect of the whole, though they are low in the formal hierarchy and tend to be neglected in formal analysis.

PRESENTATIONAL EFFECTS

We can escape this clumsy term by dividing it into *dramatic* and *narrative effects*. The "advantages" of the dramatic and narrative uses of words and the ways in which these advantages can be combined have already been discussed. Such advantages are aesthetic effects, not mimetic;[3] it is not vividness nor immediacy nor economy nor any of the other "technical" qualities attaching to visibility that constitute what I here call *dramatic* and *narrative* effects.

The *dramatic effect* includes, rather, the curiosity (and its satisfaction) about the fictional world, aroused by the way in which the fiction is revealed. It includes suspense but consists most essentially of the implied reader's interest in drawing the inferences required of him and thus tends to be intellectual. Dramatic effects can be distinguished from each other in terms of the questions the work invites the reader to raise and perhaps an-

[3]For a discussion of aesthetic effects, see chapter 8.

swer. Detective stories are obvious examples of works in which dramatic effects dominate, but they are also prominent in many works with strong intellectual appeal, works concerned with raising questions, solving problems, coping with riddles, confronting mystery. They are especially prominent in works with fallible narrators, in the inferences such works oblige us to draw.

Narrative effects, on the other hand, consist of the coloration, feeling, mood, or other quality loaned to the fiction by the presence and personality of the narrator who describes it. I mean here not the qualities in the characters or actions that the narrator's rhetoric makes us recognize but our sense of the narrator himself as an onlooker, as a companion, as a guide. If James treats Isabel Archer early in *The Portrait of a Lady* with affectionate irony, his tone may be simply a technical device to encourage us to see her with similar complexity; if, however, we become aware of him as a personality in his own right, our relation to Isabel becomes complicated by our relation to him. Though it is not a part of the fictional world that Isabel inhabits, his presence has enlarged the fictional world of the novel as a whole so as to include him as well as the world he tells about.[4] The narrative effect can be described presumably by describing the personality of the narrator and by tracing the relationship between narrator and reader as it is moved along by the narrative of the fiction.

Both narrative and dramatic effects are important in modern novels. The sequence of mysteries and resolutions that develops and our relations to the narrator as the fiction unfolds—a full discussion of the plot will not ignore these things.

MODAL EFFECTS

I take the term *mode* from Northrop Frye to designate major differences between fictional worlds. The *modal* effect is the particular claim a work makes to the reader's interest by virtue of the mode of its fictional world. It is a general effect, recognized usually early in the reading and simply deepening or becoming

---

[4]See chapter 4 and (in the same chapter) note 21 on the narrator as an independent attraction.

more definite as the reading continues. It qualifies or provides a base for the other more particular effects.

As seen in chapter 4, however, the most significant differences between fictional worlds have to do not simply with the characters' power to act, as in Frye, but also with the source of activity in those worlds—its origin, the compass of energy it expresses. Frye's five categories by no means account for them. The extremes are at one end narrator-controlled fictional worlds, at the other end history-controlled, with many varieties (including all Frye's original categories) in between. These are all differences in the relationship between the fictional world and the "reality" it claims to imitate. Hence my definition of the modal effect as "the interest generated in the fiction by the principles of invention."

Modal effects will vary as much as the fictional worlds themselves. Perhaps they can best be described according to the degree and nature of their departure from the various poles of possibility that I have suggested: from the realistic possibility, the mythic, the expressive, and so on. Thus if the work is seen as close to the historical pole, so that we read it as actual or partial history or biography, the modal effect could be summarized thus: "This world is interesting or important because it claims that it actually existed." Moving away from the actual historical but remaining still within a realistic mode, it might be, "This is interesting because it claims to *resemble* what actually exists in such and such a time and place." As the action in such modes tends to stress the relative impotence of the characters or the inexorability of the conditions under which they live, so the interest may be further specified in the conflict between individual and surroundings. Modally, such works may express our sense of ourselves as social and mortal beings, from the viewpoint of either integration or alienation.

As we move to fictional worlds more universalized, the importance lies in that universality. If the characters are "better than we are," or "stronger," their interest may depend upon our perception of an ideal, to be wished for, mourned, or perhaps feared—with variations according to the kind of remoteness from our actual experience that is supposed. As we move toward the mythic the importance depends still more on the imputation

of broad universality and deep kinship: "This is important because it joins my experience, or my fears, or my desires, to that of primitive men, or ancient civilizations, or all civilizations."

In a narrator-controlled fictional world, the modal effect will no doubt be a claim for the importance of that fictional world as a projection of the latent protagonist's concerns (see chapter 6, "Kinds of Interest"). In a rhetorical work the claim is that the importance of the fictional embodiment lends importance to the didactic message: "These characters are interesting or important (because universal, or realistic, or whatever); therefore the message they embody is interesting or important." In allegory, though the germinal interest lies in the ingenuity of correspondence between the two actions that the allegorist has brought together, the modal effect may find the importance in either of those lines, which then confers importance upon the other and upon the joining itself. In some instances (Thackeray's puppets, for instance), the intent may be to diminish importance: "Since these characters are only puppets manipulated by me, you need not take them so seriously or feel so threatened by them"—an effect useful sometimes for comic purposes. In Robbe-Grillet the interest, by the author's own theory, seems to be in the creative work demanded of the reader: "For, far from neglecting him, the author today proclaims his absolute need of the reader's cooperation, an active, conscious, *creative* assistance. What he asks of him is no longer to receive ready-made a world completed, full, closed upon itself, but on the contrary to participate in a creation, to invent in his turn the work—and the world—and thus to learn to invent his own life."[5] As I interpret this statement, in Robbe-Grillet the modal effect is a recognition of the fictional world as expressing the creative imagination: "This fictional world is important because its irreconcilable con-

---

[5] Alain Robbe-Grillet, *For a New Novel: Essays on Fiction*, trans. Richard Howard (New York, 1965), p. 156. If, however, Morissette's analyses of *The Voyeur* and *Jealousy* are correct, then the fictional worlds of these two novels are not narrator-controlled, despite Robbe-Grillet's own claims. It is important to bear in mind the distinction between a dramatized display of mental processes presupposing a "real world" outside the protagonist, so to speak, and a world that is *actually* fragmented or contradictory. See Bruce Morrissette, *The Novels of Robbe-Grillet*, trans. Morrissette (Ithaca, 1975).

tradictions remind us how the reality of our own lives is created by our own imaginations."

The *specific fictional effect* is the intrinsic interest of the subject (in mimetic plots) as developed by the principles of construction. Aristotle's "tragic effect," his "catharsis of pity and fear," provides the classic model. It is the most specific kind of interest which such a plot can have and in one sense is the ultimately controlling form of the whole. It is personal and moral, the implied reader's perception of the value and interest not of the fictional world at large but of that world as focused, of the particular sequence that the germinal subject abstracts. Even non-mimetic plots will possess a specific fictional effect of some sort, based on the fictional element in the germinal principle, though this may be subordinated to a rhetorical thesis or an expressive projection. There is always a relation of some kind between characters in a fiction and the implied reader, even if the relation is one of distance and the implied attitude is neutral, negative, or indifferent.

The attempt to discuss this effect brings us face to face with the full difficulty of explicating the emotion in fiction. The task is not impossible, however, if the effect is understood to be *within* the work and to belong to the implied (not the real) reader—that is, it is determinable to the extent that the conventions of value in the work are determinable and can be related to the construction of the work. In the remainder of this chapter I shall set forth a tentative scheme for the possible analysis of some germinal mimetic effects. My plan puts in order some useful terms and may suggest how the question can be pursued further, but it is not intended to be exhaustive nor to provide a set of categories more refined or efficient than others. The aim is rather to provide terms consistent with the kind of analysis explored in this book. The typology grows from the concept of formal principle and plot as developed here; the distinctions are those that seem most significant in this context. The typology is not to be used as a pigeonholing device, nor can it reduce in any

way the necessary inductive processes on which the analysis of all literary effects must rest.

There are, of course, many models for categorizing broadly the multitude of fictional effects. Most have traditionally begun with a distinction between "tragic" and "comic." A third category may be introduced: Paul Goodman has suggested "serious," "comic," and "sentimental."[6] Sheldon Sacks offers "tragic," "comic," and "serious."[7] Northrop Frye gives us a four-part distinction—"Tragedy," "Comedy," "Romance," and "Irony"[8]— although these are categories not of effects or forms but of archetypal patterns.

In the following discussion the categories are "families"; they can be mixed. Essentially they are "conventional forms." As such, they do not define any work, but they contribute to a vocabulary that can.

Primary Sources for the Specific Fictional Effect. Our discussion is limited at the start, for convenience, to germinal effects of mimetic plots which are *dynamic* and which have (unless otherwise indicated) a *single* protagonist—plots in which that protagonist undergoes a completed change. This restriction will enable me to establish primary terms and to defer the question of whether these terms are adequate also for other kinds of plots. Since some of the theoretical possibilities are rare or obscure in novels, I shall not hesitate, when convenient for clarity, to illustrate some possibilities with short stories.

The *Poetics* itself suggests a starting point: two different kinds of emotional interest in a plot. One is the *justice* of the action as the implied reader is directed to perceive it. The question is whether the action (whatever it may be) is made to seem just (what happens to the protagonist is deserved) or unjust (and undeserved). Either judgment implies an emotional response; the prototype is Aristotle's *pity*, defined as the emotion produced in us by the recognition of someone's undeserved misfortune.

[6]Paul Goodman, *The Structure of Literature* (Chicago, 1954).
[7]Sheldon Sacks, *Fiction and the Shape of Belief* (Berkeley, 1967), pp. 21–22.
[8]Northrop Frye, *The Anatomy of Criticism* (New York, 1967), pp. 162ff.

But fortune can be good or bad, and either possibility can be deserved or undeserved, involving different families of emotions. The judgment in any specific case depends heavily on the author's art as he manipulates ethical conventions (principles of evaluation), just as our recognition of that art and that judgment depends also upon our recognition of those conventions. The modern reader must of course be ready to cope with deliberate ambiguity as well as with complexity in these matters.

The second kind of interest concerns the degree and nature of emotional *closeness* or *distance* implied between the reader and the protagonist in the course of the action. Sympathy and distance are the opposites. Again, the prototype is Aristotle's tragic fear, defined as the emotion produced by the recognition of misfortune for someone close, like ourselves, sympathetic. There are of course several kinds of distance as well as of sympathy. Among the latter we must distinguish (formally speaking) between *sympathy* based on perceived similarity of the character to "ourselves," without a moral judgment, and that based on our admiration, approval, or even love of the character. The second kind implies, indeed, a certain distance (the character is "better than we are"), and yet we call it sympathetic because of the identification with values we regard as our own. In discussing *distance* we must likewise distinguish between the protagonist who appears to be inferior to ourselves (we have greater knowledge, or we feel disapproval, or perhaps we simply feel stronger or better off) and the one who appears to be simply different—at a remove, strange, wonderful—without moral judgment. Individual characters will often combine aspects of distance and sympathy. Characters whose adventures we are following closely, and with whom we may "sympathize" at a certain level because they are being unjustly treated or because we have such close access to their feelings, may nevertheless repel us or arouse moral objections to their behavior and in that respect be judged distant, inferior (I mean, of course, always by the implied reader, by whose standards we judge). Such relationships can change, too: a sympathetic protagonist may be removed to a distance or a distant character may be made, eventually, sympathetic.

The criteria for justice and for sympathy and distance cut

across the criteria for fictional modes. Thus, though the world of a novel by James (say, *The Ambassadors*) is to some extent idealized (all the important characters are "better than we" in certain respects, more articulate, more finely perceptive and discriminating, according to the norms of a more common realism), yet in the most significant respects Strether is "like ourselves" at least until his rarefied renunciation at the end (and Mrs. Newsome is "inferior"): his ignorance and bewilderment, crucial for the plot, put him in the same position as the reader, and our response to him depends upon that identity.

On the basis of these two criteria—which cover, it seems to me, a great range of emotional possibilities—one may set up at the start four large categories of fictional effects. As will be seen below, these are not the only possibilities admitted by our terms, but they make the most convenient starting place. I find it useful to adapt Frye's names of mythic kinds to describe these possibilities, since the designations do least violence to common usage, even though my own definitions differ from his. Tragedy, Comedy, Romance, and Irony: with wide currency as a tetrad, these terms will refer here not to mythoi, not to archetypes, but to broad categories of plots distinguished by their fictional effects. It should be understood, of course, that these effects are "final effects"—end points in the novel's development. The developing effects are composed of an unstable progression of reader's expectations, desires, temporary or passing judgments, and other responses. I cannot, below, distinguish the different configurations through which an effect might move on its way. It is the end point—or more correctly, the direction in which the effect is moving—that is most significant in distinguishing the nature of one plot from another: the end point as determinable in the implied reader, of course.[9]

Tragedy. In this scheme, tragedy is defined as the conventional form shared by any fictional work with a protagonist who

[9]The scheme that follows differs in many respects from that in my short story study, published twenty years ago—most notably in the addition of new distinctions and terms, the abandonment of the distinction between pleasurable and painful effects, and the replacement (and revision) of the term *caustic* by the term *irony*.

is or becomes essentially *sympathetic* (like ourselves) and who falls into an essentially *unjust* situation. In a fully developed plot this injustice would be manifest in undeserved misfortune, which gives us the Aristotelian formula of pity and fear. The theoretical variant on this, undeserved good fortune, is strictly speaking not possible for an essentially sympathetic protagonist.[10]

In classic tragedy the injustice is by no means unqualified.[11] The heroes fall because of errors in judgment or flaws. They bring their fates upon themselves and thus are far from innocent (especially in the case of Shakespearean tragic heroes), yet the punishment is worse than they deserve, and we pity them. But the formula also includes protagonists who suffer through no fault of their own—innocent victims who have made no notable error and yet are hurt or destroyed arbitrarily. Such plots are tragic in the broad sense, but they indicate the need for a distinction. I would use Aristotle's, between *simple* and *complex* tragedy. In the former we see suffering or pain (*The Trojan Women* is the classic example), but only in the latter is there a fully discoverable tragic hamartia, the mistake that brings the fall. "Complex" here means that the final judgment of either undeservedness or sympathy is *achieved over the strong original possibility of an opposite judgment.* We judge the misfortune undeserved, but not until we have seen the likelihood that it might be *deserved;* we recognize the protagonist as like ourselves, but only after we have been

[10]If we judge the "sympathetic" character's good fortune to be seriously undeserved, the very judgment implies a fault or lack which constitutes a distance between us that is more important than all the sympathy that surrounds it. If it is undeserved simply because we believe no human being, no matter how good, could deserve such good fortune, the injustice is unlikely to seem serious: normally good human beings or people like ourselves deserve all the good fortune they can get. If I am mistaken, I shall of course have to develop another term, for obviously "tragedy" won't do. But first I would have to find a work that actually fit that category. "Undeserved" good fortune like that at the end of *Tom Jones* is common in romance and romantic comedy—and is, of course, actually deserved. One reader has argued that Alex in *A Clockwork Orange* is a character close to us who wins undeserved good fortune. Still, closeness here (not sympathy) is subordinate to our perception of Alex's deficiencies. The plot looks to me like a complex comic plot of correction, complicated by an undertone of repugnance turning, perhaps, to irony in the end.

[11]For some interesting distinctions between Greek, Christian, and modern tragic effects in drama, see the work of Preston T. Roberts, Jr., e.g., "The Redemption of King Lear," *Renascence* 26 (summer 1974), pp. 189-206.

made aware of some important *difference* between us. The negative aspect of both emotions is provided by the hamartia, and the Aristotelian reversal and discovery are the strongest ways by which the plot can change the negative emotions into tragic ones. In the simple tragedy, on the other hand, these elements are missing: the pity and fear are simpler and by the same token potentially less interesting.

The great complex tragedy in modern fiction is *Crime and Punishment,* in which exceptional emphasis is placed upon the protagonist's discovery of his hamartia. Emphasis on the process of the fall itself is notable in the tragedies of Hardy. Tragic plots can range in magnitude from those in short, concentrated works like Edith Wharton's *Ethan Frome* to those in works such as *Anna Karenina.* Tragedy as a ruling effect is perhaps not as common in major novels as one might expect. In many works a tragic subplot is but one component in a larger structure: in *Moby-Dick,* for example, the tragic Ahab subplot is balanced by the Ishmael plot. So, too, the Gwendolyn Harleth story in *Daniel Deronda* is but a tragic part of a nontragic whole. A tragedy can, to be sure, have a compound protagonist, as *The Return of the Native* demonstrates. Yet novels dealing with suffering tend to develop other than tragic forms, which will be discussed below: "tragic romance," as in *The Scarlet Letter* or *Billy Budd* or *For Whom the Bell Tolls* or *Victory,* or "tragic irony," as in *Madame Bovary* or *Tender Is the Night* or *Appointment in Samarra* or *Studs Lonigan,* or "tragic sympathy" or "tragic discovery," as in *A Farewell to Arms.*

Comedy. Comedy may be defined as the conventional form shared by any fictional work whose central action consists of characters who receive what they deserve in situations that conspicuously and significantly distance them from us. The distance here depends on inferiority; mere difference or strangeness would not be the basis for an action in which justice would be done. Nor can the inferiority be seen as ultimately evil or seriously destructive, for such a perception would depend on our closeness if not to the protagonist at least to characters around the protagonist; thus works of vindictive or bloody justice—like "punitive" or "revenge tragedies"—cannot be called comic. Rather, in comedy distance is a positive effect, a source of plea-

sure, as is the punitive satisfaction involved. Hence comic action emphasizes absurdity or ridiculousness, with an effect appropriate to, if not always full of, humor. If the comic figure is inferior to us, the comic pleasure will lie in the perception of that inferiority combined with the perception of the actual or prospective justice of the events.

Writers of comedy long ago discovered that the kind of inferiority most natural to comedy is that in which characters claim to be more or better than they actually are. This situation most easily engages us in the enjoyment of distance. Thus the familiar observation that comic actions by and large will show affectation or vanity rather than some more serious fault. And the just deserts that befall such figures will be suitable to this vanity—embarrassment, humiliation, comeuppance—while any suffering or pain is kept from our sight.

Some further qualifications. There are comedies in which the *protagonist* is comic and undergoes comic punishment, as in *As I Lay Dying* (with a compound protagonist) or, more subtly, as in *Lolita*. In *What Maisie Knew*, on the other hand, a sympathetic protagonist acts to expose the comic foibles of others. Or the protagonist may be a rogue who exposes the comic vulnerability of others—as Flem Snopes does in a subplot of *The Hamlet*. There are also comedies in which the protagonist is exposed but also exposes others, as in *Huckleberry Finn*. A comic plot as a whole may often be looser than a tragic one; the incidents may carry much of the comic thrust by themselves, while the plot as a whole is a fairly loose principle—again, *The Hamlet* can illustrate. The comic quality of a plot is often poorly indicated by a summary of the whole, for the parts may carry greater independent weight.

Comic characters tend to be (perhaps they have to be) sympathetic in all respects except for the comic affectation. They are made comic by the distance produced by this affectation, this comic vulnerability, as it is brought to attention by the comic action. Happy endings are thus compatible with the comic effect. The happy ending may include a final comic punishment, or it may (as in *Tom Jones* or *Pride and Prejudice*) reward the protagonist for sympathetic traits of character after the affectation has been destroyed. Ordinarily both aspects of the protagonist

will be treated according to deserts: comeuppance for the comic
flaw and happy reward for the otherwise sympathetic nature.

Often, however, we meet comic characters who give every sign
of persisting in their vanities even at the end of the plot. This
may provide a sharp final comic twist: it implies that further
comeuppances like those we have seen will follow, and in this
respect our sense of justice remains satisfied. But if the character's persistence at the end overshadows this promise, we may be
moving over the line into another category—comic irony, to be
considered below. Still, room must be allowed in the realm of
pure comedy for the common character who does not acknowledge the comic punishment or recognize the comic flaw. This is
the case, for example, in *As I Lay Dying*. Our desire for comic
justice can sometimes be satisfied, apparently, by the exposure
of the character's defect to onlookers, even without that character's own recognition. We can even be satisfied when revelation
is made to no one but the narrator and the reader, if it is devas-
tating enough.[12]

A useful distinction can perhaps be made in comic plots similar to that between simple and complex tragic plots. *Simple* comedies might be illustrated by *As I Lay Dying* or *Pride and Prejudice*
or *Morte d'Urban*, a trio deliberately chosen to suggest how wide
and varied the category can be, as well as to show that a formally
"simple" comedy need not be simple in any other sense. Formally *complex* comedies, on the other hand, would be those in
which comic justice and comic distance are developed from materials that initially seem opposed to these effects. I am aware of
two kinds (no doubt there are others) relevant to modern fiction.
In one, the protagonist is eminently good—better, usually, than
any of the other characters in the book, and yet that very goodness becomes the source of the comic element: the comic flaw is a
misapplication of virtues (common in Faulkner) or a failure to
recognize them (the classical example: *Huckleberry Finn*). In the
other kind, the "ethical standard" by which a character and his
deserts are judged is raised at the end of the book to a higher
level than appeared to be the case at first. The implied reader

---

[12]The simplest clear examples that come to mind are in short stories: Joyce's
"Ivy Day in the Committee Room" and "Grace," for example.

makes judgments more severe, so that a character who at first seemed wholly admirable, threatened with undeserved misfortune, is finally seen by the stricter standard to be something of a fool, receiving a just fortune. Some of Henry James's stories and novels are of this sort—*The Spoils of Poynton,* for example. For obvious reasons, such comedy is often the subject of much critical disagreement.

Comedy as used here is a formal term. Laughter and its absence are not proof of comedy or its absence, for laughter is merely a symptom of recognition of a comic effect; the true comic effect is for the implied reader. The most important danger in analyzing comedy is that of extracting the characters from the form as one reflects upon them. If once we start thinking of them as quasi-real "people," we will destroy the essential distance in comedy. When we do so we are saying, "If this work were *not* a comedy, how would the characters look?" Not comic, we not surprisingly find. Reflection upon the characters in a comedy almost always destroys the comedy.[13]

Romance. A story whose protagonist is essentially sympathetic and who achieves justice may be called a romance in the formal sense. It may also be called—depending on the quality of the protagonist and nature of the obstacles confronted—a "heroic" story, an "adventure" story, a "sentimental" story, or an "edifying" story.

The sympathy in a romance may involve either identification with the protagonist or idealization. The satisfaction of justice may be expressed either by deserved good fortune for the protagonist or by the triumph of good elements of character. Plots of the latter kind tend to emphasize a choice or a pattern of choices that the individual makes, displaying merits, a claim to sympathy, in a striking way. The dominant effect of a romance in all these variations provides pleasure directly, satisfaction of the desire for justice, and vindication of the desire to give sympathy to the protagonist. Romantic plots are common in popular literature, since the effects can be so directly satisfying.

[13]See Elder Olson, *The Theory of Comedy,* for the most thorough and detailed analysis of comedy by Aristotelian principles.

The Mimetic Effect

In serious literature, romantic plots of good fortune can range from adventure tales in which the sympathetic protagonist overcomes dangers and rights wrongs (in works as various as *Ivanhoe* and *Intruder in the Dust*) to plots in which the protagonist's virtues receive their just acknowledgment and reward, as in *Mansfield Park*, or score a subtle moral victory over others, as in *The Wings of the Dove*. Plots of choice include those in which a partially sympathetic character—one good or attractive enough to make us want to sympathize—becomes wholly so (or, in a variation, overcomes our initial antipathy) by correcting earlier mistakes in some way, as in *The Red Badge of Courage* or, on a more extended scale, *Emma*. Or the protagonist, wholly sympathetic from the start, may demonstrate virtues by resolving a dilemma in some special manner, as in *The Ambassadors*, to take a complicated example. This type also includes plots of growth, life stories of formations of character, such as *A Portrait of the Artist as a Young Man* or, with complications, *Sons and Lovers*. A fine combination of growth and the rectifying of error is seen in *Great Expectations*.

The romantic plot can merge on the one hand with the tragic and on the other with the comic. A romantic tragedy or a tragic romance would combine the elements of vindicated sympathy or justice with the tragic element of real undeserved misfortune (*Billy Budd*, for instance, or the other examples named in "Tragedy" above). Of course, all "complex" tragedy (see above) involves an element of vindicated sympathy; it becomes tragic romance when this aspect is made more prominent than the misfortune and fear themselves. Romantic comedy and comic romance are common indeed. The most familiar kind has a comic protagonist overcoming comic weaknesses at the end and proving thoroughly deserving, as in *Pride and Prejudice*. Of course, there are many varieties.

Romances can be very easy on readers. They can flatter us and gratify us in our prejudices or in the smugness of our stereotypical assumptions. But they can also deal in the most sophisticated way with complex questions of ethical and emotional discrimination—as do most of the examples I have just named. Romances become *complex* formally when they seem to reverse their own initial assumptions concerning what characters de-

serve or what the characters' virtues are—when, in other words, they develop strenuously through some rising ethical standard, as in the complex kind of comedy discussed in the previous section. We see this tendency subtly, on a small scale, perhaps, in *The Red Badge of Courage* and, on a larger scale, but no less subtly, in all three of James's novels of his "major phase": *The Ambassadors, The Wings of the Dove,* and *The Golden Bowl.*

Irony. I use this term, borrowed from Frye, somewhat reluctantly. In rhetoric, of course, it indicates the device of intending a meaning different from or contrary to the one that is apparent. In drama and narrative, *dramatic irony* refers to meanings perceived by the reader of which the characters themselves are unaware. In Frye himself, *irony* refers to a class of archetypes and also to a fictional mode, but not to a formal effect. My own use of the word to designate a kind of fictional effect should not be confused with any of these, although it has common ground with all, a fact which makes it preferable to any substitute that I have been able to concoct.

In Frye's ironic mode, the hero is "inferior in power or intelligence to ourselves, so that we have the sense of looking down on a scene of bondage, frustration, or absurdity."[14] "Irony isolates from the tragic situation the sense of arbitrariness, of the victim's having been unlucky, selected at random or by lot, and no more deserving of what happens to him than anyone else would be" (p.41). Irony in Frye also constitutes, as I have already said, one of the four great "generic plots"; it is concerned with realism and "experience," as opposed to the ideal, and is closely related to satire (p.162).

It is necessary to distinguish *irony,* as I use it here, from Frye's term. I call a plot ironic when it involves a protagonist who is at a *distance* from us and whose situation is nevertheless *undeserved.* The emphasis is on distance, but not the kind of distance coupled with justice that gives us such pleasure in comedy; it is accompanied, rather, by injustice, which we observe, I presume, with a certain degree of bemused or concerned detachment.

[14]Frye, *Anatomy of Criticism,* p. 34. Page numbers in text refer to the 1967 New York edition.

Ordinarily the protagonist involved is inferior to us, undergoing a misfortune that, despite the inferiority, is disproportionately bad.

This definition shares ground with Frye's in the combination of protagonist's inferiority and felt misfortune. The common territory between this definition and that of irony as a rhetorical device is in the coexistence of seemingly opposite judgments that the ironic form requires, the need for us to go behind the character's inferiority to a judgment of the undeservedness of the misfortune and to go likewise behind this undeservedness to a recognition of inferiority.

I stress undeserved misfortune for an inferior character. Other combinations of distance and injustice should not be called irony. A plot of undeserved good fortune for an inferior protagonist lacks the tension of judgments characteristic of irony: the judgments of inferiority and of undeservedness simply reinforce each other. Such a plot would be more appropriately called a plot of indignation, horror, or shock ("repugnance," to be described below), if the injustice is taken seriously, or of comedy if it is not (since in that case "undeserved good fortune" is not really an injustice). Two other mathematical alternatives, those in which a character distant by virtue of difference or strangeness (rather than inferiority) experiences unjust good fortune or unjust bad fortune, also fit better in other categories: they, too, lack the necessary tension. The one is better described as a kind of romance and the other as a plot of "suffering"[15] (also see below).

Undeserved misfortune for a character who is nevertheless inferior to ourselves is therefore the characteristic situation in the ironic plot, a kind that involves a delicate balance between tragic involvement and comic detachment. It rests typically upon a sense of ambiguity: the reader's disposition to pity is undercut

[15]In both these cases there can be no connection between the distance of the character and the judgment of the deservedness or undeservedness, since this sort of distance does not involve moral judgment, superiority or inferiority. If injustice is prominent, it must be in relation to the protagonist's neutrality or innocence (qualities of sympathy and closeness) rather than to distance, which is thereby subordinated. For the case of undeserved good fortune of this kind, see n.10, above.

by a sense of the character's inferiority; a disposition to "laugh" at or condemn the character's absurdity is checked by a sense of the injustice or painfulness of the circumstances. Ironic plots often set critics to quarreling as to whether they are comic or tragic, whereas the truth is that in irony comic and tragic qualities war with each other.

Ironic plots are prominent in modern fiction, and we find them in some of our richest and most admired works. They appeal to our sense of the emotional complexity of things; they engage our interest and invite our emotional identification, and at the same time they hold us off, keep us on guard. The emotional ambiguity of the ironic plot is a positive and valuable effect that can rise to great power; it does not destroy its comic and tragic components but balances them against each other, making us aware of the insufficiency of each by itself and directing the attention of the reader to the balance.

Kinds of irony can be distinguished according to whether they are closer to the border of tragedy or to that of comedy. If the emphasis is stronger on the undeserved misfortune or suffering than on the inferiority of the protagonist, irony approaches the tragic. If in such plots the protagonists tend to bring about their own downfall, we have "tragic irony," as in *Madame Bovary, An American Tragedy,* and such other works as were named in the section "Tragedy" above. If they tend to be victims of forces that in weakness or vulnerability they are unable to combat, we have a kind of irony often called "pathetic": *Maggie, Girl of the Streets,* or *Of Mice and Men,* or the Hurstwood subplot of *Sister Carrie.* If the emphasis is on the protagonist's inferiority, the irony is closer to the comic. If the suffering is unacknowledged by the sufferer, we will have "comic irony," as in Joyce's story "Clay." The resemblance to comedy disappears when the injustice becomes more severe, even though the protagonist's inferiorities may be still more strongly emphasized, as perhaps in *Laughter in the Dark*—an effect that might be called "harsh irony." Or the elements of undeserved misfortune and inferiority may be kept fairly balanced, as in such works as *The Naked and the Dead, The Secret Agent,* or the majority of the stories in *Winesburg, Ohio.*

A distinction between simple and complex ironic plots comparable in significance to the simple-complex distinctions in the

other categories cannot I believe, be made, since the ironic effect itself is "complex," involving a tension between opposites. Of course, differences can and must be noted between different configurations of development—between, say, the pattern of *Tender Is the Night* or *Appointment in Samarra,* in which the downward path reverses a situation that initially appeared favorable (or *McTeague,* in which the emergence of the character's flaw reverses our earlier view of him) and the pattern of *The Naked and the Dead* or *Of Mice and Men,* in which the essentials are evident from the start and need only be developed concretely by the plot.

The reader fond of geometry may ask whether irony completes a circle formed by the three other categories of effect, as it does in Frye. No doubt such geometry subverts the principle of empirical readiness, yet I have to admit that comedy and tragedy do seem to be opposites; each can verge toward romance or irony, which are also opposed. Can these poles move toward each other? Tragedy can, as we know, be enhanced by comic elements—for example, the comic scenes in a Shakespearean tragedy—and perhaps the reverse is true, when materials potentially tragic dissolve in complex comedies. But is a truly balanced tension between tragedy and comedy possible—or one between irony and romance?

We have just seen that irony itself involves a tension between a tragic component (undeserved misfortune—pity) and a comic one (inferior character—comic distance). The other categories have their complex and their simple varieties, and in each case the complex introduces ambiguity into the developing effect. It is clear also that romance is emotionally the least ambiguous form, even when its moral materials are complex and sophisticated, for it ends on a note of approval and sympathy and justice. If this note itself becomes qualified—if the justice of the outcome or sympathy for the protagonist is thrown into question—we move into the categories of romantic tragedy or romantic comedy. The extreme of ironic ambiguity, on the other hand, is perhaps the introduction of a romantic element—admiration or approval for a mostly unsympathetic character—for instance, in Faulkner's treatment of Mink Snopes and others, which gives us a category of romantic irony. In general, how-

ever, ambiguity itself is to be associated with irony, and clarity
and simplicity with romance, while comedy and tragedy stand
between these extremes. Evidently, if the four terms compose a
circle, then the fourth term, irony, also invades the ground in
the middle.

I do not exclude the possibility that opposite effects may simply be juxtaposed or alternated, as seems to be intended in some
Elizabethan "tragicomedies." In such a case, however, we are no
longer dealing with an ordinary dynamic plot: the germinal
principle would specify in some way the alternating or juxtapos-
ing of the contrasting effects.

Specialized Effects. If our four major terms compose a circle, it
is not—even for "ordinary dynamic plots"—a circle that encloses
everything. The categories have been based on the development
of *two* kinds of interest for the implied reader, both developed
by the plot. There are many works, however, which develop only
one of these interests while ignoring or at least distinctly subordinating the other. As a result we may discern several more theoretical categories, not all of which can be found in dynamic plots,
nor even in novels, but we should discriminate between them
even so.

First, there are works with a great interest in the moral justice
or injustice of the action, while sympathy and distance depend
entirely on that interest. If the action emphasizes injustice or (to
enlarge the term) the largely unchecked emergence of evil, we
may call it a story of *repugnance.* The repugnance may be in the
success of an undeserving or evil protagonist (undeserved good
fortune) or in the evil or terrible things that befall an innocent
protagonist (undeserved misfortune with emphasis not upon the
suffering but upon the arbitrary evil or terror of the misfortune). The term *horror* is often though not always applicable to
such effects; in some cases *shock* may be a better word, in others
indignation, and many other variations are possible. The major
types of repugnance plots are most clearly illustrated by some
classic short stories. Thus the protagonist is the victim of the
horror in "The Pit and the Pendulum," the perpetrator of it in
"A Cask of Amontillado," Faulkner's "Dry September," and
(more subtly, if the repugnant category does not altogether give

way to the category of wonder, as described below) "A Rose for Emily." The repugnance may be caused by self-destructive behavior, as in Joyce's "Counterparts." A story of repugnance may end, like "The Pit and the Pendulum," with an escape from the evil; it then bears a superficial resemblance to an adventure romance, except that the ending is accidental and arbitrary, not integral to the dominant effect. The natural ending of a horror story is the simple exhaustion of the evil—it goes as far as it can go and then stops—as in "The Masque of the Red Death"—and the reader's relief at the end comes from realizing that it does so. Among novels, *One Flew over the Cuckoo's Nest* is one good modern example of a plot of repugnance (seen in the wanton destruction of McMurphy, the triumph of the establishment) and *Sanctuary*, with compound protagonist, another.

If the action involves mainly the correction or punishment of wrong we may call the plot *punitive*—the "punitive tragedies" of Elizabethan times furnish the most famous examples. Such plots make a rather primitive appeal to the implied reader's emotions, typically by rousing his indignation and vindictive desires and then vengefully satisfying them. They lack the emotional balance of comedy in which justice is tempered by comic distance and the potential sympathy that is satisfied by "corrective romances" in which wrongdoers reform and learn what we already know. Punitive plots differ from tragedy and irony in that no pity is permitted to dilute the punitive satisfaction—in other words, the wrongdoer's wrongs are not qualified by sympathy or by a feeling of closeness. In contrast with plots of repugnance, here the evil, dreadful though it may be, is avenged, and the primary effect is satisfaction rather than rejection of the reader's desires. Although a punitive effect may often be a component in a larger effect of a different kind (for example, in *Great Expectations*, the humbling of Miss Havisham, which turns to pity, or, most briefly though purely punitive, the destruction of Compeyson ["I saw the face tilt backward with a white terror on it that I shall never forget"[16]]), serious novels with dominantly punitive plots are comparatively rare. Punitive effects are common, however, in popular fiction, especially in the kind of mys-

[16]Charles Dickens, *Great Expectations* (Indianapolis, 1964), p. 481.

tery which combines an emphasis on finding the criminal with an interest in savagely destroying him.[17]

Opposed to such plots as these are others in which the justice or injustice, good or evil of the protagonist's case, is left either largely undeveloped and unspecified or in such a state of equivocation or balance that no judgment is possible. Instead the emphasis turns to the character's distance from or closeness to us. If the focus is on sympathy of the kind that depends on closeness—"like ourselves"—we may call it a sympathetic plot.[18] In modern fiction, especially short stories but also novels, this has been one of the most popular of these categories. The protagonist is familiar and tends to be morally "neutral", does as we would do, reacts as we would react, and is not notably victimized nor triumphant; the situation does not call for judgment as either just or unjust. The protagonist experiences something— perhaps strange or frightening or marvelous; it may have almost any quality—and by virtue of the likeness to us in his or her neutrality, we are invited to share it vicariously. There is no limit to the kinds of emotions that may be so released in this kind of pattern. The typical outcome of such a plot is discovery (the whole process is usually discovery, for that matter), which may be either emotional or intellectual, formulatable as a generalization or only in the concrete terms in which it is experienced, explicit or implicit, pertaining to the world in general or to the protagonist's own case. Outstanding examples include *Heart of Darkness*, *The Sun Also Rises*, and *A Farewell to Arms*. *Typee* and Margaret Atwood's *Surfacing* can suggest something of the range of such plots.[19]

[17]Mysteries of this kind should be distinguished from the "pure" detective mysteries described above as examples of narrational plots. Examples might be Dick Francis, *Dead Cert* (1962), and *The Lime Pit* (1980) by Jonathan Valin. The punitive effect is often strong in the movies: consider *Straw Dogs*.

[18]I take this term from R. S. Crane, who defined it approximately as I have here.

[19]No doubt *A Farewell to Arms* might be considered a simple tragedy, because of Frederick's loss at the end, but I think the organization of the whole subordinates the injustice of the specific loss (which is a direct consequence of only one aspect of the total developing action) to the general discovery that Frederick's whole experience embodies—himself alone in a world (life itself) that takes everything away. For some classic modern discovery stories, consider "The Dead," "In Another Country," "Araby," and "The Open Boat."

On the other hand, the plot may focus on behavior that noticeably distances the protagonist from us. The effect centers in the apprehension of distance, unaccompanied by any moral judgment or judgment of superiority or inferiority. Even though complex moral issues may be elaborately developed, in the end no moral settlement is allowed. I call this a plot of *wonder,* which I would define here as the interested apprehension of distance; it emphasizes how extraordinary, how amazing, how strange are the protagonist's actions or attitudes. The special tension in such a plot is in keeping us so vitally interested in what remains at such a distance. Plots of wonder may well be the most numerous of all types in the serious novel, at least in the twentieth century. Consider these instances: *Wuthering Heights* (suspending our natural tendency either to condemn or perversely to admire Heathcliff); *Lord Jim* (neither a romantic affirmative judgment of Jim's behavior nor a negative ironic one); *Light in August* (rather than tragedy or irony for Joe Christmas in his pursuit of martyrdom); and, with compound protagonists, *Moby-Dick* and *War and Peace.*

The foregoing kinds of specific fictional effects—I have distinguished eight so far—are possible organizing effects in the plots of mimetic novels. Let us complete this sketch by considering briefly five more theoretical possibilities, observable in short works but much rarer as dominant principles in works of the dimensions of a novel. The first of these would be the effect of a construction that develops the good, the ideal, the worthy or superior aspect of a character (sympathetic) without a corresponding development of the justice or injustice of that character's fortunes. The effect would be in the developed admiration or approval of the character's superiority, and we can call it a plot of *praise.* Such a plot could not be extended into a dynamic plot without becoming a romance, a kind to which it is closely related.[20] (Indeed, the effect of praise is already a component in many romantic plots.) Praise can organize a disclosure plot,

---

[20]A dynamic plot based on the good protagonist would presumably develop the character's virtues through a process of change; such growth would constitute an achievement for the protagonist indistinguishable from what we have regarded as good fortune in a romantic plot.

however: if Faulkner's *The Unvanquished* is regarded as a novel, with compound protagonist and disclosure plot, it might furnish an example.

The converse of the plot of praise is one which develops the weakness of a character (fault, flaw, limitation of some kind) without a corresponding development of the justice or injustice of that character's fortunes. The effect will be a judgment of the individual's deficiencies, and we could call it a plot of blame, or better (since blame implies consequences), a plot of *criticism*. It would differ from comedy in having no implied deflation; from irony, since the stress on suffering is absent; and from repugnance, because there is no emphasis on the destructiveness of the faults shown. These limitations make the effect unlikely in a work of novel length, though it can be seen clearly in short stories such as Hemingway's "The Doctor and the Doctor's Wife" and "Out of Season."

The third of these possibilities would be a plot that simply develops good fortune without closeness or distance of the protagonist. The good fortune in such a case is deserved, but without emphasis on that fact, for that would turn it into a romance. The emphasis can only be on the display of good fortune as such: we can call it a plot of *felicity*. It can be distinguished from other kinds of plots only by the disappearance of the character of the protagonist: a depiction of well-being without character. This becomes visible in the novel perhaps at the level of the "latent protagonist" in nonmimetic plots: it would be the implied effect of the *virtuosity* in such a plot (as, say, in the working out of an allegory or some other kind of fictional construct). It would underlie and be obscured by the more specific effects of the manifest action but would become prominent as the manifest action disintegrates, as, for example, perhaps, in *Finnegans Wake*.

The fourth possibility is the converse, a plot displaying misfortune without developing the protagonist's closeness or distance. Such a misfortune would be felt as undeserved, but without emphasis on the injustice. The stress will be rather simply upon the display of misfortune: we can call it a plot of *suffering* as distinct from a sympathetic plot of misery, such as *A Farewell to Arms*, and also from tragedy, irony, and repugnance. Again, it is

distinguishable through the disappearance of the character of the protagonist: misery without character. This, too, becomes conceivable for the novel with the aid of the concept of the latent protagonist: the fictional world as projection of the latent protagonist's vision of suffering. A possible example is Beckett's *The Unnamable*.

We must ask, finally, if there is not one further possibility: a plot that develops neither justice nor injustice, closeness nor distance—that attempts somehow to avoid a "specific fictional effect" altogether. This notion recalls Flaubert's idea of a book about nothing. Might not such a *blank* effect be possible when the mimetic interest is subordinated to some other? But what is that other interest? The difficulty with this idea is that in cases where the manifest mimetic interest is most suppressed, as in a linguistic plot, say, the latent protagonist's *felicity* will come to the fore.

At this point it may be helpful to summarize the derivations of the foregoing mimetic effects by three tables. The first table shows the compound effects, in which judgments are made as to both the justice of the outcome and the distance of the protagonist in that outcome. In this table, justice in Romance means good fortune, in Comedy it means deserved fortune, good and bad, in Tragedy and Irony it means misfortune—as we have explained above.

The second table shows four categories of effects in which the element of good or bad fortune is developed alone, with no significant development of character distance or closeness. The distinctions depend on whether the good or bad fortune is judged for its justice (deserved or undeserved) or simply with respect to the protagonist.

Table 1

Outcome	Closeness	
	Sympathy	Distance
Justice	Romance	Comedy
Injustice	Tragedy	Irony

Table 2

	Judgment	
Fortune	Ethically judged	Unjudged
Good	Punitive (justice)	Felicity
Bad	Repugnance (injustice)	Suffering

Table 3

	Judgment	
Closeness of character	Ethically judged	Unjudged
Sympathy	Praise	Sympathy
Distance	Criticism	Wonder

The third table shows four categories of effects in which the element of justice and fortune is suspended or subordinated to that of the closeness of the character. These distinctions also depend on whether the closeness entails an ethical judgment or simply one of likeness and difference.

Limitations and Applications. The thirteen kinds (families) of specific fictional effects discussed here are the basic mimetic effects. Not only do they (or some of them) organize mimetic plots, they also define the most specific qualities of the fiction as shaped by the plot in nonmimetic works. They constitute the possible relationships between the implied reader and the figures in a fiction whenever these are seen as characters in their own right engaged in situations or actions. They are distinct not only from the more general fictional effects discussed earlier in this chapter but also from the other kinds of interests that dominate nonmimetic plots as discussed in the previous chapter. In the remainder of this chapter let us consider briefly (and in a speculative way) how the specific fictional effects may be utilized and how they may be limited in various kinds of plot structures.

We may begin with the role of *subplots* in the formation of a specific fictional effect. A subplot can and usually does have its

own effect, which may come from the same spectrum of possibilities as that of the main plot. This effect is by no means usually dissolved in the main effect; in its own time and place in the novel it holds the center of our attention without reference to the rest. Thus, for example, we may read a scene involving Lena Grove in *Light in August* without feeling obliged to relate it to Joe Christmas, and we may retain in memory a clear independent image of her and her case. Apart from the mechanical connections (Brown, the cabin, the time of the encounter, the common linkage to Hightower), the Lena/Byron plot is related to the Christmas plot only through a certain ground of likeness and contrast: they are two kinds of outcasts, potential scapegoats. The common ground makes them metaphors for each other, and thus each contributes to our understanding of the other. But the Lena plot is a comic one, while the Christmas plot is a plot of wonder, transcending the possibilities it contains for tragedy or horror. Ultimately the comedy of Lena's case contributes to the distance with which we see Joe in his, the stronger plot, both during the development and at the end. It adds an important element to the definition of the world in which his bitter passion is carried out. It "places" that passion; it challenges the aspects of horror and repugnance in Joe's story and gives the final wonder of the whole a clearer, cooler, more serene quality.

Subplots always make a metaphorical comment on the main plot, and in this way alter our perception not only of the main action but also of the effect of the whole. In general a subplot will either reiterate and thus intensify as if by echo the effect of the main action or else will challenge or undermine it, by contrast or otherwise, to modify and place it. A description of the total effect must always take account of the effects of the subplots, specifying what they contribute and how they are integrated.

In plots with a *compound protagonist* the effect of the whole must be described in relation to whatever principle unites the various figures into a single protagonist and their subplots into a single plot. Let us consider the possibilities. There is first of all the kind of compound in which all the individual members are united in a common venture and have much the same behavior

and fate. The differences between them may or may not be developed, but in either case they are subordinate in importance to the common ground. The protagonist may be a town, a family, a group of individuals. The Bundren family in *As I Lay Dying* is a good example. A formal analysis will treat the members as a common "character" and at the same time will distinguish dissimilarities (in character, in behavior, in what becomes of them), seeking the common basis for these which will help unite the action. Our interests in the individuals in such a case tend to fuse into our interest in the group, for which our usual terms dealing with justice and closeness will probably remain adequate.

A second broad class of compound protagonists consists of those in which the action is a development of the relationship between the members. The action may be the formation of the relationship (creation of the compound protagonist), its growth, its survival, its disbanding (destruction of the compound protagonist), or all of these. A number of such relationships are common in modern fiction: the relationship of lovers, of enemies, of witness and actor.[21] In such cases our interest is in the relationship itself (our interest in the individuals is linked to and limited by this), and we judge its development by the same standards of good (just) and bad (unjust), close and distant, by which we judge individual actions. Thus in *The Great Gatsby* a description of the central action must account for both Gatsby and Nick: perhaps it is Nick's acknowledgment of Gatsby's wasted heroism. The effect, integrating the sympathetic plot of Nick's story and the tragic romantic plot of Gatsby's, is ultimately romantic: justice is done, the protagonist is morally united, and thereby both Gatsby and Nick's interest in him are vindicated.

A third broad class of compound protagonists is found in plots in which a number of separate stories, each with its own "subprotagonist," take place more or less independent of each other. Though there is a common ground, it would be misleading to say they are engaged in a common venture or that they constitute a significant relationship. Indeed, the unity between them may not even be recognizable until it is forced upon us by the

[21]See Peter L. Irvine, "The 'Witness' Point of View in Fiction," *South Atlantic Quarterly* 69 (1970), pp. 217-25.

convention of the organic whole. In such cases, each contributing subplot has its own effect, and the effect of the whole is the
composite of these effects as they modify each other. In a mimetic work, the principle that unites these subplots (of parallelism,
contrast, something else) will take shape as a process—such as a
shared experience, or a contrasting disposition of fates. This will
be true whether the subplots tend to reinforce each other, as in,
say, *War and Peace,* or contrast with each other, as in *Vanity Fair*
or *Sister Carrie*—actually they all always do both, and the effect
includes the perception of both aspects. The center of the effect
is the implied attitude concerning this process itself, and it qualifies the more specific effects of the subplots. For an example of
how the effect of a compound plot may be analyzed, see the
discussion of *The Sound and the Fury* in chapter 10.

The same considerations govern the effect of episodic
plots—which have a relatively loose kind of unity. Whether the
episodes are linearly related and develop a single character, as in
The Adventures of Augie March, or deal with different characters
and more radical disjunctions, as in *Go Down, Moses* (which is
beyond or at the very edges of our normal conception of a novel),
the effect of the whole will center on whatever principle unites
those episodes, and it will be less specific than the effects of the
particular component episodes.

Let us consider also how specific fictional effects may be limited by the kind of process that organizes a plot. In disclosure
plots, the effect must be appropriate to the perception of a situation held in suspension or gradually revealed. Although this
principle does not exclude any of the broad categories distinguished for dynamic plots and makes possible also effects of
praise and blame, in practice it seems to favor the ironic and the
wonderful (as in, say, *The Good Soldier* and *Absalom, Absalom!*).
Since disclosure plots in novels tend to have compound protagonists as well, their specific fictional effects will also be subject
to other limitations, as we have seen.

The distinctions in kinds of dynamic plots made by R. S.
Crane also have consequences with regard to specific fictional
effects. Although plots of action (change of fortune) may develop effects in any of our eight categories for dynamic plots,
there seem to be limitations on both plots of character and plots

of thought. In the former, the effect (I mean here the dominant effect; subplots may of course be different) will be appropriate to the perception of character change: the elements of praise and criticism are likely to be important, and the dominant effect will give these components a prominent place: romance if the plot is one of growth, irony or comedy if the plot tends to criticize, and of course wonder if it leads to a suspension of judgment. (Consider, thus: *The Ambassadors, A Clockwork Orange,* and *Lord Jim.*) Plots of character are not likely, on the other hand, to be dominantly tragic, or punitive, or sympathetic. Plots of thought are even more limited. These are most likely to be either discoveries (movements from ignorance to knowledge) or demonstrations (the protagonist displays knowledge or some intellectual process), although only the former are common in novels. In both kinds the protagonists are more or less neutral as characters; even if their discoveries include the uncovering of mistakes or weaknesses or worse in themselves, still they are like neutral observers with respect to these discoveries, and we share their viewpoints. As a result the specific fictional effect of most plots of thought is what I have called sympathetic—though it may be enriched by other effects, depending on what is discovered and how.

In nonmimetic plots, specific fictional effects will tend to be subordinated to other interests. In rhetorical plots they will serve the rhetorical interest. No doubt, any of the categories listed may be useful to some rhetorical purpose, though a subordinated tragic effect is less likely in a rhetorical novel than a subordinated ironic, repugnant, or comic effect (suitable to satire) or a romantic or sympathetic effect supporting a positive rhetorical statement. Like the tragic, the effect of wonder cannot usually serve well in rhetorical plots. And since the fictional effect is subordinate, there is no reason to assume it will be developed coherently or be pulled into a unity in its own terms.

In creative, narrational, and linguistic plots, the specific fictional effects are subordinated to the interests of the latent protagonist as these have been described in the previous chapter. In creative plots, since the ostensible autonomy of the fictional characters has been destroyed, fictional effects depending upon that autonomy are undermined, challenged, or replaced by the

effects of regarding these characters as projections of the latent protagonist's imagination. The effect of Joseph K.'s story as he tries to deal with his trial, or of Quentin's as he tries to reconstruct Sutpen's story, or of Skipper's as he recounts his "victory" over horrors, is altered by our perception that that story is an expression of the "vision" of the inventor of Joseph K.'s or Quentin-Sutpen's or Skipper's world, and it is subordinated and contributes specificity to the "modal effect" (designating the kind of importance that the fiction has as an expression of such a vision). The dominant interest of the work as a whole is a unity of this modal effect and the virtuoso creative effect which the creative emphasis expresses. For one possible analysis of the effect of a creative plot, see the discussion of *Pale Fire* in part 2.

In narrational plots, the specific fictional effects are not quite so undermined unless the fictional world is actually disrupted, but they are subordinated to what I have called "dramatic" or "narrative" effects: curiosity like that of the pure detective story or interest in the narrative personality. These effects are the interest which the fiction acquires as it expresses the virtuosity of the latent protagonist of the narrational plot.

Finally, in the linguistic plot (if I may speculate on the basis of such a scarcity of examples), the fictional interests are subordinated, as I have said, to the virtuoso verbal interest. A fragmenting of the fictional effects is required, and if it were carried far enough we might perhaps arrive at the "blank" fictional effect postulated by Flaubert. Such an effect would pertain only to the fictional elements in the work, of course. It would lie under the linguistic or stylistic interest, which would thereby be given an unobstructed view.

So much for this rough, speculative, quite tentative beginning of a vocabulary of fictional effects. I have said nothing at all about the interesting but not formal question of the psychology underlying our pleasure in these kinds. I have said enough, though. I would reiterate that the terms here, like the names for other kinds of genres, are better regarded as designating ingredients than categories of works—even though in my examples I have tended to treat them in the latter way. I would also repeat that the "typology" of effects offered here is indeed only a vo-

cabulary, and vocabularies are never fixed, never final. In analyzing a novel it is more important to describe truly what one sees in it, using whatever terms one can, than to try to fit it to a set of predetermined terms. This point is more important than anything else said in this chapter, which is offered mainly as a convenience until more finely discriminating language can be developed.

[8]

General Formal Values

Thus far I have developed the idea of the formal principle according to the assumption that the novel is a self-contained art and that art in general is "making." I have inspected the construction of the novel in this light, pursuing the formal principle until I could identify its elements—the germinal principle, the plot, the various kinds and major aspects of plots. My analysis depends on that original assumption: *if* that is true, *then* the formal principle of the novel should have such an appearance and such significance. But the validity and usefulness of the first assumption still remains to be considered.

We must therefore look more directly at the values we as readers normally expect to find when we perceive the formal principle in a novel. It is time to ask to what extent, if any, our perception of formal unity actually contributes to the pleasure or esteem of a novel we admire. The analysis so far has suggested two possibilities, extreme and opposite. Perhaps the value of a novel lies in what I have just been calling its interests, especially the effect of the display of its fictional world, the attachments we form or the significances we find in our relations to its characters, its actions, its problems, its themes. Or the value of the novel may lie where we placed it at the beginning of discussion in chapter 2: in our appreciation, for whatever reasons, of the mastery, the skill, displayed by the novelist in the construction of the form. Until recently most criticism of the novel has concerned itself with the first sort of value. Our emphasis on the analysis of form has been based on the second. It concluded, however, with an examination of fictional interest,

the first kind of value, after all, which I located in the form. Has my argument therefore undermined itself, leading us away from the formal values we started out to find and depositing us finally in the nonformal values of the fictional world?

To be sure, I took care in the preceding chapter to distinguish this fictional interest, the effect, from the "aesthetic values" of the work. The interest, we saw, was part of what the imitated form displays, part of the object of imitation rather than a primary value of that form itself. The possibility remains, however, that those aesthetic values might be largely imaginary, or at any rate, as E. M. Forster felt, relatively trivial, and that in the novel (if not in other arts) the great values that make the novel so much admired, are after all in the object of imitation, in the characters and the life, in the fictional world. If so, the novel would be to some extent a kinetic art rather than a self-contained one—a "less pure art," say, than music—and the thematic and didactic critics would be right: the only reason to study form is as a means to an end. No doubt such study would still be a useful activity for some purposes—to help novelists develop their skills, perhaps, and even to aid critics and readers in correlating their descriptions of novels under discussion—but it would be far less important than other critical activities.

What, then, are the "formal values" in a novel? How important are they in its total scheme? On this question hinges the real value of formal study of the novel and the general usefulness of the concept of the novel as self-contained art.

The formal values we seek must be found in our perception of the form as such—not as means to some other end but as end in itself.or as manifestation of the skill or mastery of its maker. Our task is to determine which of the numerous values we find in novels can be called formal in this sense and to distinguish them from the various nonformal values which novels admittedly also possess. The question does not require us to probe psychology but only to inspect the various fictional components already analyzed so as to relate them to the familiar values of recognizable experience—or to the values traditionally attributed to the novel. Our aim is not to discover new experiences in novel reading but to determine to what extent the appreciation of form is an actual part of the experience we all know and enjoy.

General Formal Values

The values we seek are sources of esteem, admiration, approval, which may be attached to the various properties of a work. In some sense they are benefits to the reader. Formal (or aesthetic) values are benefits the reader finds in the direct perception of form as manifestation of artistic skill.[1] Let's not hope to find all that are possible; it will be enough to find some, if these are important enough. Let us pursue them through each of the major elements in the formal hierarchy we have seen—in the fictional world, the language, the presentation, and the formal principle as such—distinguishing everywhere between the obvious nonformal values possible therein.

The specific values of the *imitated form*—the values in the effect, or interest, of the fictional world—are, as I have just been arguing, *not* formal values. They are, to be sure, necessary to the analysis of the form, as we have seen in the preceding chapter, for we need to specify these effects (presentational, modal, specific fictional, as well as didactic and creative) in order to describe it.

Although these specific interests differ in every novel, they partake of certain general values. Some of these should be noted, since they are so prominent; they need to be distinguished from formal values. There is a general value often appreciated in "learning about reality," or more correctly, in believing that we do—of whatever kind and at whatever distance, in the distortions of whatever mode. This value is not restricted simply to didactic effects but may inhere in any construction we recognize as an "imitation." We are persuaded of realities or we learn of possibilities. We learn how hard things were for farmers in the 1890s; we learn that crime does not pay—or perhaps it does; why such a kind of pride may fall; or what fine and noble discriminations are possible to a highly developed moral sense. Related but different is the enhancement of our own experience that comes through attending to a fictional experience of some sort: the adventure of a character (including the excitement of suspense, the shame of defeat, the exhilaration of triumph, the

---

[1]Though the function of the form is not to benefit the reader but to manifest art, our question now asks how this display of art benefits the reader.

exercise of judgment) become part of our personal history. As the values of new experiences in real life are infinitely various, so are the values of the fictional experiences that become our own through reading.

Though scorned for a number of reasons by many modern critics,[2] such values have obviously been a major part of the enjoyment of many devoted novel readers. They are, as I have said, nonformal. But we can also find formal values in the perception of the imitated form, and these constitute, I believe, a larger part of our normal appreciation of novels than we may often realize. These formal values lie in our perception that the imitated form is a created form and an integral part of the form of the whole. We are aware that our attention is being called to the fiction as a created entity; this awareness, this consciousness of our attention, provides the specifically *formal* value of the fictional world.

What is this value among the familiar values of novel reading? It has, I think, two sides. One is the enhanced sense of worth which the self-consciousness of attention confers upon the abstract imitated forms that enter into the fictional world: what critics used to call the "naming" function of art, what Shelley described as the stripping away of the veil of familiarity, what the structuralists call "defamiliarization." We are made to see everything more sharply, to notice what we have become accustomed not to see. We must ask exactly what is made unfamiliar and thus enhanced by this act of attention. I think it must be the whole constitution of the fictional world—not only the forms of reality of which it is composed (the "stones made stony"), but the

[2]The strongest reason, as I understand it, is that the illusion of reality we may draw from fiction is naive, a manifestation of the prison house of language, of the conventions we take for reality. The intelligent reader of fiction, who distinguishes the conventions of fiction from those of history, might still reasonably believe that some fiction can afford access to reality of a kind distinguishable from that of history, but the argument cited above attacks the reality of both fiction and history as illusions. Although realistic fiction claims, as a matter of convention, to be presenting some reality, doubtless the truth is, generally, that rather than *give* us reality such fiction confirms ideas we already have or persuades us to modify these. The claim is, however, a necessary part of our experience in the reading, whether we accept it provisionally, for the sake of the game, or literally.

nature of the perception itself, that is, its relevance, its effect. Our habits of perception themselves, of recognizing distance and closeness, of making judgments, of fully recognizing interest in the fiction—all these habits are also defamiliarized, called to our attention, when we recognize the fiction as a fiction.

The other side is the value conferred upon the fictional world by the sense of community which this act of attention implies. A common ground of experience is created between us and others whose attention we know has also been directed in this way—first of all the author and also all other readers we may imagine. Such attention breaks down the barriers of our existential isolation: there is a consciousness of sharing.

Defamiliarization and the sharing of attention in a community are thus the two most prominent general formal values arising from our perception of the fictional world. They do not require a full perception of the formal principle, to be sure—to that extent they are not likely to be the primary formal values—but they do depend essentially on the perception of form as form, of formal relationships as such, of the relationship of part to whole.

Values residing in the use of *language* offer some readers some of the strongest appeals a novel can make. To be sure, they are not equally esteemed by all readers (nor even all writers): as we have seen, it is quite possible for clumsily written books to gain recognition, and even some highly regarded novelists have been surprisingly indifferent to the way their sentences actually read.

It is of course through the language that we perceive the form, in all its detail, its richness, its complexity. When we are perceiving a form, the minimum virtue we can demand of the language is that it enhance our perception of the form, that it be apt. This statement refers to something more interesting than Aristotle's plain dictum that the diction be "clear and not mean." The appropriateness of language to form extends to almost any kind of virtuosity in language that does not actually create a disunity, since the concept of the form itself includes its linguistic vitality. The virtues we particularly appreciate in a given use of language—its power to shape and even create thought and to concentrate and intensify and enrich meanings (with immense economy, as, for instance, through the multiplication of secon-

dary meanings and qualifications of meanings), to arrest attention upon every successive detail, to render vividly states of mind
and attitude in the speaker, the vitality and motion and play of
thought and intensity of feeling, along with the purely sensuous
qualities of the words and phrases themselves, of the rhythms,
the sounds, the "free-floating imagery"—these virtues are all
(except the sensuous ones) of the same kind as the values we
shall see below in the conventions and principles of construction
by which the larger forms are built. And if these virtues are to be
fully appreciated in a text, there surely must be a full comprehension of the significance of their context—which is the
perception of the form of the whole.

Still, it is clear that a writer may easily develop such virtues in a
fragment, and just as plainly a reader or critic may appreciate at
least some of them in a passage taken out of context—
independent of the form, as we see whenever a critic isolates a
passage for praise or blame without mention of its surroundings.
When so handled, linguistic values must be regarded as nonformal values. It seems clear, however, that the linguistic values
of a text can never be fully recognized apart from a perception
of the form of the whole—which makes them dependent on the
form if not directly formal values themselves.

If there are specifically formal values in our perception of the
presentation, the "execution" of the form, we should find them in
the work's use of conventions, since it is through conventions
that the form is executed. But conventions have two aspects:
they are agreements and they perform functions. It is clear that
they may contribute values to the work in both aspects but not
that both kinds of values are formal.

The mere fact that a convention is a convention—that it is
related to other works—itself attracts many observers. Such a
value—that contributed by the convention as an agreement—is,
however, clearly not formal. As agreements, conventions precede the perception of the form, existing in a sense outside the
work. The recognition of a convention can be a source of delight, even though it has nothing to do with the specific artistic
nature of the work and requires nothing more than a superficial
understanding of it. The delight may arise from the power of
conventions to exclude audiences, to create elite or select

groups—for conventions, both traditional and original, are the source of the unfortunate capacity of art to support snobberies. Or it may arise from the feeling of security that traditional conventions may give us (the recognition of the familiar, as in a style or genre or period), or it may arise from the feeling of shock (with the promise of pleasure to come when the convention is mastered) which the original conventions may give us.

None of these values, though important in the experience of most novel readers, is formal. But what about the values in perceiving the function of conventions? Let us distinguish here between values in the conventions and the values of the forms created by those conventions. The popularity of studies of "technique" in the novel implies that the functioning of conventions is valued in itself to some degree, and the addressing of many such books to an audience not of writers trying to learn a craft but of academics eager to understand it suggests that this value is not merely practical but in some way a part of the general audience's appreciation of the art. But is it a formal value?

We can pursue this value by considering restrictive conventions. To perceive execution as such, technique or presentation as such, is to perceive the restrictive conventions against which the created forms struggle. In the novel these begin with the restrictions on the narrator and language and extend to every restraint. Like the rules of a game, they provide the terms and measure for a display of specialized virtuosity. They differ from games in that each new work sets up new rules: the artist invents his own tests to define his own skill. Each novel measures itself against its own narrative ground rules, its own restrictions on the fictional world, on the action, on the language.

In a competitive game the object is to win within the rules.[3] What is the analogue of "winning" in the novel? If the aim is to create a form in the process of becoming visible, victory would

[3]Competitive sports of course imitate combat and have ritualistic and expressive functions as well, and the sports fan probably derives chief gratification from these aspects. Still, in many games, the victory itself is understood as a manifestation of the winner's superior skill, and even the partisan fan would not like a team's victory to be achieved through cheating or default or by changing the rules of the game. Obviously the appreciation of skill for its own sake is a profound value for nonpartisan and partisan fan alike.

be measured by the extent to which this process is made difficult (yet not actually prevented) by the restrictive conventions.

The artistic virtue developed in this way is *economy*, concentration and efficiency: the maximum use of the means available within the restrictions set. The principle of economy is relevant in every part of the work, since restrictive conventions operate everywhere; it is the common virtue of all good technique. The display of Isabel's great discovery in the single concentrated scene of her "midnight vigil," or the use of Henrietta to provide dramatically certain lights on Isabel while at the same time moving the action forward, or the use of Gardencourt as a framing site for beginning and end, enriching the implications of both scenes—these are only some clear and obvious examples in *The Portrait of a Lady*: the quality can be discerned, no doubt, in every scene, every paragraph, perhaps virtually every sentence in the whole long novel. Economy is certainly, preeminently, a "formal" value—a criterion directly related to the display of skill which the work of art intends to manifest. It is evident, too, that though particular economies may be observed in fragments, a full appreciation of economy is not possible without a clear perception of the whole, which provides its measure.

To many of us an appreciation of a novelist's economy seems intrinsic, absolutely essential to all appreciation of his work. But is this really true for the so-called nontechnical reader, not a writer or trained in the study of the writer's art? I suspect it is, that even for the lay reader the recognition of economy is important. Nor is it merely that a lack of economy would obscure the form and hence create annoyance or boredom. Economy is positive; we appreciate it wherever we recognize it, in arts other than our own and in kinds of writing other than our own specialties. Students who are not writers appreciate economy in writing when it is pointed out to them. Critics assume that it will be appreciated when it is observed, with no need to demonstrate why.

Why do we value economy so much? How do we benefit when we discover it? Most obviously, economy is an achievement, a conquest of a difficulty; the recognition of such a conquest apparently strengthens us, becomes in a way our own. Have we a need to identify with achievement, or perceive what makes it

possible? Our perception of economy is just this, the beginning of a diagnostic analysis of an achievement. Economy in art is also a display of abundance, wealth, even power—the mind holds all these goods in its clear grasp, and we gratify ourselves when our minds, following, experience that same power. It also intensifies our perception: the fictional world, images, thoughts, people, the whole panorama of existence, are distilled into perception for us by the author's restrictions and words in particular, consciousness concentrated in those restrictions, magnified by the terms that confine it.

But what of the *formal principle* itself? Of course, perception of it helps us to discover and appreciate the values I have been describing. It enhances our enjoyment of the fictional world and is essential to our enjoyment of the economies of the presentation. But is it a value in its own right?

No doubt every analyzable aspect of the formal principle is a source of possible value, but some of these values appear to be rather specialized. The aspect of singleness, for instance (the germinal principle or, even more abstractly, the design principle) is valued more by some than by others. This is the issue in debates between critics and partisans of the "well-made" work and the novel of full life, between Henry James and E. M. Forster. These debates show the relatively narrow attraction of singleness as such. No doubt a fondness for symmetry, for balance, has deep psychological roots, yet some people care more for it than do others.

The opposite virtue, copiousness, is also rather specialized, as a formal value. To appreciate a novel for its "teeming life" is to appreciate the interests of its fictional world, enhanced by its magnitude. We value copiousness for extending the limits of those novelistic values that can be so drawn out.[4] This extension in itself is not a formal value. To appreciate, on the other hand,

[4]Copiousness is a value especially addressed by gigantic works: *Don Quixote, War and Peace, Ulysses* and, on the contemporary scale, *Gravity's Rainbow.* To some degree, however, it seems to be an intrinsic novelistic value (why we choose to read a novel instead of a short story), though when carried to the gargantuan extreme it is obviously a specialized one (not everybody who likes novels cares to read such works), just as tight unity is. Let it be noted that as a value copiousness is not necessarily antipathetic to economy as the latter term has been defined here.

how copiousness has been developed from a simple germinal idea is to appreciate principles of construction. This value is formal, involving awareness of the very process of composition, but it seems to be specialized, since it requires not merely knowledge of the art and its difficulties but also projection into the imagined psychology of the author as he or she creates from who knows what beginnings? It is the sort of appreciation, perhaps, that novelists often give to their colleagues—"novelists' novelists."

Appreciation of the formal principle as such may include specialized values, but it goes beyond them. The most general value directly arising from the perception of the formal principle is probably that which is associated with *synthesis*. This value we find in the display of manifest relatedness, of inner logic, of complex consistency, in any kind of joining together, most especially and significantly in the conversion of chaos into order. It differs from economy, though the two virtues will always be found, I think, together.[5] Whatever value the novel has as synthesis results from the formal principle, which expresses the synthesizing power that holds the novel together.

Our pleasure in the perception of synthesis must surely be one of the most important of all the novelistic values. Its importance in poetry and in art in general has long been recognized: it is implicit in the very conception of organic form. For Coleridge synthesis was the essential function of the primary poetic faculty, the imagination: "that synthetic and magical power" which expresses itself in "the balance or reconcilement of opposite or discordant qualities."[6] It is implicit in expressive theories such as Croce's intuitive form and Langer's expressive form. Synthesis felt in every detail is the defining feature of the language of poetry as it is understood by the New Critics.

[5]We appreciate economy when we see how much has been achieved with so few or so concentrated means, synthesis when we see how intimately or essentially one thing is related to something else seemingly different. To appreciate Isabel's vigil for how much and how dramatically she learns in that scene is to appreciate economy; to appreciate it for its contribution to our understanding of the story as a whole, for its place, given what has preceded and what will follow, is to appreciate synthesis.

[6]Samuel Taylor Coleridge, *Biographia Literaria* (London, 1934), chap. 14 (p. 166).

Compelling evidence for the value of synthesis in the novel can be found in the very process of reading itself. I have stressed the importance of the act of reading—so much more central to our pleasure than any subsequent reflection can be. It would be hard to imagine better evidence for the importance of the value of synthesis in the novel than this most fundamental delight all readers take in the patient, slow, orderly process of watching the novel grow together, piece by piece, step by step, part by part. We are most conscious of the process by which form is synthesized when the form is not clearly visible. When elements of seeming disorder remain—this is when we most desire to watch that active synthesizing power; when previously unaccountable parts become predictable, then we are most conscious of it. The "process of discovering the form," as I have called it, is nothing other than the process of synthesis itself.

Of course there are other possible explanations for the patience in us which the act of reading so beautifully demonstrates. We read in order and complete because this is how the work of art is displayed to us, how we experience whatever the values of the novel may be. But would we do so if synthesis were not high among those values? I have been able to think of only one other value which might compel such high respect for the order in which the novel unfolds and such passion to follow through to the end: namely, the vicarious pleasure we take from participating in the *mimetic* experience—in brief, the "suspense." The lover of fiction says, "I read because I am interested in these people, in what happens to them and who they are and how they feel, and I have to read it in order—from beginning to end—because if I don't I won't be able to follow." Yes, but still we can ask, what is it that intensifies your interest as you approach the end, makes you so restless that you do not stop until the finish? "I have to know what becomes of these people"—is this the reply?—"I can't leave them all unsettled; their story's not over until the end." But what do such answers show except how much of the value of the experience results from its being unconfused and complete: ordered, coherent, clear—and synthesized. Which brings us back to the same point: the pleasure in discovering the synthesis seems to invade even the vicarious mimetic experience itself as it compels us to go through the slow process

of reading the novel, with such patience in the hope of such rewards.

Two suggestive comparisons help support my claim. First, other arts—notably music—also develop a process which for their devotees is as compelling as the process of fiction yet contains no vicarious mimetic experience at all. Second, other kinds of literary works, not fiction, also compel us to a similar patience (well-crafted works of philosophy, of history, of science, when we respond to these works as literature), again without the vicarious mimetic experience. Our willingness to submit to the author's organization, not to skip about nor to skim but to wait and find out, our readiness to be shown the possible importance of even the most seemingly minor details, and our hopeful assumption that their proper places will be found—this attitude shows the high importance we give to the value of synthesis in the literary work.

Here I differ, of course, with those who, like Longinus, find the highest value not in the whole but in the sublime moment—that which "flashing forth at the right moment scatters everything before it like a thunderbolt, and at once displays the power of the orator in all its plenitude."[7] The difference must be conceded, although I think an argument might be made to reduce even this somewhat by showing how much sublime moments may resemble manifestations of the formal virtue of economy. A modern critic might also make an argument,[8] which would have to be against Longinus's explicit view (as also Matthew Arnold), to show that the sublime moment cannot be quite so independent of its context as the method of quoting out of context implies. Such arguments are not needed, however, if our aim is to show not that synthesis overshadows all other values but only that it is important in itself.

The emphasis on synthesis is also contrary—or looks so, anyway—to the argument that the true value of the literary work is in discontinuity, disruption. I have spoken of this view before.

[7]Longinus, *On the Sublime*, trans. W. Rhys Roberts, in *The Great Critics*, ed. James Harry Smith and Edd Winfield Parks, rev. ed. (New York, 1960), p. 66.
[8]For an example of this kind of argument, see Elder Olson's demonstration of how the power of the "Tomorrow and tomorrow and tomorrow" soliloquy in *Macbeth* depends on its context (*Tragedy*, pp. 114-25).

Discontinuity, it is claimed, fixes our attention, makes the work call that attention to itself. Unquestionably discontinuity is an attraction, a genuine artistic value. Yet, except for the political (and perhaps symbolic) values that some critics attach to it, the values of discontinuity seem to me not contradictory to but actually expressive of the values of synthesis and indeed directly linked to them. I mean here not that discontinuity has to be based on a ground of conventional coherence, as everyone acknowledges, but rather that synthesis itself is not possible without discontinuity first: the attempt to overcome the latter constitutes the attraction of the former; discontinuity calls attention to the synthesizing process. Discontinuity is of course the same as the delay and the difficulty mentioned above, which enhance the synthesizing process, but actually it does more than enhance, it is essential. Contemporary critics, to be sure, deplore the idea that the discontinuity could ever be resolved; they protest the banality that ensues when we "naturalize" prematurely the difficult contemporary novel.[9] So do we, though we cannot stop pursuing the synthesis: because at the point when the synthesizing process finally stops, when the form is fully seen and there are no more problems to be solved—at that point the synthesizing value ends and the form does indeed become banal.

Can we explain why we find such attraction in the synthesizing process? Order and chaos are phenomena of perception; as the formal principle imposes order, so the observer's confusion changes into control. The working of the formal principle is simply (and literally) the reader's own mastery of the work presented. We value this experience. Why? Is it that the artistic experience exercises our faculties so that we can better cope with the great disorderly world and the mess of our minds? Or is the activity of understanding—which the process of synthesis constitutes—sufficient in itself, intrinsically pleasing because it is the natural exercise of the human mind? Does the guidance of

[9]"Such novels [the most radical modern texts] act by becoming thoroughly banal when naturalized and showing the reader at what cost he has purchased intelligibility" (Jonathan Culler, *Structuralist Poetics: Structuralism, Linguistics, and the Study of Literature* [Ithaca, 1975], p. 200), summarizing what Stephen Heath "has admirably demonstrated" in *The Nouveau Roman* (London, 1972), pp. 137-45.

an artistic principle enable us to master more complex perceptions than we can elsewhere, thus making us feel more sentient
than we ordinarily do? Or does sharing the perception of the
form with others (with artists and other members of the
audience—a sharing which art always implies) confirm our sense
of belonging to a community of sentient beings? Or are we made
aware of our sentience without regard to others: is our sentience
affirmation that we are alive? However we describe it, certainly
we all want to enlarge and enrich the activity of our consciousness as much as possible, and so we gather experiences of creative perception—synthesis—for ourselves and to share with others.

And we value the skill that is manifested in the synthesis. This,
too, is enhanced by the delay in the perception of the form
through the act of reading. We are most aware of the artist's skill
when we are most aware of what that skill is doing. The delay in
the process makes our consciousness of that skill active. It leads
us to participate in the forming of the novel, labor akin to the
novelist's. The values of the visible form are values we have
worked for. The artist's mastery is a mastery we ourselves have
worked to perceive, and thereby to achieve. Perhaps this effort is
the source of that personal attachment that makes us feel that
the work of art belongs quite privately to us (how generously we
share it with the rest of the world) and leads us to identify so
strongly with the artist as maker of the form.

No doubt we have just answered a question that might otherwise perplex the cynical reader: why should we, self-centered
as we are, care so much about somebody else's skill, anyway? Are
we so generous of spirit, after all, that we can explain our intense
devotion to certain books and other works of art as the admiration of someone else's ability? Does the artist's skill make us feel
better about the human race (without envy, too)? Does it speak
to us of what we might have been (without envy)? If this seems
unlikely, consider those other activities besides self-contained art
whose aim is to display skill. If the goal of art were so simple, we
would distinguish it with difficulty from games, acrobatics, other
virtuoso performances, puzzles, and the like. Skills are always
specific, however; the specific skill in the art is devoted to the

making of original things, and that added particular takes precedence over the general specification.

The specific value of the original form as a self-contained entity must be not that it *displays* the artist's skill but that it makes us partake of or exercise an analogous skill ourselves. I mean not that we admire the author's mastery of disorder by order; we move ourselves from the one to the other as we take hold of the form. It is the same with our perception of economy and the other formal virtues: to perceive the economy we must at least feel the difficulty that has been so economically resolved, and in so doing we, too, become its master.

Participation of the reader in recreating the form has been implied throughout this book. The idea has been recognized by critics in a number of contexts—beginning with Longinus, who, of course, conceived of it in relation to the perception not of the whole work but only of the sublime moment. For Croce, however, and for Collingwood, the reader reproduces the expressive experience of the artist in reconstructing the integrated work of art. The notion has become especially popular nowadays—it is apparent not only in the general conception of "recuperation" or "naturalization" of a text, which is seen by the structuralists as the reader's task, but also as a kind of ideal objective for a literary text, as in Barthes's conception of the true "writerly" text and Robbe-Grillet's assertion, in the passage quoted more fully above, of the author's "absolute need of the reader's cooperation, an active, conscious, *creative* assistance."

So we must revise our words in the beginning about the novel as a work of self-contained art; its function is not after all simply to display or call attention to the art of its maker but to make us participate as if the art were our own.

The primary values of economy and synthesis and the secondary values of defamiliarization and shared attention—no doubt there are other "general formal values" in the novel besides these, and certainly these could also be described in other ways, approached from other viewpoints, given different names. The point here is only that they are indeed "formal"—they arise in our perception of the form, what it is, how it works—and they

are important. It would be wrong, of course, to insist that these are the primary novelistic values in an absolute sense and in every reader's experience. Who can speak of every reader's experience? And who is the critic who can tell "every reader" which are the true novelistic values in that reader's experience and which are not? Even so, apart from the values of vicarious mimetic experience, which have been severely attacked by so many contemporary critics and are obviously of great importance to so many real readers—apart from these, which cannot be dismissed, I find it difficult to think of any significant novelistic values or interests—ones that are generally applicable, those which I expect to find in any good novel, values strong enough to put the average or the good reader to the work of reading a whole novel—that are not here included. They show how central is the idea of form, and how useful in taking us to what counts in the art of the novel.

FOUR NOVELS

Introduction

A "formal analysis" of a novel studies how its parts relate to the whole. It requires a conception of the whole and implies a formal theory of some kind, of which it is an application. A formal analysis applying the theory of this book would study the novel's formal hierarchy—the principle that governs it and the relationship of parts to that principle. It would begin with and focus on what I have found at the center of the formal principle, what I have called plot.

It is curious that this process does not quite correspond to any of the categories of possible operations on the text that Todorov has described.[1] It is not projection, commentary, description, or interpretation, all of which attempt to translate the text into other terms. It is not poetics, which treats the text as an example of a system. It is close in its aims to what he calls reading, which seeks to "relat[e] each element of the text to all the others" so as to "dismantle the system of that text" but rejects the concept of a unifying principle. Does it then belong to the kind of circular operation for which Frank Lentricchia has recently castigated the New Critics: "The New Critic tends, first, to ascribe, *a priori*, special objective properties to literary discourse (it is inherently ambiguous, or symbolic, or organically whole), and then, with circular logic, to describe the critical act as consisting in the location, that is, the *finding* of those qualities, wherever they may be"?[2]

[1]Tzvetan Todorov, *The Poetics of Prose*, trans. Richard Howard (Ithaca, 1977), pp. 234-41.
[2]Frank Lentricchia, *After the New Criticism* (Chicago, 1980), p. 107.

The formal critic's answer is that although he does indeed start with the abstract conception of an organic whole (which is, we have seen, a *convention* of the novel, as of all self-contained art), what he seeks is a specific and quite unique principle of wholeness. He does so not to prove that a principle is indeed there but to use that principle to articulate (and perhaps facilitate) his perception of the work. He tries to put into words an essential part of the reader's experience: a perception of what the work *is*, in terms more comprehensive and freer than the limiting terms of interpretation or commentary. The values of this procedure are many and obvious. If the formal analysis can actually describe the work artistically, its conclusions will be useful for anything else we may want to do with the text: to make it more accessible to others (that is, "teach" it), for instance. Or if we want to understand it in the context of literary history or of genre. In general, a clear perception of the form and a good articulation of that view seem to be prerequisite to any intelligent communication between one reader and another about a work, the question always being, "What work are we talking about?" And certainly a critic who wants to judge, to make evaluations, for good or bad, ought to have a clear idea of the form he is criticizing.

As for the danger of circularity, we look for wholes because we are expected to. The search is a fundamental convention of art. Is there a fear that in my eagerness to find a whole I will impose on a work a unity that is not there? Oddly enough, this danger does not worry me, provided I am able, if someone produces a better hypothesis, to recognize its superiority. If I am unable to do so, the problem is not in the intrinsic circularity of wholeness but in my stubbornness or vanity.

The stubbornness can be chastened, perhaps, if we reiterate that there is no such thing as a definitive formal analysis, not unless the work has died—become banal, as judged at least by whoever calls the analysis definitive. For the form of a novel is not an inherent, intrinsic, provable either-or fact, which you see or you don't. The reader while reading, and while reflecting afterward, expects to discover wholeness. A formal analysis is an attempt to describe that expected principle, and its very incompleteness, its very tentativeness, are signs that a full perception

has not yet been reached and the work is still alive. It is likely, too, that as the reader's view grows clearer, his expectations will change and the form, still an expectation, will change accordingly and will continue to elude him.

For the writer, the case is similar. What he writes is a construction meant to suggest the likelihood that a principle of wholeness may eventually be discovered. Whether the writer himself has found it is less important than that the work be able both to arouse and to avoid terminating the reader's expectation. (I shall consider how this question appears to a writer, from my own personal point of view, in the last chapter of this book.)

To be sure, the reader's pursuit of that perception is not totally free. We acknowledge a standard of some sort when we admit the arguability of our hypotheses. The standard is in part set by the criterion of "explainability" (the superior hypothesis is the one that accounts for more and so has the greater integrative power) but also and more significantly by the conventions in the work, gathered together in the concept of the implied reader. If we the readers do not actually know all these conventions, we nevertheless accept the idea that they exist when we agree that misreading, or overreading or underreading, is possible. This agreement qualifies our conception of the form: it is the principle of wholeness which the implied reader expects to perceive and which we, following, expect to see over his shoulder, so to speak. It is what we anticipate finding when we have acquired a full knowledge of the work and of the conventions that compose it.

This statement, too, needs a qualification, since most of us read novels for our own interests rather than for historical ones. (See chapter 6, "The Limits of Analysis.") We tend to accept as legitimate those readings that adapt the implied historical reader to some contemporary standard of competent reading (the "implied contemporary reader"). Thus many of us will accept as more interesting, and legitimate, a reading of "The Turn of the Screw" that defines its subject as the neuroticism of the governess than an interpretation of it (what James appears to have intended) as a simple ghost story. In general we accept as competent a reading that introduces ideas which could not have been explicitly known in the original (Freudian psychology, for in-

stance), as long as such a view is not actually incompatible with the norms of the implied historical reader.[3] This procedure of course tends to keep open and extend indefinitely the process by which a form continues to recede before us.

Each chapter in part 2 of this book studies the plot of a specific novel. The aim is partly to make the analysis of the formal principle more specific by demonstration and partly to show the light that such an analysis can shed on particular works.

No doubt *The Portrait of a Lady* is one of the most worked-over of novels. For this reason (and others) I have used it frequently for illustration in the foregoing discussion. By choosing it for the first plot study I hope to pull together and perhaps correct what I have already said about it. *The Portrait* is also convenient as a type for the traditional—a classic novel, tightly unified, on a large scale.

The three other studies demonstrate some ways in which the concept of the formal principle can be adapted to works that depart from the central tradition. Each case illustrates in a distinctive way some problem of a kind especially important in modern fiction. For this purpose I have preferred not to use the most revolutionary novels of our time (not *Ulysses* or *Gravity's Rainbow* or *Naked Lunch* or *Ada*), taking rather works whose innovations are more modest. Those treated here are formally radical in some specific and limited ways—a characteristic which makes them more useful for showing the adaptability of the theory than a revolutionary work with many-sided innovations would be.

[3]The "implied contemporary reader" might be described as the range of possible (though of course unforeseen by the author) knowledge and opinion which might enter into the reading of the work after its own time or outside its own implied audience which is, or appears to be at any rate, compatible with the conventions, the knowledge, and opinions, of its "implied historical reader." I propose the compatibility test uncertainly. We do seem to accept some departures from the strict implied historical reading, yet we don't accept all. At some point we will object, and if we do allow a reading beyond that point we will qualify it by admitting that we have ourselves in some way revised the work. What is the standard by which we make this distinction, if not that of compatibility with the initial assumptions of the work?

Similarly, the fact that the novels are well known permits me to keep the focus more securely on the question of form; the problems of interpretation at the basic "grammatical" level have presumably been solved. I have not attempted to incorporate every refinement of meaning critics have found in these texts: the "orthodox interpretation," largely reflecting conclusions agreed upon by good, intelligent readers, is less likely to obscure the nature and usefulness of a plot study.

In limiting each study to plot (since the analysis of the formal principle of any novel could be almost infinitely extended), I have set as the minimal requirement that the analysis abstract the germinal subject and show it in its main embodiments. Although each study focuses on a different formal problem, bringing into use different terms for analysis, none develops the lower elements in the formal hierarchy. Nor have I attempted to spell out the compositional principles used in my explication of the theory—terms such as *principles of construction* or *invention,* which are used to compose the formal principle, as distinct from terms such as *germinal principle* or *plot,* which concern the formal principle as composed. A complementary analysis of compositional principles, valuable in showing how an artist works, and for the study of poetics, can come only at a later stage, when a conception of the form composed by such principles has been attained.[4]

The most important limitation, however, results from the fact that the *process of discovering* the form, and its continuing nature, can scarcely be shown at all in a short formal analysis. True, plot studies like these tend to develop a kind of dialectical organization, and this tendency may reflect in a reorganized way the nature of the discovery process. But the actual process is concealed, and as far as I can tell, it cannot be otherwise. In every one of these studies it is tacitly assumed that the form described is not a thing completely viewed, although the formal analysis can describe it only as if it were. The analysis thus presents a

---

[4]It is with the possibility of an analysis of the compositional principles that the formal critic of this book comes perhaps closest to the interests of the structuralists—and maybe such analysis would also be what Todorov calls reading. The structuralists' terms for distinguishing such principles are, of course, very different.

model that we would expect to find confirmed (filled out, made more concrete, qualified without being altered) if we were to pursue it further, a view hypothetical in an essential and necessary way, a station on the way toward full visibility. As long as the work lives for its critic, there will always be more to discover.

[9]

Dynamic Plot:
The Portrait of a Lady

Perhaps no other major novelist was so explicitly concerned with unity, order, or form as Henry James. And of his larger works, *The Portrait of a Lady* was, by his own judgment, "the most proportioned of his productions after 'The Ambassadors.'" It was a large edifice built "brick upon brick" upon a "single small corner-stone," which was, as we have seen, the "conception of a certain young woman affronting her destiny."[1] Having already used an imaginary version of this most deliberately unified work to help us develop the concept of the formal principle, let us now return to the real thing.

This analysis must be confined to the dominant element in the formal hierarchy, that is, the plot—the "germinal subject as developed by the principles of construction." First, however, we must sketch the primary subordinated commitments—to fictional world, narrative, and language (which I have already outlined for the imaginary case in chapter 7). Unfortunately, I shall be able in so short a demonstration to suggest only roughly how plot actually controls these subordinate parts.

The most significant feature of the fictional world (which I described earlier as "realistic, contemporary, international upper-class") is that it manifests a high civilization in which social evils have been by and large stripped away. The people are exceptional rather than normal, more capable, stronger of intellect, more articulate than usual in modern realism. Isabel is

---

[1]Henry James, *The Art of the Novel* (New York, 1946), p. 52, 48.

superior to "nineteen out of twenty women." Madame Merle is famous for the "perfection" of her social manner, the "cleverest woman in the world"; Pansy is the paragon of childish innocence and filial obedience; Warburton, Goodwood, and even Osmond epitomize qualities that we shall consider later. These features help bring into focus such essential traits as Isabel's inner suffering and Osmond's malignity, which might otherwise be less visible.

The primary narrative commitment is to a voice that I described in the hypothetical case as "outside the fictional world, having an independent personality, a point of view with broad privilege, close to Isabel but not always so, with dramatizing restrictions, an attitude of mild irony and sympathy, and so on." This narrator is notable for his leisurely and gradual development of the story, for moving easily between narration and dramatic scene, for careful preparation and fullness of development, and for his sympathetic, affectionate, yet critical attitude toward the protagonist.

The stylistic commitment ("Jamesian language with all that implies") is to a simpler kind of language than that which James later developed. It is nevertheless capable of great elaboration. Its most significant feature is its capacity for making fine distinctions ("With all her love of knowledge she had a natural shrinking from raising curtains and looking into unlighted corners. The love of knowledge coexisted in her mind with the finest capacity for ignorance.")[2] In addition James shows a constant tendency to use, and sometimes develop at length, metaphors, especially for mental, emotional, and moral states and states of character (the curtains and corners in the passage just quoted). A third major feature is frequent irony, generally quiet and subtle, often just barely suggested in the tone of the language (as in the expression "finest capacity for ignorance"). Fourth, the novel shows James's notorious indirectness, a preference for avoiding the forthright statement of an action, a motive, a fact. This aspect is related to the metaphors and the irony, both of which reflect it. Then, too, the language is meticulous, self-

---

[2]Henry James, *The Portrait of a Lady*, New York Edition (New York, 1908), 1:284. Page references in the text refer to this edition.

conscious about usage (James often places words in quotation marks), and distinctively informal—including colloquialisms, even slang (though seldom the vernacular), suggesting conversation in its vocabulary if not always in its construction.

Commitments to these features are in a sense independent of the plot yet secondary to it, made to serve it in the formal hierarchy. Disregarding the hypothetical germinal principle used for argument in our imaginary case, let us approach the plot by analyzing the action. There is a clearly identifiable center—a protagonist, Isabel Archer—and our impressions support James's claim that the other characters exist for the sake of their "contributions to [her] history." The terminal points of the action are easily located; the beginning is roughly Isabel's decision to go to Europe, and the end is her decision to return to Osmond in Rome. Events before this beginning (Isabel's earlier life, for instance) exist as "background," part of the given complex from which the central action springs rather than an integral part of it. Between these points, Isabel loses things of value—her freedom, her beloved Ralph, her hopes. She also changes; perhaps she grows. These changes evolve through an elaborate series of problems and resolutions. We may begin to grasp the structure of this series by observing how the movement from beginning to end is divided.

There are two distinct parts, unequal in length—the second is shorter than the first—but with balance of a kind. In the first part Isabel is on a quest. Having been taken up by Mrs. Touchett, she pursues a double end: to find a worthy destiny and to form (more or less deliberately) her character. In the midst of this search she unexpectedly inherits great wealth, which sharpens her problems and also makes her exploitable. In this part of the plot she refuses possible commitments (in the form of offers of marriage) until the end. Her choice of Gilbert Osmond, obviously a great error, culminates her quest in the first part and becomes the chief source of her subsequent difficulties.

The second part develops after a three-year hiatus and displays through a couple of extended episodes the consequences of Isabel's mistake: her suffering, her awareness, growing in stages, of the various aspects of her error, and dilemmas caused

by her discoveries. This section concludes with a choice—the decision not to escape from her constricting and humiliating marital situation.

Let us look more closely at the divisions. The opening chapters of the novel define the protagonist's character at the outset. A detailed portrait establishes her intrinsic distinction, her general superiority of intelligence and perception, what the narrator calls her "fine organisation." Isabel is motivated by a powerful desire to know as much about life as she can and to be involved in it, a desire that does not exclude the possibility of unhappiness. Her most important motivation is her self-esteem or pride, evident in her desire to control her fate and her striking concern for independence. Equally striking is her wish to shape the growth of her own character: "She was always planning out her development, desiring her perfection, observing her progress" (1:72). Although "she had no talent for expression and too little of the consciousness of genius[,] she only had a general idea that people were right when they treated her as if she were rather superior" (1:67), but she needs to confirm or consolidate this view of herself. Gradually we learn how she conceives superiority. It is a matter of intelligence and good manners, of kindness, of cultivation and taste, knowledge of the values of civilization, freedom from vulgarity. The superior person is open and appreciative and tolerant. Heroism and courage are important ("Sometimes she went so far as to wish that she might find herself some day in a difficult position, so that she should have the pleasure of being as heroic as the occasion demanded"[1:69]). Most important of all, however, is moral perfection ("She had an infinite hope that she should never do anything wrong" [1:68]). Much later, in the midst of her suffering, she sums up, in her idea of the "aristocratic life," the needs of the superior being: "simply the union of great knowledge with great liberty; the knowledge would give one a sense of duty and the liberty a sense of enjoyment" (2:198). The phrase is similar to that with which James in the Prefaces characterizes the "free spirit": "finely aware and richly responsible."[3]

Despite the criticism in the narrator's gentle irony in the early

---

[3]James, *The Art of the Novel*, p. 62.

chapters, Isabel is presented mostly with sympathy. She is approved for her honesty, her generosity, her good intentions, and the nobility of the qualities for which she would like to be admired. The narrator's own carefully qualified admiration is fortified by the almost unqualified admiration of the other characters we meet early in the book—especially Ralph.

Given such a character, whose chief aspirations are to find a worthy destiny and to mold her own character, it is not surprising that the primary suspense will be not the question "What will happen to her?" but rather "What will she do?" The major events in the first part are choices she makes. There are four of these, all in response to offers she receives as a result of the extraordinary attraction she exerts. This magnetism—itself an effect of her character—is "given" (present from the beginning, not produced by the action), an involuntary power that her superiority lends her, and it must be reckoned along with her choices as a major cause for the development of the plot. It is partly responsible for the fortune bequeathed to her by Mr. Touchett, a bequest that simply increases her attractiveness to people like Osmond and Madame Merle.

The first of the four choices is the beginning of the plot: her acceptance of Mrs. Touchett's invitation. It expresses her desire to live and to know and her belief that for this she must go to Europe, the center of civilization and the repository of history and art. The second and third choices—her rejections of Warburton and Goodwood—both resolve dilemmas caused by her attractive power. Each of the offers proposes an answer to her quest. Each is rejected because she believes something better is possible. What it might be she does not yet know, but it appears when she makes her fourth choice and accepts Osmond. To be understood, this final choice must be measured against the other two; it indicates her preference for values represented by Osmond over values represented by the other two. Her decision shows that she has been learning to discriminate since the beginning of the novel. I say she has "learned" this, since she had not been able to envision the choice until Osmond presented himself, while her rejections of the other two were forged from her feelings, only partly articulate, at the time the offers were made. The dilemmas, in other words, more than merely illustrate how

she decides; they force her to choose and to discriminate between values as she had not previously done.

Obviously she chooses Osmond because he offers (so she supposes) what the others could not. Each of the suitors seems the perfection of certain admirable traditions. Caspar is the flowering of American industry, of self-sufficiency, of the forceful man. Warburton epitomizes the British aristocracy, the grace and gallantry of the chivalrous man. Osmond, however, transcends nationality. In him we see—or, rather, Isabel thinks *she* sees—the culmination of international culture. He is the man of art, the man of taste, liberated from vulgarity. (He was, by his own judgment, "the first gentleman in Europe" [2:197].) In preferring him to the others, she expresses her preference for truth and beauty over wealth and status, over power and prominence, over the parochialism of country.

But doesn't this description ignore the emotional basis for her choice? No doubt her action does include a rejection of sexual emotion and romantic feeling, of the energy she fears in Caspar and the untapped responsive force she fears in herself. It is said, also, that she "loves" Osmond and did not love the others. And of course she is cleverly manipulated toward him. The emotion is scarcely dramatized, though; unexplained, it is easily reducible to a warm response she feels to the high good things she selects in Osmond (an emotional expression of rational choice). The manipulation is not discovered until later—so that from her own point of view her discriminations seem as I have described them. Together they express Isabel's chief desire, to become (and live the life of) the most highly civilized being possible, a desire that has taken her to Europe, made her reject the most brilliant roles in the best societies of America and England, and led her to choose instead the supranational world, where all that is base and vulgar has been refined away, where the highest values are knowledge and beauty.

A major complication here is Isabel's acquisition of a fortune between her third and fourth choices. The death of Mr. Touchett, "accidental" in Isabel's story, enables the author to *delay* the full emergence of Isabel's dangerous attractiveness. This delay is useful chiefly for "rhetorical" considerations: by making her inheritance follow her rejection of Warburton and

Goodwood, the author preserves the attractiveness of the rejected proposals and emphasizes her disregard for such advantages. The timing also brings out another aspect of Isabel's choice: her preference for giving great gifts (and choosing people who deserve them) rather than receiving them. The best life includes, she thinks, being of great use. It is her fortune that makes her errors so serious.

The consequences of these errors are developed in the second part through two major episodes. Both concern Isabel's relationship to Osmond, the first as affected by the Pansy-Rosier-Lord Warburton triangle, the second by Ralph's death and its aftermath. Both episodes bring intense and growing suffering for Isabel. There is also a sequence of discoveries of mistakes, which contribute to her distress. And the choices she now makes, to cope with the situation caused by her errors and discoveries, differ from those made earlier. Now she must choose not between positive values but between evils that must be faced.

Isabel's suffering results from her errors, and the discoveries in this part reveal those errors. First, she learns that she misjudged her husband's qualities—this discovery has developed gradually during the three years between the two parts and is brought to full consciousness in her "midnight vigil" by the fire. The crucial mistake was her failure to recognize the egotism concealed beneath his pretended indifference to the world, his absolute concern for appearances beneath his pretended superiority to them. In the perfection of his taste, she now recognizes, he lacks all generosity, humor, compassion, vitality. Contrast of him with Ralph makes these deficiencies clear, since Ralph actually does possess the virtues she had attributed to Osmond. The latter's faults are terrible for Isabel because they make him want to destroy her intellectual freedom; he wants her to be without ideas of her own: "Her mind was to be his— attached to his own like a small garden-plot to a deer-park" (2:200). She retains her freedom of mind in spite of him, but in so doing she incurs his hatred, which has "become the occupation and comfort of his life" (2:201). His perfect taste and love of tradition are now seen as slavish worship of forms and conventions. As Ralph later says, she is "ground in the very mill of the conventional"—an ironic fate for the girl who, in the beginning,

wanted to know the "things one shouldn't do," not so as to do them but "so as to choose."

She also becomes aware of the moral disorder concealed by Osmond's attitude: she is offended by his assumptions, which seem to her "hideously unclean" ("Did all women have lovers? Did they all lie and even the best have their price? Were there only three or four that didn't deceive their husbands?" [2:200–1]). Her discovery of Osmond's cynical morality is brought home when Osmond tries to make her use her power over Lord Warburton to secure him for Pansy. Isabel's awareness is complete at the end of the Warburton episode when Osmond accuses her of stopping Warburton's letter: the accusation reflects his own baseness of spirit, and she thinks of him as "going down—down; the vision of such a fall made her almost giddy" (2:275).

This episode also initiates Isabel's gradual discovery of her error in judging Madame Merle. She first recognizes a connection between Merle and Osmond in the famous scene in which Osmond is seen familiarly sitting while she is standing. Then, after Osmond's "fall," when Madame Merle chastises Isabel for the loss of Warburton, she realizes that Madame Merle has manipulated her into marriage. Here, too, she perceives a moral question in the case and tries to make a moral judgment: was it "wicked," what Madame Merle did to her? If not, it was at any rate "deeply false . . . deeply, deeply, deeply" (2:329). It remains for her to learn the motive: Madame Merle's relationship to Pansy, which is not revealed until Countess Gemini tells her near the end.

Isabel's final discovery of error concerns Ralph's role in her life. In her last meeting with Madame Merle she learns that her inheritance was actually a gift from Ralph, and in Ralph's deathbed scene she becomes aware of his love and of how well he has understood her.

Except for the relationship between Madame Merle and Pansy, the reader knows all Isabel's errors long before Isabel discovers them. (I speak, of course, of the "implied first reader.") We are privy to Ralph's request that Mr. Touchett change his will, as well as to several scenes in which Madame Merle "conspires" with Osmond. This knowledge also tends to

divert our interest from what happens to Isabel to what she knows and how she chooses. The primary impact of her discoveries lies not in the shock of the facts they reveal but in the satisfaction of seeing Isabel's awareness catch up with our own.[4]

Though they move Isabel toward moral discovery, the mistakes that she discovers in this part are not moral but judgmental. In the first place, she has misjudged people by their appearances. What she has most disastrously missed is the capacity for evil in people like Madame Merle and Osmond. Her error results from her failure to discriminate between her highest values: her assumption that Madame Merle's perfect social manners and Osmond's freedom from vulgarity imply corresponding moral virtue. The discovery of these mistakes thus *continues* the process of discriminating between values observed in the first part. Now she learns to distinguish between art, taste, and manners, on the one hand, and morality and humanity, on the other. When they clash, she will sacrifice the artistic to the moral.[5] And at the same time she relinquishes (though it is not so explicitly stated) that general faith in human perfectibility that she so vigorously defended earlier against the gibes of Ralph.

In the second place, she has misjudged her own ability to judge people. It is not merely that she mistakes Madame Merle and Osmond; she misunderstands and rejects the wisdom of the friends who warn her. All her friends except Warburton are opposed to Osmond at the time of her engagement. Their very

---

[4]This explanation does not justify the narrator's trick in withholding from the Merle-Osmond conspiracy scenes the truth about Pansy's birth. I am not sure the trick can be justified except as it intensifies the dramatic effect of the final scene between Countess Gemini and Isabel. This scene has other functions—but the surprise in it for the reader is not necessary for them. I suspect James was anxious to avoid an anticlimax here, but the device gives to the conspiracy scenes an air of trickery (on the author's part), a bit of fussywork that I wish he had found some way to eliminate.

[5]Even in the beginning she was prepared to do so, although apologetically: "She was fond of . . . looking at historical pictures—a class of efforts as to which she had often committed the conscious solecism of forgiving them much bad painting for the sake of the subject" (1:45). Her support of Henrietta, vulgarity and all, shows again her preference for humanity, when good, over aesthetic perfection. But good taste might conceal corruption—a fact that she did not know until Osmond demonstrated the possibility.

opposition only strengthens her determination. She is thus arrogant in thinking herself a free spirit. She does not fully recognize this mistake until Ralph's deathbed scene, when she abandons her attempt to hide her unhappiness from him. By this time she knows that her quest for freedom has led to her loss of freedom and that her assertion of free choice has played into the hands of her manipulators. The chief cause for this misfortune has been her pride. Although many of her errors arise from inexperience and ignorance, and so can arouse full sympathy in the reader, her pride qualifies everything. Like that of many another tragic or heroic character, it is presented as morally complex: we can admire it and at the same time see it as a fault that needs to be chastised. Much of the strong emotion in the final scene with Ralph certainly depends on the long-awaited collapse of Isabel's pride, which she acknowledges in her confession of need for his love and her own love, feelings which she has never before been able to admit.

All her discoveries, then, show moral evolution on Isabel's part—the continuing discrimination of high values and the acknowledgment of her own moral complexity. As in the first part, however, the chief events of this part are not the attainment of awareness but the choices she continues to make. Three are important, the controlling points in this section of the plot. They are (1) Isabel's response to Osmond's request to secure Lord Warburton for Pansy, (2) her decision to visit Ralph on his deathbed in defiance of Osmond, and (3) her decision to return to Rome at the end, thereby renouncing escape from her marriage.

In the first, Isabel performs a delicate balancing act, typical of Jamesian heroines. With Pansy she carries out Osmond's instructions to the letter, even though doing so means frustrating the young lover Ned Rosier and ignoring Pansy's own desires. With Warburton her behavior is more complicated. Though she avoids directly discouraging him, she refuses to use the power that Osmond wants her to use: she avoids allowing Warburton to think she would welcome his marriage to Pansy so as to have him near. The distinctions she makes indicate that she is trying to follow Osmond's wishes, but there is a limit beyond which she

cannot go.[6] She is stopped not by love—she is quite ready to ignore Pansy's love and concedes that Warburton need not be "in love" to marry Pansy, as long as he is "sure" (2:220)—but rather by honesty, a rejection of falseness or deviousness. In effect, her compromise means that she does not positively act in this case at all: though she does not obey Osmond, she does not defy him either. Her rule here seems to be to try to avoid deception of any kind.[7]

It is never stated to what extent Isabel is directly responsible for Warburton's departure, but the reader is encouraged to suppose that though she has prompted his self-inquiry, he would have come to the same conclusion sooner or later on his own. The most important thing, therefore, is not Isabel's accomplishment but how she tries to deal with it, and the most important consequence is not Warburton's flight but what happens between Isabel and Osmond. The baseness of Osmond's accusation in the end (namely, that she has intercepted a proposal from Warburton) is accentuated by the irony that she disobeyed him in order to avoid deviousness. The full contrast between their moral natures emerges vividly here.

The two final decisions also turn on conflict between Isabel's duty to her husband and some other claim. In each case the dilemma seems insoluble until a specific discovery tilts the balance and enables her to act. Both discoveries thus become extremely important to our understanding of the decisions. In the first—Isabel's decision to go to the dying Ralph—Countess Gemini's revelation that Madame Merle is Pansy's mother breaks the deadlock and apparently justifies Isabel's flight. Since Isabel makes her decision instantly, under the stress of strong emotion, it might be taken as simply an emotional—unreasoned—rather than principled act. The narrator says as much, in fact: "Her

---

[6]Note this complication in her attempt to heed Osmond's wishes: "There were directions of his which she liked to think she obeyed to the letter. Perhaps, as regards some of them, it was because her doing so appeared to reduce them to the absurd" (2:214).

[7]Note the ironic implication here that such avoidance is never really quite possible. In her attempt not to deceive, Isabel might be accused of deceiving everyone.

coming itself had not been a decision. On that occasion she had simply started" (2:421). In the context, however, it is impossible not to read Isabel's action as an expression of preference, a moral choice whose nature is clarified by what she has just learned. The motivation is emotional, yes, because it is no longer impeded by moral scruples. Something has been settled by the Countess's revelation.

Apparently the disclosure has given Isabel for the first time the right to violate her husband's express command overtly. In the Warburton case, earlier, though she was checked by her scruples, she obeyed as far as she could; now she openly defies. Why should the Countess's words so liberate her? Not because she knows that she has been manipulated and treated falsely by Madame Merle; she already knew that. But Countess Gemini has confirmed it; she has also explained the motive, which was previously lacking. Furthermore she has implicated Osmond himself directly in the conspiracy, although Isabel has already realized that he married her for money. But now she sees exactly the role that she was meant to fill in his life; she can see the full extent of her deception.

Her action here may become clearer in the light of her final decision—the renunciation that takes her back to Rome after Ralph's death. Here again the choice is precipitated by a discovery—in this case the "white lightning" in Caspar's kiss or, more completely, the recognition that he has real aid and comfort to offer her: "The world, in truth, had never seemed so large. . . . She had wanted help, and here was help," and she feels "each thing in his hard manhood that had least pleased her . . . justified of its intense identity and made one with this act of possession" (2:435–36). Yet earlier she did not know whether to return. To Pansy, Isabel had promised that she would, but she was unsure of the reason or whether she would honor it. Evidently, then, what prohibits her escape at the end is not the promise to Pansy but the need to avoid what Caspar has to offer.

For most post-Freudian readers Isabel's deepest problem will thus seem to be her fear of sexual feeling—and I shall have more to say about this fear later. First, however, it must be understood in its context—namely, the progression of Isabel's moral discoveries as she tries to form her character and find a worthy destiny.

There is also an external context—parallels to renunciations in other novels by James—a legitimate appeal to Jamesian conventions that may help our understanding here. These contexts suggest that Isabel has discovered a fundamental morality that she shares with a good many other Jamesian characters. It is a system of moral priorities whose underlying idea is that of "keeping faith," of respecting contracts, commitments, vows. Except under special conditions, this principle takes precedence over all others; it is the special conditions that provide the interesting moral tests. Isabel's dilemmas in the second part confront her with such tests: first is the conflict between breaking faith with Osmond and abetting the deception of (or breaking faith with) Pansy and Lord Warburton, which she meets by a delicate compromise that avoids taking sides. Then comes the conflict between her duty to Osmond and her duty to Ralph. Here the resolution (in favor of Ralph) seems based upon the discovery of Osmond's original deception of her. Apparently this deception voids her contract with him. The appearance of Caspar complicates matters, however; it nullifies the escape and reimposes her original obligation. The reason seems similar to the reasons for the renunciations of Strether in *The Ambassadors* and Fleda Vetch in *The Spoils of Poynton:* though one may legitimately break a contract because of conflicting obligations or because it was fraudulently drawn up, one must not show personal gain in doing so. This rule is not explicitly stated; it is, however, so common in Jamesian renunciations[8] that it can safely be applied here. It is not, of course, a popular morality in our time. Strether's obedience to this principle has been criticized as being nothing more than a concern for appearances.[9] It seems clear, however, that such characters see themselves as affirming faith in moral principle *as such:* one must neither profit nor appear to profit, because doing so would cast doubt on one's belief in contract. I have suggested elsewhere[10] that such a morality implies a great value placed upon social organization—the primacy

---

[8]As also in other American fiction of the late nineteenth and early twentieth centuries. See my discussion in *The American Short Story in the Twenties* (Chicago 1961), pp. 114–18.

[9]Yvor Winters, *In Defense of Reason,* 3d ed. (Denver, 1947), pp. 334–35.

[10]*The American Short Story in the Twenties,* p. 147.

of contracts and the conspicuous, public affirmation of this principle constitute a morality (endorsed by many writers of James's time) useful to the functioning of society. From this point of view Isabel's renunciation may represent the final success of her attempt to become a fully civilized being in a high civilization.[11]

Let us now consider what principle best unifies the action I have been describing. Two alternative possibilities appear.

1. From great hopes and expectations Isabel falls into misery, the more or less tragic victim of her errors and the selfish duplicity of others. The conclusion maximizes her misfortune—it completes her discovery of its extent (the last and worst blow is the loss of Ralph) and marks the final loss of all possible relief. Her dilemmas and choices in the second part (necessary choices between evils) are signs of the trap she is in, showing the depth of her misfortune. The final renunciation could be interpreted in either of two ways: as required by the integrity of her character (which is bound by a morality that I have just described) or as the effect of her impotence, her fear of convention and sexuality (fear that is the root cause of all her misery). The first interpretation gives us a fairly classic kind of tragedy—with hamartia, suffering, and discovery, redeemed at the end by the character's nobility—what I would call a romantic tragedy. The second interpretation gives us a distinctly modern "neurotic tragedy"— the causes lying deep and undiscoverable within the character's unconscious—not strictly tragedy at all but "tragic irony," in which pity for the protagonist is the strongest element.

2. Or possibly the primary interest is not in the misfortune and suffering but rather in Isabel's action. Of course, I have already suggested this possibility in the preceding analysis. If so, Isabel's renunciation is not merely a sign of her misfortune but the end toward which the plot has been moving, the final solution to a dilemma. Her suffering, on the other hand, is not the end but simply an important condition in her choice. Whereas the first hypothesis emphasizes the steps by which Isabel's suffering grows, the second stresses the sequence of her decisions. Since

[11]I do not mean to suggest that she has developed a theory of society or of morality or that her story is in any way a didactic disquisition on such abstractions.

such decisions express character, the second plot is essentially a "change of character," whereas the first is a "change of fortune."[12] (I say "change of character," not "revelation of character," which is different.) Both alternatives are dynamic plots. Both include in their formulas the threefold movements—from error to discovery, from happiness to misery, from comparatively unformed to formed character—but they differ as to the ruling principle.

My preference for the second of these plots has already been made obvious and rests mainly on two grounds. Despite its intensity, Isabel's suffering is too special to be an end in itself. It depends too much on her character; if she were even a little different, she would find escape from her misery easy—if not in flight, then by acceptance of Osmond. Her suffering directs attention to her character. Second, the episodes are most coherent, as my analysis of the action shows, when seen in terms of Isabel's choices. The three-year gap between her marriage and the resumption of her story supports my view: it suppresses exactly what ought to be most important if her developing unhappiness were of primary interest.

Isabel's "change of character," motivated by her desire to become fully civilized, centers in the refinement of her moral consciousness. Originally well intentioned and potentially superior but ignorant and foolishly proud, she develops a fine discriminating morality which she heroically supports. Her errors and consequent suffering provide the measure of this growth and the proof of her heroism. Though her development is traceable through the progressive discriminations that I have outlined, the most important aspect is the progress not of her moral understanding but of her moral emotions, so to speak—most notably the discovery and collapse of the moral arrogance that was so strong in the first part. Accordingly, the most powerful moments in the plot (other than the final renunciation) are the great discovery scenes in the second part: the midnight vigil, which dramatizes the discovery of her mistake about her hus-

---

[12]This novel is R. S. Crane's example of a "plot of character" ("The Concept of Plot and the Plot of *Tom Jones*," in *Critics and Criticism*, ed. Crane [Chicago, 1952], p. 621).

band, and the deathbed scene with Ralph, which completes the surrender of her pride. These two scenes are the two parts, widely separated, of a great "reversal" that brings the plot almost to its conclusion. The makings of the "specific fictional effect" are implicit in the description of this plot as a growth of character. Clearly (on the face of it, at least) Isabel is judged from the beginning as mostly sympathetic and admirable. At the same time, we are made conscious of her errors, the blindness of her pride, the foolishness of her arrogance, with an irony which, though affectionate, is definite and strong. We are shown the trap into which she is falling, and sympathy and fear are qualified by our wish that she discover her mistakes. Thus the first part establishes a familiar and strong kind of effect: the desire that the character vindicate the sympathy we wish to give her by overcoming her faults. In the final part our fears are amply justified—now she is potentially tragic, pitiable—but our sympathy is even more amply vindicated, our admiration justified, by the picture of her growth, fortified by the hostile picture of her enemies.

In Ralph's deathbed scene, Isabel is probably closer to the reader than ever before: now at last she has recognized her faults. She knows everything we know and judges and feels as we have wanted her to. Vindication of sympathy is complete. The final renunciation, however, changes matters. Here she repudiates the course of action that I think most readers and probably the implied reader, too, would favor—what Henrietta and Mrs. Touchett and Caspar think she should do. This decision removes her again to some distance. In view of the context, the pattern of moral growth, I suspect the renunciation is meant to be judged as austerely admirable. Modern readers have trouble with this notion, but I am unable to square any other view with my sense of Jamesian conventions.[13] At this point she becomes "better than we are." We understand the principle behind her act; we see why any other course would be less acceptable (the

---

[13]Not that all Jamesian renunciations are to be admired. I suspect that Fleda Vetch in *The Spoils of Poynton* is judged as having gone too far. The circumstances are different, however, and the conditions for that judgment are clearly presented (including her own admission).

promise to Pansy is significant here). At the same time it is rather awesome in its self-denial: we admire, but with less sympathy than before.

The hypothesis I have been describing has the advantage of giving us a coherent movement from beginning to end: we see Isabel grow into an austerely superior human being. It is the germinal principle of a large-scale, serious *complex romantic plot,* with a secondary tragic component on which the romantic justification is based, and it moves toward *wonder* at the very end. If the description is sound, it should make possible (in combination with the principles of construction and presentation—which may or may not need to be spelled out) an explanation of anything in the novel, an explanation superior, at any rate, to any of the alternatives we have seen. It is still tentative, of course, for better explanations will appear, and the form itself will become still more visible.

This description of the plot should acknowledge the prominence of Ralph Touchett. Next to Isabel, Ralph is certainly the most important character in the book, a position for which my proposed germinal principle may not have prepared us. He is so important not merely because Isabel needs a benefactor, for Mr. Touchett could have acted on his own. Nor does Ralph merely supply a generous and humane alternative to Osmond as supranational product of high civilization. A superior antithesis to all her suitors, Ralph understands and appreciates Isabel best. He also provides a concrete measure of her ignorance, her errors. Most important, as the object of the strongest emotion that she ever displays, he validates for the reader the depth of Isabel's growth and also prepares us to distinguish between her emotional needs (expressed to him) and the moral austerity she attains at the end: how different—how much colder—the effect would have been if Isabel had had to reject Ralph rather than Caspar or if no warm scene with Ralph had immediately preceded the renunciation. Ralph's view of Isabel is close to the reader's throughout, and the reader's judgment of her is tied closely to her own perception and understanding of Ralph.

The question arises, why is Ralph presented as fatally ill? No doubt the role I have attributed to him could not be filled by a character free to act openly upon his love. His illness is conven-

ient, too, as it sharpens Isabel's conflict of obligations with Osmond at the end. More significantly, it makes an ironic comment about Isabel's aspirations: Ralph is more like the "free spirit" that Isabel would wish to be than any other character in the book, but his freedom is bought by his illness. It is a physical counterpart to her imprisonment with Osmond. No doubt also it reflects symbolically the corruption in the highest civilization—the physical counterpart, here, of Osmond's moral corruption.

It has been suggested that Ralph's concealed gift to Isabel is nearly as destructive and manipulatory as anything that Merle and Osmond do. True, he suffers guilt as a result. No doubt James could easily have made us judge Ralph's act severely, but he distinctly refrains from doing so. When Ralph says of Isabel's error in marrying Osmond, "I don't believe that such a generous mistake as yours can hurt you for more than a little" (2:417), he seems to be expressing also the attitude the implied reader is expected to take toward Ralph's own mistake. Ralph embodies in the fictional world the reader's interest in Isabel, projecting concretely some aspects of her situation, including some of its sharpest ironies, and providing the standard and measure of her growth.

I must now recognize some objections to such an interpretation that have been pressing all along. In our times it is difficult, not to mention unfashionable, to admire "awesomely superior" moral people. The "rich Jamesian ambiguity" is threatening, and some account must be taken of it. Briefly, it is possible to interpret the action and hence the plot in at least two ways different from mine here. Both imply a form that has become "more visible," with more complexities or ambiguities, than the straightforward one I have described. How do we interpret this particular kind of increased visibility?

In the first place, it is possible to see Isabel—as some commentators have done—as motivated primarily by fear of sex. Her fine moral consciousness is merely a screen. The author himself seems to suggest such a possibility—most strikingly when he makes Caspar's kiss the precipitating cause of her renunciation, with "each thing in his hard manhood that had least pleased her" (2:436). Indications early and late of Isabel's fear of hard manhood and buried forces make this view impossible to refute. But

if sexual fear and a repressed potential for passion are components of Isabel, what becomes of my hypothesis?

Such a view of Isabel complicates and fortifies our conception of her motivations, without altering their essential significance. The notion that if Isabel is sexually motivated her conscious reasonings must be self-deceptions strikes me as anti-Jamesian. If such a judgment is intended, it is taken for granted, undeveloped in the text—a way of handling moral issues quite uncharacteristic of Jamesian convention and of James (who always regarded "overtreating [as] the minor disservice" as opposed to undertreating.)[14] The narrator's irony is clear and moderate. Isabel's sexual fear adds emotional force to her reasons for doing as she does. But it is intended to strengthen, not undermine, the picture of her moral consciousness. In Isabel's eyes the sexual force is savagery, whereas she is pursuing the highest civilization. From her point of view, it is right to keep this force under control, and I see no evidence that the implied author (the conventions of evaluation) disagrees. Twentieth-century readers who feel differently must distinguish their own judgments from that of the implied reader. The picture of repressed sexuality is there, certainly, but the negative judgment which we are accustomed to associate with it in twentieth-century writing is—very probably—no part of James's form.

In the second place, the moral issue in Isabel's development may not be as unambiguous as my description suggests. I have spoken of the discovery of her pride, but might not her return to Osmond be regarded as the most egotistical act she has yet performed? Is not her early naive desire "that she should never do anything wrong" stronger than ever at the end, as she deliberately does the most perfectly moral thing she can conceive of? Does not her fine moral consciousness conceal, just as Osmond's fine disregard does, the serpent of her egotism? Her suffering is as full of hatred for Osmond as his is for her; it is fed to a large degree by the fact that he does not recognize her superiority; is there not therefore a much greater similarity between the two than she is willing to admit? Is not Leon Edel right when he describes Isabel and Osmond as "mirror images of power," see-

---

[14]James, *The Art of the Novel*, p. 57.

ing each other "as objects they wish to subjugate and possess," so that the novel "in its deepest sense...[is] about a group of egotists, and power and egotism is the real subject of the book"?[15] And is not F. R. Leavis, too, correct when he identifies Isabel with Gwendolyn Harleth in *Daniel Deronda* (differing only in that she is seen through the sentimentalizing eyes of a man)?[16]

Unfortunately such statements extract the characters from the book, treating them as real people rather than as parts of a form. If the narrator says that Isabel is different from Osmond, we have really all we need to know that she is different. We learn more, of course: great care is taken to distinguish between Isabel and Osmond. While it is true that Isabel's ego is involved in her renunciation, as it is in her suffering, it is not true, I think, that James expects the presence of her ego to undermine our admiration. The case against Osmond has been so intensely drawn that we cannot sympathize with him against her. If her ego pursues moral perfection, for James as well—for this implied author—moral perfection is to be admired, it seems. There is no sign at the end that Isabel wants others to recognize her superiority (Osmond will never acknowledge it), and the battle to which she returns is too grim. The perfection is for herself only, and I see no reason to think this fact cancels the *implied* reader's admiration. As with the sexual question, a part of the form has become more visible, but not to change the implied judgment that is also part of the form. Our perception of Isabel's lonely private egotism probably acts chiefly to increase the distance at the end—to enhance the awesomeness and the wonder. An appropriate end: having justified herself, Isabel escapes us. It is curious how little need I have ever felt to pursue her back to Rome, to speculate on what awaits her there. The distance introduced by her renunciation severs her ties with us.

The next step in the plot analysis would be a demonstration through details of its unifying efficacy. Here I must stop, since the process could go on indefinitely. It would be a pursuit of the actual form of the work, an attempt to convert the hypothesized,

---

[15]Leon Edel, introduction to *The Portrait of a Lady*, by Henry James (Boston, 1963), pp. xii–xiii.

[16]F. R. Leavis, *The Great Tradition* (New York, 1963), pp. 79–125.

the expected, into the actual, found form. Such a further dem-onstration would attempt to show, in general, how the chief commitments and dependent details in the various subordinate categories (noted at the beginning of the analysis) relate to the hypothesized plot. At the minimum it would try to show the *compatibility* between these commitments and the plot; a tighter unity would be achieved if it could show their actual *dependency*.

In the case of the fictional world, dependency has already been suggested in my discussion. The magnitude of this world, the elaboration of detail, enlarges Isabel herself, intensifies her problem. Isabel's importance derives from the fact that she is not merely conceivable but conceivable in a conceivable world—hence the realistic basis. The superiority of this world, its ideal quality, which is nevertheless associated by name and particulars to real places, provides a proper setting for her superiority, her ideal quality as a character meant to discover and distinguish values of the highest civilization.

The narrator plainly exists to display this Isabel. The use of dramatization, of narrative summary, is a means to both vivid-ness and magnitude. The flexible point of view enables us to see beyond Isabel's own limitations, so necessary to the wonder of her eventual achievements. The affectionate irony and basic sympathy of the narrator's attitude is appropriate to develop the balance of sympathies which the plot has designated, leading to the final wonder. The gentle, wise, civilized personality of the narrator guides and supports the reader's tolerance and ap-preciation of Isabel in her world.

Further demonstration would be especially concerned with the efficacy or appropriateness of the language itself, in its de-tail, for of course the idiosyncratic Jamesian style has much to do with the individuality of this novel. The demonstration would show, as far as possible, how this idiosyncrasy is made functional in the plot. For example, the indirectness and the distinction-making features of the style tend to magnify the importance of any action taken (action is directness), making it seem both dif-ficult and consequential—necessary for an adequate apprecia-tion of the intensity of Isabel's "mild adventures." More particu-larly, these stylistic aspects fortify her values and their subtlety, linguistically supporting the concern for fine discriminations

which is epitomized finally in her renunciation. These features also tend to imply further unspoken meanings (again, the passage about Caspar's kiss and the hard things of his manhood is an example) and thus prepare us for the psychological complexities of Isabel's case. The informality and high-class colloquialisms help to humanize the narrator and characters who are involved in such questions and to support sympathy. The concrete metaphors extend the context of Isabel's (and the others') experience, so to speak, and increase its importance. The demonstration would make the plot more concrete by specifying the kinds of contexts which these metaphors supply.

Finally, the demonstration would want to deal with the changes in the text effected by James thirty years later for the New York Edition. These revisions are mostly in matters of style; for the most part they intensify by introducing new metaphors or concrete images or by developing further images already there. They create a form slightly different from the original, although with one exception no change is large enough to affect the hypothesis of plot described in this chapter.[17] The exception is in the last revision:

> "Look here, Mr. Goodwood," she [Henrietta] said; "just you wait!"
>
> On which he looked up at her—but only to guess, from her face, with a revulsion, that she simply meant he was young. She stood shining at him with that cheap comfort, and it added, on the spot, thirty years to his life. She walked him away with her, however, as if she had given him now the key to patience. [2:437-38]

The revision added everything in the last paragraph from the dash on, thus removing the hint in the original that Isabel might yet change her mind and leave Osmond after all. That hint was, to be sure, sufficiently undermined by other circumstances to remain highly questionable, but it did exist and received a strong emphasis from its placement at the end. By eliminating that hope the revision magnifies Isabel's withdrawal from us (as from

[17]See the discussion of James's revisions of *The Portrait of a Lady* by Anthony J. Mazzella in the Norton Critical Edition of that novel (New York, 1975), pp. 597-619. F. O. Matthiessen's earlier discussion in *Henry James: The Major Phase* (1944) is also reproduced in this edition.

[216]

Caspar and Henrietta), and the comments about Caspar's disappointment doubtless transfer to our own view of Isabel and enhance the austerity of what she has done (as does the irony directed to Henrietta). James's alteration deletes the ambiguity and increases the final distance on which wonder is based—now so much more strongly and coldly than before.

I have said nothing here about those abstract qualities of symmetry so often cited when critics speak about form in James—the balance between the two parts (actually not symmetrical) and the circular movement that begins and ends in Gardencourt. As kinds of material unity, these features contribute to the irony which intensifies the effect. They enhance our general impression of good order, but they are not themselves the primary manifestations of form. Such manifestations are to be found, as I hope I have shown, in the strong unifying plot, large, rich, complicated, complete.

[10]

Disclosure Plot:
The Sound and the Fury

What possible kind of plot could be conceived as the unifying principle for Faulkner's *The Sound and the Fury*? Certainly not a dynamic plot of any traditional or familiar kind—not given the radical disruption of chronology. The division of emphasis among three or four major characters is also a problem—only somewhat less vexing. It has been argued, in fact, that the novel is deliberately disunified. The movement is "away from order and coherence," not toward it; we end in the same state of "suspension" in which we began. Any comprehensive or unifying statement about the novel can be confuted, for a deliberate confusion is part of the intention.[1] This is a minority view, but it reflects the difficulty which the novel presents to the formal critic.

The most coherent descriptions of the form have been "thematic," locating the novel's unity finally in the exposition of a theme, as in Hyatt Waggoner's analysis: "Theme and structure are one thing in *The Sound and the Fury*. Both assert the possibility of achieving a difficult order out of the chaotic flux of time."[2] Or in Olga Vickery's: "The theme of *The Sound and the Fury*, as revealed by the structure, is the relation between the act and man's apprehension of the act, between the event and the interpretation."[3] Or Cleanth Brooks: "The novel has to do with

[1]See Walter J. Slatoff, *Quest for Failure: A Study of William Faulkner* (Ithaca, 1961), chap. 10, also p. 147.
[2]Hyatt Waggoner, *William Faulkner: From Jefferson to the World* (N.P.: University of Kentucky Press, 1959), p. 59.
[3]Olga W. Vickery, *The Novels of William Faulkner* (Baton Rouge, La., 1964), p. 29.

the discovery that life has no meaning."[4] It may or may not be true that, as Irving Howe says, Faulkner is "a writer who particularly requires and tempts thematic analysis."[5] Such analysis is of course useful when one is trying to find common ground between diverse works. But it seems doubtful that a consideration of universals or thematic implications plays much part in the immediate pleasure of reading this vividly concrete novel. Recognized universals help us perceive and judge particular characters and situations, as in any good fiction (they are material conventions, abstract imitated forms). But I do not think we read *The Sound and the Fury* for its themes.

The best studies give full attention to the vividness and emotional power with which the Compson story is brought to life. Yet an implicit gap tends to remain between the discussion of particulars, including principles by which the novel is ordered, and the thematic discussion of the unity, with another gap usually between these and consideration of the book's effect. Most critics agree that a primary principle of order is the gradual movement from obscurity to clarity in the exposition of the Compson story. Other principles qualify the first: a movement from the "concrete to the abstract,"[6] an "unfolding of consciousness and comment,"[7] a movement from a private to a public view, a progression from characters who cannot cope with time to one who can.[8] These sequential developments bring out the full emotional and moral implications of the Compson story, producing an impact that is either, as in Howe, "tragic"[9] or, as in Swiggart, a mixed or double judgment.[10]

[4]Cleanth Brooks, *William Faulkner: The Yoknapatawpha Country* (New Haven, 1963), p. 347.

[5]Irving Howe, *William Faulkner: A Critical Study*, 2d ed. (New York, 1962), p. [v].

[6]Waggoner, *William Faulkner*, p. 57.

[7]Howe, *Faulkner: A Critical Study*, p. 166.

[8]Perrin Lowrey, "Concepts of Time in *The Sound and the Fury*," *English Institute Essays*, 1952, ed. Alan S. Downer (New York, 1954), pp. 57–82.

[9]This is "one of the three or four American works of prose fiction written since the turn of the century in which the impact of tragedy is felt and sustained" (Howe, *Faulkner: A Critical Study*, p. 174).

[10]"The reader views events with a double vision: on the one hand he recognizes the sordid Compson reality for what it is, and on the other hand he raises the family tragedy to a universal status" (Peter Swiggart, *The Art of Faulkner's Novels* [Austin, 1963], p. 107).

True enough. Yet the focus of the Compson story remains unclear. Who among the Compsons is tragic or quasi-tragic—all of them, some, or just one? What is the tragic experience? Is it the fall of the family or somebody's perception of the fall? Does the tragic experience have a beginning and end? Symptomatic of the vagueness is the problem some critics have had with Quentin: the claim, for instance, that Quentin and his problem are unable to carry successfully the weight that Faulkner "intended" them to carry—as if Faulkner had really meant Quentin to be the protagonist of the book.[11]

The unquestioned power of *The Sound and the Fury*, accumulating to the finish, is strong intuitive evidence that the novel is truly unified and that the disorder of which Slatoff complained (he does acknowledge the power of the ending)[12] cannot somehow be a flaw in the form—at least not a serious one. Once this power has been felt, however, it is difficult to find the terms to clarify it, given the disappearance of the familiar conventions of unity: the absence of the single identifiable protagonist and of the unfolding and finally completed (dynamic) action. Faulkner's own remarks about the novel's composition offer little help with this particular problem.[13]

The following hypothesis attempts to find terms. It depends heavily upon the interpretations of critics—Vickery, Swiggart,

[11]Howe, *Faulkner: A Critical Study*, pp. 169-70.

[12]"It is a powerful ending and a fitting one in its focus on Benjy and its application to the general theme of order and disorder running through the novel. But it is an ending which provides anything but a synthesis or resolution, and it leaves us with numerous conflicting feelings and ideas" (Slatoff, *Quest for Failure*, p. 157).

[13]From one of Faulkner's accounts: "They were three boys, one was a girl and the girl was the only one that was brave enough to climb that tree to look in the forbidden window to see what was going on. And that's what the book—and it took the rest of the four hundred pages to explain why she was brave enough to climb the tree to look in the window. It was an image, a picture to me, a very moving one. . . . And the symbolism of the muddy bottom of [her] drawers became the lost Caddy, which had caused one brother to commit suicide and the other brother had misused her money that she'd send back to the child, her daughter. It was, I thought, a short story, something that could be done in about two pages, a thousand words, I found out it couldn't. I finished it the first time, and it wasn't right, so I wrote it again, and that was Quentin, that wasn't right. I wrote it again, that was Jason, that wasn't right, then I tried to let Faulkner do it, that still was wrong" (Frederick L. Gwynn and Joseph L. Blotner, eds., *Faulkner in the University* [New York, 1965], pp. 31-32).

Disclosure Plot: *The Sound and the Fury*

Brooks, others—who have clarified much that once seemed obscure. My essay goes beyond these views into the stubborn problems of form only tentatively.

Noteworthy at the outset is the adaptation in *The Sound and the Fury* of the narrative and language to each other and to some aspects of the fiction. The most striking feature of the narrative is its division into four large discrete segments—four episodes, each dealing with a part of a day, each related by a different narrator. (To these was added in the later edition the appendix, really a fifth narrative, which raises special problems.)[14] The initial three are told in the first person (by Benjy, Quentin, Jason); the fourth is an external narrative. The language of the first three is adapted to traits of the narrators considered as characters: Benjy suggests his idiocy by means of simple diction in which the inability to form abstractions is suggested stylistically by occasional circumlocutions around simple concepts (for example, "hitting little" for "putting" in golf); Quentin's elongation of sentences, breakdown of grammar, and interweaving of

[14]I relegate to a footnote the problem of the appendix, not added until 1946 nor placed at the end until 1966. Essentially it is an epilogue with two functions: (1) it adds information about the protagonist's fictional milieu, of two kinds—historical and "future" (it extends the time range to 1945, many years after the publication of the original version); (2) it makes explicit a number of particulars implied in the original and reiterates or confirms others. Neither of these additions alters significantly our perception of the plot except to enlarge the fictional context of events. The appendix has a distancing effect (Quentin and the others recede into the background of their ancestors as into the future of their forgetting), which is appropriate to the plot's final effect as described in this chapter. The appendix is thus a final confirming and reiterating "episode" in the disclosure. Unfortunately this description ignores the fact that on several points the appendix contradicts the novel (especially with regard to Jason's business arrangements and thefts). I am unable to discover a principle of coherence capable of rationalizing this contradiction which is at the same time able to give as interesting an account of the rest of the novel as the hypothesis developed in this chapter. I find it impossible therefore not to attribute it to Faulknerian inadvertence. If so, it provides a striking example of genuine (and distracting) "disunity" in an otherwise powerful form. (If the appendix is in the beginning, as when it first appeared—placed there according to Faulkner's own wish at the time [per Joseph Blotner, *Faulkner: A Biography* (New York, 1974), 2:1208]—it functions in a different way, comparable to a "frame narrative" like the opening of *Heart of Darkness* or *The Turn of the Screw,* to establish the broader milieu at the start and reduce some of the initial obscurity—again without significantly altering the plot principle.) André Bleikasten (*The Most Splendid Failure: Faulkner's "The Sound and the Fury"* [Bloomington, 1976], p. 243) insists that the appendix is "no organic part of" the novel—a simple resolution to the problem.

fragments, with material ranging from the elaborate poetic-philosophical discourse of his father and long fragmented passages of dialogue to the relatively straightforward (simple sentences, chronological order) account of his adventures in the present, all suggest a stream of consciousness in which present action and past memory run together; Jason's vernacular language, full of ready phrases in the manner of speech addressed to a listener, suggests his defensive mode of thinking. The language of the fourth narrative is comparatively formal, straightforward, precise and fully developed in its descriptions, concentrating on detail of objects and actions, vivid in imagery.[15] By such means a fictional world is presented which lies within the broad confines of modern realism (contemporary, localized, with ordinary people like ourselves—or, no doubt, inferior to ourselves as we think of ourselves), but notably "stylized"— meaning that the salient features of characters and society are heightened, made conspicuous by reiteration and "exaggeration":[16] Benjy's idiocy, Jason's meanness, Mrs. Compson's self-pity.

The total known action so presented in *The Sound and the Fury* occupies a time span from the late 1890s to 1928.[17] There is much "background," an elaboration of the *given* conditions from which the main action of the novel arises. The focus, however, is on the four episodes treated directly by the narratives: three days in April 1928 and the day of Quentin's suicide in 1910. Certain remembered episodes are also emphasized: especially

[15]Note that none of these narratives makes much use of the idiosyncratic Faulknerian style (as in, say, *Absalom, Absalom!*), though there are suggestions of it in Quentin's recollections of his father's talk. The appendix displays this style, however.

[16]By "heightening" or "exaggeration" I mean our impression of the extreme, sometimes the outrageous, when we notice, for instance, that almost everything Mrs. Compson says and does manifests her self-pity. There is a norm here, though what we think of as the lifelike may be derived more from so-called realistic literature than from actuality—although I would hold that the norm is not entirely divorced from our perception of "ordinary life" (our own lives); otherwise it would never have occurred to us to find one kind of fictional world more "realistic" than another. The Aristotelian distinction between fictional objects "like ourselves" and those "unlike ourselves" (whether "better" and "worse" or "stronger" or "weaker," as in Frye) is still useful.

[17]Or from 1699 to 1945 in the version with the appendix.

the childhood incident at the branch when Damuddy dies and the incidents associated with Caddy's "fall"—her promiscuity, marriage, disgrace, banishment.

Caddy's fall is the beginning of a sequence that the reader gradually discovers which includes Quentin's suicide and Jason's blackmail and does not end until Miss Quentin escapes from the Compson household. This action is sometimes spoken of as the "plot" of *The Sound and the Fury,* and its nature is fairly clear: it shows the disastrous consequences (for the family) of the initial event. It can be regarded as a battle between Caddy and her family that destroys the family—literally as well as morally. In summary, Caddy wounds or provokes her brothers, who in reaction wrench the family apart. At the end Miss Quentin has become Caddy's surrogate; her flight completes Caddy's break from the family.

Important as it is, however, this action cannot be the *plot* of the novel, not its germinal subject. Not only is its chronology fragmented, but its protagonist, Caddy, disappears backstage, behind the experiences of Benjy, Quentin, and Jason. The true action, the basis for the plot, ought to be at the center of our attention, having more to do with what is directly dramatized in the four narratives. Yet except for the third and fourth, the narratives are not linked causally and, of course, are not chronological.

Internally each episode is strung on a chronological thread, but in all except the last, memories are so important that they cease to be entirely subordinated in the reader's mind to the sequence of "present" action. This effect is sharpened by the seeming obscurities in the first two sections, requiring the reader to work hard to disentangle the remembered events. Consequently past events become almost as vivid as the episodes in which they are remembered.

As Olga Vickery says, the narrative episodes are "static";[18] they don't describe changes. Brooks observes: "Jason's section does prepare us for what the girl Quentin is going to do, but much of it is simply typical of almost any day in the Compson

[18]Vickery, *The Novels of William Faulkner,* p. 29.

household for the last year."[19] Benjy's episode is also "typical," and though Quentin's brings us almost to the point of his suicide, it too is static—for the suicide decision has already been made before the episode begins and is never reconsidered. Only the final section involves significant change, but only in the part that deals with Jason's comeuppance. The part concerning Dilsey is, again, typical of what is constant, although Dilsey is aware that a great change has indeed taken place when she says, "I've seed de first en de last."[20]

Both the order of the episodes and their internal arrangement thus help destroy the sense of an action developing in time—at least until the final section. As if deliberately to make sure of this effect, the author reverses the chronology of the two narrated days just preceding Miss Quentin's escape, so that Benjy's, placed first, follows Jason's in time—and the two are separated, of course, by Quentin's day, eighteen years before. All signs indicate that the movement from one point of view to another is more important in this novel than the movement through time.

Moreover, we are virtually forced to look for a compound protagonist. Such a concept tempts the critic to vagueness, in this case to speak loosely of the whole Compson family as protagonist—a temptation likely to encourage our thematic tendencies. Better to limit the composite character to the narrowest possible, which would here be the trio of narrating Compson brothers, Benjy, Quentin, and Jason. Their sister is a separate character.[21] If the protagonist is the composite of the three characters, then the unifying action is their common experience. The narrated episodes are, as I have said, static, illustrative. The relationship between them is not sequential but parallel. The central unifying action is presumably a composite of the static situations that the episodes illustrate—the common ground of action or experience that they share.

[19]Brooks, *William Faulkner,* p. 345.
[20]William Faulkner, *The Sound and the Fury* (New York, n.d.), p. 371. Page references in the text refer to this (the Vintage Books) edition.
[21]Swiggart, *The Art of Faulkner's Novels,* pp. 88–89, has tried to put Benjy in a role comparable to that of Dilsey, distinct from those of Quentin and Jason. But such a role is probably too restricting. It raises awkward problems when we try to explain the emphasis placed upon Benjy and why his narrative section is as prominent as the others.

In consequence, like the individual episodes, the "action" of the novel as a whole is static and the whole Caddy-to-Miss-Quentin sequence, noted above, is a *given* condition in the novel's world rather than part of its central action. Formally speaking, the entire sequence of events that can be reconstructed and put into a chronology may be regarded as a "cause" for the plot, even though Quentin doesn't live to see its end. Since the germinal subject is not a completed change of any kind, it is therefore in a sense not an "action" at all. It is rather an "activity," performed by a character in an unchanging situation—one whose beginning and end are no essential part of what is being depicted. The "beginning and end" that bound the germinal principle and give formal unity to the work are determined not by events in the object being imitated but by the requirements of exposition of the qualities of the depicted situation.

A plot so organized—with such a germinal principle at its heart—is a *disclosure plot*. Such plots are more common in short works than in novels of this magnitude. Action is not lacking, but the actions that do appear, the sequences, the episodes, the incidents, exist for the sake not of a larger change to which they contribute but of the *constants* that they display.

The analysis of a disclosure plot should distinguish those constants as well as the principles which make them manifest. First, however, certain peculiarities in the novel must be taken into account. One is Quentin's death and the time lag between his version of the common experience and those of Benjy and Jason. Does not his death break up the protagonist—destroy it—before the common experience can be experienced? Does not his death also condition the Benjy and Jason episodes by introducing an element not present in his own episode? But of course, Quentin's death *is* present in his own episode, too, and hence the second of these objections falls down. Each brother affects the others—this is part of what they have in common: Quentin's death, Benjy's idiocy, Jason's meanness, each plays its part in the lives of the others.

Quentin's death is not, of course, an actual part of his dramatized experience, which is essentially static. The time lag between his episode and the others makes clear that the time of the com-

mon situation is not fixed, that the situation is a quality common to various and separate moments rather than to the conditions of a particular time. One of the most prominent problems shared by the three brothers is the struggle with the sister, but for Quentin this struggle is manifest in Caddy's "fall," whereas for Jason, Caddy is represented by her daughter. Apparently the typifying episodes have been placed in time so as to show the extreme of each brother's characteristic response to the family condition. The full meanness of Jason's response to Compson womanhood ripens into the third generation, whereas Quentin's intolerant romanticizing cuts him off in youth.

Another difficulty for the hypothesis of a disclosure plot is the function of the final episode—Miss Quentin's flight and Jason's pursuit. How does this episode with its emphasis upon great change relate to a disclosure plot in which things do not change? The Caddy-to-Quentin sequence is now over; Jason has been balked; Dilsey has seen the beginning and the end, as if the Compson history itself had come to an end. Such elements enhance the effect of closure, the finality of the novel. Yet they cannot change the formal principle into a dynamic plot—not in view of the difficulties previously observed. The chief significance of the final events is in what they reveal about the unstable situations dramatized earlier. Young Quentin's flight relates to Jason's episode much as Quentin's suicide does to his episode. They complete the *definition* of their respective situations. The same is true of Benjy's appearance in the final section: he is taken to church by Dilsey, which further defines the situation presented in his own section. The disclosure plot reveals the parallel situations of the three brothers in their own narrated episodes. It also shows what is potential there but not yet attained, by showing the aftermath of the unstable situation: Quentin's suicide in the Benjy and Jason episodes, Benjy's "redemption" and Jason's comeuppance in the final episode.

The primary cause of the situation revealed by the disclosure plot is the moral misfortune that has befallen the Compson family. The most striking sign is Caddy's problems, but Mrs. Compson's neurasthenia and Mr. Compson's alcoholic impotence also contribute. The misfortune is also internal to the protagonist:

each of the brothers has inadequacies of his own, and the protagonist as a whole is divided and in conflict with itself. The
essential disclosed situation, however (the "subject" in the germinal principle), is not this moral misfortune as such but the
protagonist's response to it, shown to consist in feeling and behavior (activity) rather than an event. This activity is represented
by the three typifying episodes—each allotted to one of the three
members—and is completed by the fourth.

The essentials of this common activity are made visible by the
parallels and contrasts between the episodes as well as by their
order. There is no room here to repeat all the connections that
have been noted, but some of the most obvious should be
named, beginning with the character of the protagonist himself.
"He" is incomplete, crippled by the insufficiency of his faculties
and unable to cope with his situation. Benjy's insufficiency is
intellectual; it renders him incapable of action or judgment, leaving him only sensory perceptions and a capacity for strong but
quickly passing feelings. Quentin's is practical, the result (or
cause?) of an excessive moral idealism that is unable to cope with
the realities of his world. Jason's is moral, the result (or cause?)
of an excessive desire to manipulate, directed by his self-interest,
conceived in the narrowest way. Jason's conception of his self-
interest reflects another important lack in the protagonist: he
has an inadequate conception of himself. Benjy, of course, has
no conception of himself at all. Quentin and Jason are both
impractically proud, but Quentin's pride is expressed by his
identification with moral and romantic absolutes (if they fall, he
must, too), while Jason's appears as a jealous personal need to be
respected, feared, and obeyed. There is also a general distortion
of the protagonist's capacity to love. Benjy's love of Caddy, his
most important feeling, is innocent, but his idiocy makes it totally demanding, dependent, childish. Quentin's love of Caddy is
a distortion of his love of family and self, caused perhaps by his
subjugation of love to moral idealism. Jason's love of Caddy is
distorted into hate, which he transfers to her daughter, the result no doubt of the frustration of his desire for power and his
resentment of being disregarded. It is worth noting that the
whole protagonist, and not just Quentin, is deeply motivated by

incestuous feeling, another sign of its failure to cope with the world. Both incest and idiocy are, of course, popular stereotypes to suggest the degeneracy of inbred aristocratic families.

Each of the brothers suffers. Sometimes cruel outsiders are to blame (Luster, Dalton Ames, Gerald Bland, the sheriff in Jefferson, the man in the train). At a deeper level the Compson parents are at fault. The most significant direct cause of their suffering is Caddy, who wounds Benjy by growing up and leaving him, Quentin by failing to protect her honor, Jason by losing him his job in the bank. The brothers also hurt each other: Quentin takes Benjy's pasture and receives the education Jason is denied; Benjy's idiocy is an annoyance to Jason and contributes to Quentin's sense of family decline; Jason, his mother's treacherous pet, contributes to Quentin's alienation from his mother and has Benjy castrated,

What is most important here is the protagonist's response to his suffering. This response has been much studied. The common motive of all three brothers is an attempt to gain some control over the cause of the suffering, which is expressed in two ways: on the one hand, by deeds—Benjy's bellowing, Quentin's preparations for suicide, Jason's manipulations—and on the other hand by constant mental activity. It is this mental effort—essentially an attempt to master the situation by consciousness—that the novel most directly dramatizes by means of its successive self-characterizing narrative voices. It is at least as important as the protagonist's external acts.

In all cases this mental process involves the imposing of memories upon the present. Benjy does this automatically by association, without being aware of the distinction between past and present—it is a rudimentary effort by his limited mind to understand his surroundings.[22] Quentin deliberately dwells on memories in his effort to "destroy time," subordinating his consciousness of the present to that of the past. Jason utilizes memories as material for self-justification, which is the primary labor of his mind. These mental activities relate differently in each case to the

[22]Does "making an effort" seem too much to credit Benjy with? Still, even the simple making of associations is a more advanced activity of mind than mere brute perception of the present.

character's acts. In Benjy the mental activity is far more important than the occasional bellow to which it gives rise. In Quentin it aims at the same objective as his planned suicide and seems meant to enforce his will to act.[23] In Jason the rationalizations in a sense *follow* the acts, in that they offer specious reasons for things already decided upon or done. In each case, thus, the mental activity gropes toward the very kind of consciousness in which the individual is most deficient, and it displays this deficiency vividly. Benjy gropes for simple understanding of relationships, Quentin for the practical consciousness that makes action possible, Jason for the moral consciousness that makes action justifiable.

Seen in this light, the most important feature of the protagonist's activity, in both deed and mind, is its futility. "His" effort to gain control of the situation by consciousness is a failure: Benjy has no understanding of events, Quentin conceives only of self-destructive action, Jason's morality justifies only corruption and deviousness. The failure of each to control time exemplifies the general shortage of consciousness. And the protagonist's acts are equally futile. Indeed, they worsen his situation in at least two cases. As an expression of despair over the

---

[23]Though Quentin considers change to be terrible and thinks the past better than the present, the memories he dwells on concern not the superior past but rather his discovery of terrible change—the events that have determined him to kill himself. The imposition of this remembered *recent* past upon the otherwise prosaic Harvard present seems meant to propel him to act. Swiggart's analysis of Quentin's aims is pertinent here: his suicide is called, "not an act of deliberate self-destruction, but an attempt to free his consciousness from the inevitability of change and decay" (*The Art of Faulkner's Novels*, p. 95) and an attempt to preserve his despair in the belief that the threatened loss of moral fury would be intolerable—motives made clear in Quentin's imagined discussion with his father just before the end of the section. I cannot accept Swiggart's belief, however, that "the point of view from which Quentin narrates is the moment in which his death has, as he anticipated, destroyed time without depriving him of consciousness" (p. 96). Although it may be true for Quentin that "with the elimination of time, every object of perception, whether in the past or in the present, has equal reality," the much-discussed problem of Quentin's use of the past tense strikes me as unreal. Swiggart's view seems to imply a double layer, memory of the past within memory of Harvard. It seems more natural to regard the past tense of the whole as a simple convention (one of the most natural in all fiction) and to assume that Quentin's memories of the past occur to him at the times during the day with which they are associated. Analogously, no one asks at what time the dead Addie gives her narration in *As I Lay Dying*.

Compson degeneration, Quentin's suicide hastens that degeneration; it makes possible all the conditions that eventually cause young Quentin to be so hard and bitter. Jason's futility is shown generally in his universal unpopularity and specifically in his failure to protect his money or to control Miss Quentin.

The real germinal situation, then (what the disclosure plot reveals), is the diversified but futile effort of the compound protagonist to cope with his family's and his own disintegration or degeneracy. The subject consists, however, not merely of this situation but also of the process of disclosure and the specific fictional effect that it is calculated to produce. This process is developed through the sequence of narrated episodes, which constitute its major steps. It is important therefore to consider the progression of the episodes.

The episodes produce the following major movements: (1) An increasing grasp (by the implied reader) of the facts of the given situation—an exposition that, except for Jason's comeuppance and some gains of explicitness, is roughly complete by the end of the third section. The movement starts not with mere ignorance or emptiness but with actual confusion—an obstructive obscurity which motivates the movement of the plot toward its eventual clarity.[24] It is a nonchronological process that describes by means of incidents, presented originally as fragments which the reader gradually pieces together, and it contributes also toward the development of the other movements. (2) An increasing understanding of the moral milieu in which the protagonist lives, epitomized by the progressive *deflation* of the moral stature of the Compson family as we move from one viewpoint to the next. This deflation is essential to our full understanding of the protagonist's failures and affects our judgment of them. (3) An increasing understanding of the nature of the protagonist himself, which has two aspects: the process by which the problems of the individual members are revealed, from the most innocent and sympathetic to the most corrupt and unsympathetic, and second, in some ways the most important strand of all, the pro-

---

[24]Just as *characters* motivate or provide "probability" for the action in a dynamic plot.

cess by which we come to identify the protagonist as such, culminating in the recognition of all the parallels between the three members. (4) A progression of specific fictional effects. Viewed as independent units, each episode has its own individual protagonist, each of whom is judged differently, so that there is a sequence from the possible pathos of Benjy to the tragic horror (perhaps) of Quentin to the ironic comedy of Jason—effects added to each other and preparing the way, cumulatively, for the effect finally achieved in the last section.

The unity of these processes can be shown more concretely by tracing them through the individual sections, paying special attention to the way the specific fictional effect is developed. In the opening section, although it is customary to speak of Benjy as pathetic, the pathos is sharply limited by Benjy's own unconsciousness of suffering and even more by the initial obscurity of the narrative. The section establishes the possibility of pathos, but the full pathos is not seen until later when we have a clearer view of the case. At the start, the reader's strong impression of Benjy's pitiful confusion is inevitably subordinated to curiosity about what he does not understand. Our interest is drawn to the world surrounding Benjy—especially to Caddy—as much as to Benjy himself, a fact that may help us later to accept a compound protagonist. We are prepared for the ultimate deflation of the Compson family by the fact that to Benjy the Compsons are like gods—and Caddy the goddess—all-powerful, the source of everything. The reader knows better, of course, and can guess at the Compson weaknesses and desire their exposure; nevertheless, Benjy's view gives them a look of mystery and power. The conditions are created here for an unstable effect of pathos (the undeserving victim, a kind of irony), but it is only potential, not fully developed until later, retrospectively, and the curiosity characteristic of a *dramatic* effect is strongly launched.

In the Quentin section, the tragic possibility reaches its fullest development. Quentin approaches the tragic through the intensity of his suffering and the nobility (as he believes) of his desires. The tragic form so approached is tragic irony rather than true tragedy, however, since there is no discovery or acknowledgment of the hamartia—the radical misjudgment of his world

that destroys him—and it tends toward moral shock, rather than pity and fear: the "good" character willfully destroys himself for insufficient cause. This quasi-tragic effect, whatever it may be, is mitigated, however, by its juxtaposition upon the opening section. We are conscious of Benjy's presence in the background of Quentin's world; of his pure innocence in contrast to Quentin's consciousness of corruption; of his view of Caddy, corrective to Quentin's; not to mention our inferences as to what will *follow* Quentin's suicide—the coming of the young Quentin, the implication that history will repeat itself. These facts warn us against giving too much sympathy to Quentin; they prepare us for the possibility that Quentin's romantic illusions, which seem in the immediate context so tragic or painful, may ultimately look silly, vain, comic. The implied reader indeed sees through those illusions and wishes them to be exposed. We also know that Quentin alone cannot be the protagonist, for we know how early in the Compson history he removes himself from the scene, and we may already be prepared for the possibility that an analogy between the romantic Quentin and the idiot is in store for us. Meanwhile, the expected deflation of the Compsons' stature has already advanced, for to Quentin they do not possess the omnipotence they have for Benjy. They still are, however, romantic symbols of the great abstract values—honor, tradition, virtue— and the Compsons' degeneration (which we now see through Quentin's eyes) has great moral significance, since it implies the death of those values. This is indeed the very source of Quentin's problem, of the enormous importance he attaches to Caddy. As in the Benjy section we see beyond him—we see especially Caddy's simpler humane virtues, which to Quentin are trivial. His own moral fear of the deflation of the Compsons' stature is of course the essential motivation for his suicide. In this section, the Compsons still retain a romantic aura, but we are prepared to see it disappear.

In the Jason section, the emphasis is now squarely on the moral inferiority of the character (Jason), underlined in every incident, scene, and line of narration. The stress is here rather than on his suffering or misfortune; it is a caustic comic effect, and whether the reader finds Jason funny or hateful, whether

he is amused or indignant, is perhaps a matter of temperament, since the two qualities here seem to merge.[25]

We read the Jason section in the light of the two preceding ones. Our previous attention to Benjy and Quentin, the unfavorable view of Jason and Mrs. Compson generated there, along with the favorable view of Caddy, all help to intensify the hateful and absurd in Jason. The shift to Jason places Quentin at a remove (just as the shift to Quentin distanced Benjy), and it also permits Benjy to regain some of the prominence he lacked in the Quentin section. The shift confirms our expectation that none of the brothers alone will be the ultimate center of interest. The outlines of the compound protagonist are taking shape, and the fact that Jason is ironic-comic seems to prepare us for an ultimately comic or ironic conclusion. This effect is enhanced by the increasing clarity of the picture, accompanied by decreasing sympathy for the characters who are the foci of attention. We have been moving "through" the protagonist from innocent to corrupt.

The process of the Compsons' deflation has received a rapid thrust, for to Jason the Compsons are all as individuals reduced to the level of contempt, although he still cares for the status conveyed by the family name. Perhaps we even condemn Jason for deflating the Compsons too much. His biting contempt as well as his attention to the weakest and most sordid aspects of his family (seen in the increased prominence of Mrs. Compson and young Quentin, as also in his constant attribution of low motives to everyone) effectively robs them of the qualities attributed to them by Quentin. Yet in an important sense he, too, is overvaluing them still. His contempt is the expression of his hatred, which is proof of the importance he still grants them as enemies of consequence. They still have "weight" for him, though lacking the moral and romantic significance that Quentin attaches to them. The implied reader is likely to resist this sort of hostile

---

[25]"Caustic comic": comic tending toward the purely punitive (rather than the romantic): an inferior character gets what he deserves, with emphasis on the inferiority, largely unrelieved by positive qualities. This meaning for "caustic" differs somewhat from my usage in *The American Short Story in the Twenties* (Chicago, 1961).

overvaluation, by which Jason denies them human dignity, just as we resisted Quentin's denial of Caddy's virtues, and we await the exposure of that illusion.

Three matters are emphasized in the final section of the novel: first, the detailed look, centered mostly on Dilsey, at the routine work of getting this family moving on a not-too-typical Sunday morning. Second, Benjy's trip to church, escorted by Dilsey. Third, Jason's discovery that he has been robbed, with his futile rush to the sheriff and to Mottson before giving up the chase. And there is the very end—Ben's ride in the buggy with Luster and the momentary outbreak when Luster takes the wrong turn around the monument. These components develop a contrast in dignity and sympathy between Dilsey (an "ethical norm," as some critics have said) and the remaining Compsons. Jason's chase becomes a full-fledged comic punishment and converts the episode of his narrative into a completed comic sequence. Benjy's trip to church, as I have earlier suggested, also terminates the Benjy episode, with testimony by Dilsey to his worth as a human being, to his soul, redeeming his idiocy: "You's de Lawd's chile, anyway" (p. 396). It completes the pathos implicit in the Benjy section.

The critical problem is in determining why these elements are a fitting conclusion to the novel as a whole, a question that challenges not just the analytical critic but any reader as he finishes the book and looks back. The question forces him to consider the matter of unity; he is prodded by the convention of unity into making the necessary inferences to discover the full impact of the disclosure plot.

The plot's impact depends in part upon the completion of the deflating of the Compsons—a process important less for its own sake than as it punctures the illusions of the brothers. The outside look at Jason, Benjy, and Mrs. Compson (including the physical descriptions) by an external observer, the public humiliation of Jason, the contrast with Dilsey's dignity and goodness, strip the Compsons of even the weight that Jason's hatred had given them. True, the only Compsons (other than Benjy) who are directly seen in this episode are Mrs. Compson and Jason, and no doubt we remember, as from long ago, the more attractive people who have gone. Even so, the deflation

continued here has to embrace the whole family, not just Jason
and his mother. The display of Mrs. Compson's stupidity as well
as selfishness and of Jason's futility reflects upon all the previous
narratives, in which for all their faults these characters seemed
more formidable than they do here. One wonders how even
Caddy and Quentin might have looked in clear daylight—would
even they, for instance, have treated Dilsey with much decency?
When Dilsey takes Benjy to church—showing respect for him
that only Caddy, we know, has approached—it calls to mind the
limitations in even Caddy's care for Benjy, important though
this was to him. Finally, there is a deflating effect in our recognition that we are now witnessing the last stage of the decline of
the Compsons, that the only Compsons who remain are fools.
Indeed, in the final section it is striking how the past and its
figures have been stripped away, as if young Quentin in leaving
had taken them with her—Quentin, Caddy, even Mr. Compson.
The real source of this effect of family death is, of course, the
shift from Jason's mind to an external narrator, for Jason's mind
was still peopled with the memories of those who have gone.[26]

The deflation of the Compsons does not destroy our appreciation of their virtues and suffering, but it is essential in the exposure of the protagonist's delusions. The most important effect of
this final section, however, is the recognition forced upon us of
the true identity of the protagonist. With the shift in narrative
viewpoint, Jason recedes from the center of attention. In his new
perspective, distanced, shrunken in stature, humiliated, he
ceases to be the villain he was, becomes more distinctly a mere
fool, capable even of stirring pity in some critics' sympathetic
hearts.[27]

We are now prepared for the inferences we must make at the
end, by which we can grasp what the real "story" is and the light
in which we are meant to see it. We see that Quentin's moral

[26]A further result is to emphasize the split of the Compsons into Bascombs and
true Compsons; the Bascombs outlast the Compsons despite their foolishness, a
further reflection upon the Compsons' futility.

[27]Waggoner says, "Perhaps a part of the secret [of what makes Jason a successful character] is that ... we are invited to pity rather than hate him" (*William
Faulkner*, p. 53). Faulkner, however, described Jason as "the most vicious character in my opinion I ever thought of" (Robert A. Jelliffe, ed., *Faulkner at Nagano*
[Tokyo, 1966], p. 104).

romanticism has been juxtaposed upon Benjy's idiocy and Jason's selfishness and impotence, and we see the spreading analogies among them all, the similar delusions and futility in their attempts to deal with the Compson decline. We find the qualities of all three present in all three, and we see the sense in which all are idiots, all are impotent, all are selfish, all have illusions.

What then is the final, specific fictional effect implied by this analysis? No doubt the general movement is toward a last rather detached perception of the protagonist, one in which the implied reader's particular involvements, "emotional attachments" to the individual members, give way to more intellectualized recognition of their common ground. Certainly of the four progressions listed above, the identification of the protagonist is the most important of all. The dominant effect might thus be "dramatic"—the more or less intellectual pleasure in drawing inferences. The first of the four sorts of progressions—the disclosure of the facts—would also contribute. Yet the final effect is not simply dramatic, not simply intellectual, not simply the satisfaction of curiosity. It has an emotional dimension. The specific fictional effects of the various sections (Benjy's pathos and so on) are undermined, qualified, or better, stabilized (resolved, catharted) by the progressive deflation of the protagonist. In the end is a disengagement. Like the final effect suggested in *The Portrait of a Lady*, this, too, can be described as a kind of *wonder*, though it has been reached through a very different route and has a very different sort of object.

I define "wonder" as the interested perception of unbridgeable distance between us and the characters in their situation. It is "interested" in that it involves some keen sense of the potential importance, or interest, of the characters, the desire to penetrate to them, to come close with sympathy or hatred, to understand, to bridge the gap. Yet the effect of a plot of wonder is to frustrate this wish, to confront us finally with the mystery, the strangeness of the fictional case. Such an effect differs from both comedy and irony (other effects that also depend on distance) in that it suspends all judgment of deservedness or undeservedness in the situation, all judgment of good or bad. It lacks or cancels the pleasure that we normally take in the distance displayed in

comedy and the pity or condescension that may accompany our
perception of irony.

In *The Sound and the Fury*, the effect of wonder is reached
from a potential effect of comic irony. It is ironic in that despite
the distance between us, the protagonist appears to be caught in
a situation undeservedly or excessively unfortunate. It is comic
because of the ambiguity in this, the real possibility that the
protagonist's misfortunes are a just and proper punishment for
his vanities and errors. The conflict between these two
possibilities—the refusal of the plot to tilt toward either justice or
injustice—turns us toward the unjudging contemplation of distance, the effect of wonder.

A root for the possible comic irony could be found in a common abstractable "error" that the protagonist makes, which
could be called either "comic" or "ironic." This error (or vanity)
lies in the protagonist's assumption that his evaluation of the
family's problem and his judgment of the correct action to take
are better than any others. It may seem unfair to accuse Benjy of
this mistake—surely we cannot accuse him of "vanity or
affectation"—yet he partakes, insofar as he is capable of perception at all, in his absolute failure to question his perceptions or to
realize that anything is missing in what he sees or understands.
This is idiocy, not vanity, but it parallels significantly the vanity
of the others. Quentin's vanity lies in his conception of the moral
importance of the family's decline and of himself as spokesman
and defender of that morality, and Jason's is, as Vickery has said,
"his pride that he has no illusions about his family or himself."[28]
But the most important aspect of the protagonist's mutual vanity
lies in the contempt Quentin feels for Jason and Jason for Quentin, the superiority both feel to Benjy, Benjy's own ignorance
that he is their brother, and the universal failure to see what they
have in common. This failure opens the final distance between
protagonist and implied reader at the end as the latter is forced
(by the conventions of unity) to make these discoveries.

Yet all seems to be qualified by compassion—an effect
achieved through our partial recollection of the live suffering of
Quentin and the muted suffering of Benjy—which extends even

[28]Vickery, *The Novels of William Faulkner*, p. 42.

to Jason in our next-to-last view of him as he sits defeated in his car in Mottson waiting for someone to drive him back to Jefferson. The irony is relieved of its harshness, the comedy is nullified, and we focus finally on wonder, here the compassionate perception of distance. The compassion is our acknowledgment that the Compson brothers are important enough to deserve our attention and to make this display of their folly an emotionally significant experience.

The final incident reinforces this effect. Benjy is taken around the square in the wrong direction, howls outrageously, but calms down as soon as he is taken the right way. Why should the novel have this ending? By now the reader is aware of the compound protagonist. Our inferences about the protagonist will inevitably incorporate this final appearance of Benjy, as if it represented the protagonist's most important qualities. If his earlier visit to church implies the fundamental innocence of the family on a cosmological scale despite hysteria and corruption and delusion, then the incident in the square may symbolize still more vividly the difficulty all the brothers have shown in adapting to change and disorder. Order is restored for Benjy by the simple expedient of reversing tracks and going around the statue in the customary way; it is a superficial or specious order, but it satisfies him:

> The broken flower drooped over Ben's fist and his eyes were empty and blue and serene again as cornice and façade flowed smoothly once more from left to right; post and tree, window and doorway, and signboard, each in its ordered place. [P. 401]

So, too, the order that Quentin has attained in death, and Jason by ridding himself of the others (as the appendix will confirm), is specious. But it is peaceful, too, even "serene," and this quality we are invited to look for at the very end in *all* the brothers. It liberates the novel, despite its title, from an effect of despair or bitterness.[29]

Formally speaking, *The Sound and the Fury* is unique in modern

[29]Wonder is an effect treated often in Faulkner, notably in such works as *Absalom, Absalom!, Light in August*, and many short stories.

fiction—radically different from other novels, a work of exceptional originality. Large-scale disclosure plots are, as I have said, rare. In theory they are likely to be less economical than conventional dynamic plots with comparable materials. There is likely to be an effect of looseness which might easily turn the work into a collection of episodes or stories. *The Sound and the Fury* has a certain looseness of this kind, no doubt; a critic concerned with form might easily be troubled by its big, almost discrete segments, its heavy joints. Yet this is no real fault and a small price to pay (if a price at all) for the vivid complexity that is achieved. The advantages of Faulkner's disclosure plot can be seen if we try to imagine the same materials worked into a conventional dynamic plot. The most likely way of making the conversion (without adding to or changing the material itself to make a different novel—one like, say, *Sartoris*) would be to rearrange the episodes in chronological order: Quentin, Jason, Benjy, and the final episode. But see how little we would gain and how much we would lose by such a shift. We would gain a more or less dynamic view of the family decline—the fall between Quentin's suicidal miseries and Dilsey's "de first en de last," eighteen years later. But in every respect except the actual unfolding, that fall is fully before us in the disclosure plot. We would lose, on the other hand, all the various progressions I have described. The fine coming together of the compound protagonist would be destroyed. The focus would be blurred, the effect of wonder diffused. As the next step in the analysis would attempt to demonstrate (I shall, again, stop short here), the disclosure plot appears to govern an extraordinarily rich array of complex materials—fictional, narrative, linguistic—in a most subtle sort of unity. *The Sound and the Fury* is a triumphant display of formal originality in its time.

[11]

Rhetorical Plot:
Invisible Man

Midway through Ralph Ellison's *Invisible Man*, the unnamed narrator, who has just joined the Brotherhood, realizes that he must sever his ties. He will be giving speeches, but under a new name, and his old identity must be concealed. Briefly he worries about this switch, his worry extending to the motherly Harlem woman who has been sheltering him in his need: "But what if someone from the campus wandered into the audience? Or someone from Mary's—even Mary herself? 'No, it wouldn't change it,' I heard myself say softly, 'that's all past.' My name was different; I was under orders. Even if I met Mary on the street, I'd have to pass her by unrecognized."[1] A reader concerned for realism might object. The Brotherhood is a fictional cousin to the Communist party, yet though we may associate stereotypical communism with secrecy, it is difficult to understand the particular secrecy indicated here. The Communist may have to conceal his membership in the party, but the narrator and his Brothers are about to become public figures, and it is not their Brotherhood which is to be concealed but their non-Brotherhood past. Why? The narrator's past is politically innocuous; he is not a criminal or a spy. Why should he deny Mary Rambo in the street? The ban makes no sense except by analogy to a religious order in which the novitiate is required to break earlier ties for the sake of discipline.

[1]Ralph Ellison, *Invisible Man* (New York, 1972), p. 254. Page references in the text refer to this edition.

Although the situation is unrealistic, most readers will find it intelligible at another level, a level at which we have been trained, long before reaching this point, to read the book. This is the symbolic, or allegorical, level. It is important for the narrator to deny Mary Rambo because his entry into the Brotherhood signifies the adoption of a "new personality" and the rejection of the old. He is given a new name by the Brotherhood, which represents a much deeper change: "The new suit imparted a newness to me. It was the clothes and the new name and the circumstances. It was a newness too subtle to put into thought, but there it was. I was becoming someone else." (p. 254).

Invisible Man is full of such devices: mimetic conventions violated or disregarded for the sake of other conventions typically associated with allegory or didactic forms. For example, the narrator begins and ends his narrative in a new residence—a "hole in the ground," illuminated by stolen power from Monopolated Light & Power, with 1,369 bulbs in the roof. This hole in the ground cannot be understood realistically; it is fantastic and requires symbolic reading. So, too, do the paint factory and hospital episodes—of which more later. Again, there is the seeming difference in character between the violent angry man of the opening, who almost kills a stranger on the street for a racial slur, and the much more moderate and careful man whom we follow into that hole at the end. The contrast is difficult to accept realistically, since the narrator of the beginning (the angry man) has presumably begun to write soon after the events described at the end. The contrast is easily explicable, however, in terms of the dialectic of the argument that has developed from the beginning. There is also the problem of the indefiniteness of time in the narrative,[2] as well as the vagueness of many names and places (the unnamed narrator, the unnamed Founder, the unlocated and unnamed college, the unnamed Brotherhood), which contrasts so strikingly with the specificity of the concrete detail of ordinary life, especially in Harlem. There is the selectivity of the narrator's represented experiences. We notice that several of his public speeches, as well as the speeches of others, are given in

[2]Most details would locate the action in the early 1930s, but there are a number of anomalies.

full. On the other hand, though the story is concerned with his growth, his childhood is almost nonexistent; the only remembered details reflect the culture in which he grew up. We know virtually nothing about his parents. His great difficulty in the book is summed up in the figure of the "invisible man," which is presented as a social and, specifically, racial problem: he is invisible, as he seems to say, because he is black. From his opening address to the reader, we are encouraged at every point to read the narrator as typical, as representative. Care may be required to define just what he stands for—it is probably not the ordinary "black experience," since he has special talents, education, and ambition—but that it is something beyond himself is unquestionable, especially when he speaks directly to the reader. The last words are explicit: "Who knows but that, on the lower frequencies, I speak for you?" (p. 439).

All these elements are signals pointing to the possibility of a rhetorical form, which has led me to select this novel—so powerful and important in our time. My label in no way involves a disparagement of the book's artistic integrity. It should not be necessary to say this, except that the concept of rhetorical art ("didactic") is so often taken as pejorative. Ellison himself has on occasion objected to "ideological" judgments of his fiction, asking that it be judged as "art."[3] It must be understood, therefore, that although a novel may resemble active rhetoric (aimed at persuasion), it is no less a novel for that, no less a work of self-contained art. Artistically, it can be understood as an "imitation"

[3]In later discussions of this novel Ellison often emphasized the "artistic" as opposed to "ideological" interest: "I can only ask that my fiction be judged as art; if it fails, it fails aesthetically, not because I did or did not fight some ideological battle" (Ralph Ellison, *Shadow and Act* [New York, 1964], pp. 136-37). Also: "I think that the writer's obligation in a struggle as broad and abiding as the one we are engaged in, which involves not merely Negroes but all Americans, is best carried out through his role as writer" (p. 132). His most specific comments about the work tend to refer to its mimetic aspects, as, for example, his frequent stress on the irony in the portrayal of the hero, his comments about the division of the book into parts (three parts, representing "the narrator's movement from . . . purpose to passion to perception" [*Shadow and Act*, pp. 176-77]), and his comments about the style (shifting in the three parts from a "naturalistic treatment" to an "expressionistic" to a "surrealistic" style [p. 178]). On the other hand, Ellison also insisted: "Now mind! I recognize no dichotomy between art and protest" (p. 169).

of a piece of rhetoric, so to speak—principles of evaluation (instead of principles of fictional invention) occupy the privileged position in the germinal subject. The designation simply proposes that the concept of a rhetorical plot will do better justice to its art than some other hypothesis might.

None of the signals I have mentioned is sufficient by itself to make *Invisible Man* rhetorical. Together they make a strong circumstantial case which should be compared with the best mimetic alternative. Like other major rhetorical novels of this century, *Invisible Man* displays a full and rich development of the fictional conventions, techniques and materials, of its time. Like others, it approaches the borderline between the two principles. Since this is a rhetorical *novel*—that is to say, the form is based on novelistic materials—the analysis of the plot itself will depend heavily upon the analysis of the fictional stuff of the work.

Mimetically, the plot is best described, probably, as centering in a discovery for the unnamed narrator, framed and completed in the prologue and epilogue, written in his hole in the ground. The protagonist-narrator is an educated young black man with ambitions to be a leader of his people and a specialty in speechmaking. His discovery is accomplished through the various episodes that constitute the action and is explicated quite fully, especially at the end but also, in part, in advance, in the prologue. Its core is stated in the novel's opening sentence: "I am an invisible man." After the prologue has postulated the metaphor of invisibility and has indicated some of the suffering it entails, the novel moves back into a conventional narrative in which the events leading to this conclusion are unfolded.

Invisibility is a metaphor for the narrator's social and psychological condition, felt in his relations with society and in his attitude toward himself. The metaphor indicates his failure to be recognized by others as an autonomous individual with an independent identity and mind. The people around him see him not as he is but as they preconceive or wish him to be. There are two sides to his condition: the blindness of others and the man's own submission, his surrender of self to the identities others would impose upon him. He becomes aware of his invisibility only gradually. Before recognizing it, he is subject to the manipulation and image-making of others; in this state (for two-

thirds or more of the book) he is fearful, anxious, dependent. He tries to shape himself to fit the stereotypes offered by others. This is ultimately impossible, however, for he has a heritage within him, an unrecognized "true self," racial and cultural in origin, which is betrayed by his attempts to adapt himself to imposed roles. He cannot rid himself of his tastes, his links with the slave past, his connections with the black culture in which he has grown up. Whatever identity he tries to adopt, he is forced into the position of betraying his people, as he regards it, and his anxiety is intensified by guilt.

The narrator's discovery is not merely a personal one, however. In briefest terms, the root cause of his invisibility is the white man's refusal to grant the black man full human identity, combined with his own fear of asserting it. The consequences are bad not merely for the narrator but for his people—not only because of the personal degradation but because such a situation prolongs and exacerbates the poor social conditions under which most blacks live. The worst evil here is not poverty or destitution but the threat of violence caused by the denial of black pride and dignity. The riot at the end makes this evil explicit and drives home the importance of the issue.

By the end of the novel, the narrator is conscious of his invisibility and recognizes three alternative courses of action. One is to accept his invisibility and exploit it. This course is taken by Rinehart, the con man, who is the extreme case: he splits himself into a variety of identities—gambler, lover, runner, preacher—and so makes his living. But clearly Bledsoe, the President of the College, does the same; this acceptance is what the narrator's grandfather has proposed ("overcome 'em with yeses, undermine 'em with grins, agree 'em to death and destruction" [p. 13]), what the narrator himself finds so shocking, so offensive to his integrity. The opposite is to withdraw completely from society, as the narrator does when he retreats into his hole. The third alternative is to confront his invisibility in a socially responsible way. This requires not only acceptance of what he knows—of his invisibility and of the social diversity that gives rise to it—but positive action in society. Although the kind of action needed is not stated, apparently it is most important to make others also conscious. Though in the epilogue the narrator

claims that he is now ready to emerge from his hole, that he will now enter society and begin to "act," the indications are strong that he has already acted most powerfully by writing the book. He has become, indeed, a writer—changed, in Ellison's words, from a "ranter to a writer."[4] This writing is presented in the epilogue as a self-conscious act, a process in the course of which his emotions have changed and his consciousness has grown, action which seems implicitly (although he never admits the possibility) to have made him at last visible.

The final element in the plot is thus a choice by the protagonist. In contrast to the decision that ends *The Portrait of a Lady,* however, this choice is significant as a sign not of character but of knowledge; it marks the final step in discovery, a recognition of the appropriate attitudes and behavior in response to what he has learned. We remain "close" to the protagonist, our attention focused upon his reasons, his thinking, not so as to judge him for them but so as to understand them in themselves.

The plot process develops the protagonist's discovery in two ways. First, events lead him to it directly: a sequence consisting of the two most extended episodes in the book, involving first the College and second the Brotherhood—parallel experiences, both of which take him a long way toward knowledge. In each case he seeks to develop a certain identity, is betrayed and disillusioned. Each episode begins an attempt by the narrator to prepare for a position of leadership. He is ambitious for himself and wants a career that will benefit his people. Inspired in each case by a fatherlike leader who exemplifies such a career, he hopes in the first case to become an educator and in the second a revolutionary leader. In both his opportunity for leadership is offered by an institution (the College, the Brotherhood) dominated or supported by whites. In the first case, the leadership is within the established society; the benefactor Norton wants to raise Negroes "up" to take their places within that society, for his own personal gratification. This step requires the rejection of black culture and gratitude on the part of the benefacted Negroes. An opportunity for personal gain presents itself for blacks

---

[4]See Abby Arthur Johnson, "From Ranter to Writer: Ellison's *Invisible Man,*" *South Atlantic Bulletin* 42 (May 1977), pp. 35-44.

like Bledsoe who understand what is wanted and can manipulate the white benefactors so as to let them see only the kinds of blacks they want to see. When the narrator makes the mistake of allowing Norton to meet not only the field Negro with his outrageous and colorful story of incest but also the insane blacks of the Golden Day, he himself is pushed aside by Bledsoe, the real power in the institution, for not playing the game. From disillusionment he turns eventually to his second alternative, the Brotherhood, which offers a chance of leadership through political activity, the objective being to bring about social justice by overthrowing the status quo. The difficulty is that the Brotherhood pretends to deny racial differences, and the narrator's concern for blacks is criticized for being racist. He is punished for being too successful with his own people and is required for a while to abandon Harlem and instead lecture on the Woman Question (a comic interlude that gives him insight into sexual invisibility but strikes me otherwise as a relatively weak part of the action, vague and unrealized). Ultimately he concludes that blacks are being sacrificed by the Brotherhood for the sake of larger political ends. The Harlem race riot with which the book ends is interpreted by him as the result of deliberate provocation by the Brotherhood—hence a murderous act—intended to hurt the blacks. Hence there is no essential difference between Brother Jack, the Brotherhood leader, and Bledsoe and Norton: all in their various ways try to keep the Negro down, in his place, "running."

In both cases, thus, the narrator's desire to become a leader of his people runs aground on the discovery that the leadership sought requires the denial of his people. He himself is invisible to those who would direct his new career, in the sense that he is being used to serve their ends—Bledsoe's and Norton's and Jack's. His people are also invisible to them in that they are disregarded, and the narrator partakes of their invisibility, too, when he tries to take their part. His conclusion, reached in the epilogue, is that black identity (which includes the free acceptance of the black heritage in all its diversity) must not be sacrificed to either of the great objectives to which the narrator temporarily committed himself—neither to the goal of elevating blacks to take their places in the status quo nor to that

of finding justice for them in a revolutionary program that would eliminate racial identity. Instead identity must be preserved with full consciousness, on the one hand, of the value of the differences between one individual, one culture, and another, and on the other hand, of the interdependence of all parts of the society.

These two major episodes provide the main action of the novel. They teach the protagonist directly by frustrating his purposes and exposing his illusions. A second way in which he learns is through symbolism and allegory; several episodes which do not directly advance the primary action just discussed express aspects of the protagonist's discovery in symbolic form. In addition, many parts of the major events themselves are full of symbolic significance.

The chief episodes which contribute to the discovery primarily through their symbolism are the battle royal episode, which begins the narrator's adventures, and the factory-hospital episode, which occurs midway and is developed at length between the College and Brotherhood episodes. Although both sections manifest the hero's invisibility and contribute to his disillusionment, they do not mark steps in the dialectic of his education as the others do. Instead, they symbolically replay or foreshadow his learning experience. In the battle royal scene, indeed, the narrator's awareness does not seem to advance at all. The reader learns much, but the meaning of the episode is not really clear until later events show the scene to have been highly symbolic. Similarly, the factory-hospital sections are more important for symbolically anticipating than for what they teach the protagonist at the time.

The allegorical nature of these scenes is obvious. When the black boys in the battle royal scene are made to fight each other blindfolded for the entertainment of the whites, they prefigure many of the later struggles in the novel and most notably the final riot: blacks blinded to reality, unable to see each other, made to attack each other (blindness and invisibility go together) for the pleasure of the white power structure. The worst outrages—the blonde temptress and the electrified coins on the rug—show how the white culture tempts blacks with values that it punishes them for pursuing. The shocks given by the coins

(like the shock therapy in the hospital scene) are metaphors for the moral jolts which form the substance of the narrator's disillusionments—most especially, perhaps, his betrayals by Bledsoe and Jack. With the conclusion of the scene—the narrator's prize speech praising humility, which expresses the black response taught by the College and exemplified (ostensibly) by Bledsoe—the whole section anticipates both the College and the Brotherhood lessons.

The factory and hospital scenes develop a complex system of symbolic schemes, only a few aspects of which can be suggested here. For example, the factory apparently represents American industrial society ("You just aren't prepared for work under our industrial conditions" [p. 187]). The paint manufactured by the factory symbolizes American illusions: of liberty ("Liberty Paints"), of American purity and superiority ("Keep America Pure With Liberty Paints" [p. 149]), of white supremacy, of white America, of white government ("If It's Optic White, It's the Right White" [p. 165], "the purest white that can be found" [p. 153], "as white as George Washington's Sunday-go-to-meetin' wig and as sound as the all-mighty dollar" [p. 153]).

In the Kimbro scene, which comes first, the illusory nature of the whole project is symbolized in an elaborate allegory in which, finally, the addition of a certain black dope to white paint makes the paint seem whiter to the white man, Kimbro, but gray to the narrator. In the Brockway scene which follows, we see the making of the "vehicle" for the paint, produced in the basement by an ignorant but skilled black laborer. He represents the lowest level of the laboring world, but the whole industrial society (the factory) depends on him. He is selfish and reactionary, jealous of his job, violently prejudiced against the younger workers and against the union. He defends vigorously the idea that the black man should be grateful to his white employers. The vehicle he produces is filthy and foul. It is also colorless; the coloring is added upstairs. The implication is that it represents the *disposition* to prejudice, a compound of ignorance and hatred and sadism (foul natural things, all) manufactured by industrial society exploiting the ignorance and prejudice of its laborers and converted into fine-looking dreams and illusions, especially the American Dream of a pure white "free" society. The explosion

which concludes this scene also shows (like the riot and the battle royal) the violence of blacks struggling against each other, in this case the illiterate old-timer fighting the newcomer who might want to change the status quo.

The hospital allegory that follows is in part a symbolic replay of the change in the protagonist that results from his disillusionment in the College episode. In retrospect Brockway is a caricature of Bledsoe, the explosion in which he injures the narrator a replay of Bledsoe's betrayal. The result is shock and amnesia. The narrator's literal inability in the hospital to remember his name symbolizes his loss of identity, of goals, of attitudes, of illusions, as a result of this betrayal. The aim of the treatment is to restore his identity. It means, as the doctors say, making a new man out of him: the hospital scene parallels the larger problem. He is treated by machine—imprisoned in a box and subjected to shocks. The treatment does not work, however, though the white doctors do not notice its failure. He remembers who he is when the doctor who is releasing him casually mentions his name. Again, as with Kimbro, there is the blind white assumption that something has been done to the Negro that in fact has not been done. Yet the machine treatment has accomplished a change of which the doctors are unaware: it has released the narrator for anger. "And suddenly my bewilderment suspended and I wanted to be angry, murderously angry" (p. 181). The anger is not yet available, though; first he must leave the machine—that is, withdraw from it, from the factory, from industrial society, from the "system." Later, when he sees the couple being evicted and makes the speech that begins by counseling restraint and ends by challenging the law, he is full of the rebel's rage. Thus the hospital scene foreshadows his entry into the Brotherhood and his readiness to attack the establishment, of which he has always before (like Brockway) been afraid.

The sections just discussed are allegorical as the two major episodes are not. Within the fictional world they function as symbolic of other elements within that world. My description here can only hint at their complexity. Indeed the whole novel is striking for its allegorical richness. There is scarcely a detail that does not seem to acquire symbolic resonance of some kind—not only the obvious symbols like the cast-iron Negro doll-bank

which the narrator breaks but cannot get rid of, or Tarp's chain link, or the narrator's briefcase, which he carries everywhere, or the hole in the ground, or Tod Clifton's paper doll. It is certainly significant that the narrator is made the Harlem spokesman in the Brotherhood on April Fool's Day. Light and darkness, sight and blindness, clustering around the central figure of invisibility, are always meaningful, not only in such obvious matters as Brother Jack's glass eye and the blindness of the Rev. Homer A. Barbee, who delivers the eulogy to the Founder of the College, but in the references to vision throughout, reaching a curious symbolic complexity in the narrator's discovery of the effect of Rinehart's dark glasses on both others and himself. All references to color are likewise significant, not only black and white, but the green grass of the College and Brother Jack's red hair. Machinery is symbolic—in the factory, in the hospital, in the robot that threatens to take over after the narrator's painful castrating disillusionment in his last dream—suggestive always of the industrial society and of inhumanity and rigidity of thought and feeling. With such a profusion of symbols, the reader is encouraged to look deeply into almost every emphasized image that is not merely connective in the thin but necessary thread of mimetic coherence: in the blueprints carried by the man with the cart, in the pounding of the steam pipes at Mary Rambo's, in the "dangerous animals" in the Central Park Zoo (p. 227), even comically in the "partly uncoiled firehose hanging beside the entrance" (p. 309) at the beginning of the seduction scene when the narrator is diverted to the Woman Question.

Similarly, most of the characters become significant to the narrator less for what they do than for what they represent. This is especially true of those who seem to represent certain kinds of black traditions. There are Bledsoe, the Negro educator, and Barbee ("part of Dr. Bledsoe" [p. 91]), who articulates his tradition in the form of the legend of the Founder. There is Trueblood, the sharecropper, who represents the "field nigger" heritage that the educated blacks in the College would like to disown (a rural equivalent to Brockway, but without the latter's competitiveness and jealousy) and who articulates through his extended narrative a tradition of bawdy folk humor. There is Ras

the Exhorter, who represents the black revolutionary alternative to the nonracial Brotherhood, articulates most effectively the black resentment of the narrator for subordinating black interests to those of the Brotherhood, and is judged finally to be ridiculous but dangerous, primarily because of his pretensions and lack of means to carry out his aims. (The absurdity of Ras is emphasized symbolically by his appearance on horseback carrying a spear and is made explicit in the conversation of two citizens who are overheard ridiculing him.) Especially significant is Tod Clifton, whose primary function in the mimetic action is to drop out of the Brotherhood, to be killed in a run-in with the police, and to become thereby the occasion for the funeral ceremony which ignites the passions of Harlem, prepares them for riot, and precipitates the narrator's break with the Brotherhood. Tod's reasons for dropping out are plain enough: he is disillusioned with the Brotherhood, much as the narrator himself will soon be. It is also clear that Tod's despair provokes him to arrange his own death deliberately at the hands of the police. Somewhat less apparent, perhaps, is why he chooses to do it by becoming a street peddler selling paper dolls that mock blacks, a bitter gesture, presumably, that mocks his lost illusions. The reason is probably less important, however, than the consequence, in which Clifton's chief function is evident: ultimately he represents the man who "drops out of history," who "falls into obscurity"—the ordinary black man, unnoticed, unknown, a mystery. This is the meaning of the funeral speech, in which the narrator finds himself able to do little more than repeat Clifton's name and recite the facts of his death. Clifton represents all ordinary black people who are trampled and killed by the white society just as they are ignored by revolutionary movements with an eye on history. Symbolically, it is right that he have done something inexplicable and disgraceful, for the narrator's point is that all the disgrace and mystery disappear in the light of his simple humanity. He is also associated with both youth and the beauty of the black race, a connection emphasized by Ras himself, who cannot kill him. As Ras explains it to Clifton:

> It took a billion gallons of black blood to make you. Recognize you'self inside and you wan the kings among men! . . . You six foot

tall, mahn. You young and intelligent. You black and beautiful—
don't let 'em tell you different! . . . I'd have killed you, mahn. Ras
the Exhorter raised up his knife and tried to do it, but he could not
do it. Why don't you do it? I ask myself. I will do it now, I say; but
somet'ing tell me, "No, no! You might be killing your black king!"
[P. 282]

In his death Clifton emerges as the most important of the
figures who symbolize the black culture and tradition. He represents most particularly the bond of blackness itself, the feeling of
beauty and pride voiced by Ras, and his funeral brings the community together in their greatest display of shared emotion. His
drop out of history is a surrender, the most extreme abandonment of the ideal in the novel, more extreme even than Bledsoe's. Significantly, this behavior, which the members of the
Brotherhood predictably call a betrayal, is the work of the character who is then in death most explicitly "forgiven" by the
narrator, pardoned because of the intrinsic worth and beauty of
the humanity that has been crushed.

In a mimetic analysis of the plot, these symbolic and representative elements are explainable as means both to facilitate the
narrator's discovery and to articulate it for us. Even so, their very
prominence, and the heavy dependence of the plot upon such
features, add to the other signals noted earlier in suggesting that
some other principle might provide a stronger hypothesis. Let
us examine further, then, the difficulties in the mimetic conception that we have been considering.

First, there are certain problems of believability at the realistic
level, such as the question I noted at the start concerning the
strictures on the narrator's life when he joins the Brotherhood.
Time is another problem, not so much because of its indefiniteness as because of the speed with which changes in the condition
and morale of the Harlem community are noted in the last
stages of the book. The motivation of the narrator's enemies is
sometimes obscure or inconsistent: it is difficult, for instance, to
find a consistent thread to account for all aspects of Brother
Jack's behavior, and even Bledsoe's deceiving letter seems odd if
one tries to regard it from Bledsoe's own point of view (especially his sending the letters by way of the narrator himself,

trusting that they would not be opened); in both cases evidently the narrator's discovery that he has been betrayed is more important than an exact and clear understanding of the motivation for the betrayal. Again, the sarcastic arguments of the Brotherhood members as they criticize the narrator and each other seem relatively weak mimetically, as if the convincing creation of a realistic scene were sometimes less important than a forceful demonstration of the narrator's problems. There is a seeming mixture of fictional modes, ranging from the realism of most of the scenes in Harlem to the somewhat surrealistic effects of the Golden Day, the Rinehart, and the hospital episodes—a mixture of possibilities not easily explained by the discovery plot so far considered. And as we have seen, mimetic fidelity seems often to be sacrificed to symbolic suggestion.

Another kind of difficulty lies in the fact that much of what the narrator experiences, hears, and says seems intended primarily for the reader rather than constituting a real part of the narrator's own discovery. This is true of much of the symbolism, including those allegorical scenes which I have already described. The direct and extended presentation of various speeches and tales also shows this tendency. (I do not mean to say that incorporation of a narrative within narrative reduces mimetic coherence. Such a presentation does, however, introduce other interests besides those of the action in which it is embedded, and those interests will somehow have to be accommodated in one's hypothesis of a form.) Most striking in this regard, however, is the narrator's own direct address to the reader, notably in the prologue and epilogue, and his evident effort to make his point clear, as explicitly as he can—as if to imply that a straightforward narrative of the experience itself is not sufficient without an explanation of, as he calls it, "the lesson of my own life."

A third difficulty with the mimetic hypothesis lies in the emphasis which I have observed on the representativeness of everything. This emphasis includes not only the major characters discussed above but the narrator as well. The symbolic and allegorical components especially drive it home. The narrator's representativeness is suggested by such devices as the withholding of his name and the selectivity and nonspecificity of his

childhood—just as the general representativeness of the story is supported by the lack of a name for the Founder or for the College (as well as by "meaningful" names like those of Trueblood, Bledsoe, Norton, and Emerson). The narrator's representativeness is enforced, of course, by his role in the action: the fact that as a character he is, so to speak, morally neutral, that he enters his world innocent, that though he wants to act and has abilities, what happens to him is determined mostly by the external world, social conditions and social attitudes, to which he reacts in normal and innocent ways. Such a character could, of course, be the protagonist for a sympathetic mimetic discovery plot, exactly as proposed by our first hypothesis. The representativeness of what he learns, however, is emphasized by his own treatment of it, his ways of categorizing the people he deals with and his great concern to explicate what happens in general terms. His last words, as I have already suggested, forcefully make the point.

The narrator's discovery itself is of a kind that tends to divert us from a primarily mimetic interest. His invisibility is, as we have seen, a social condition (the result of social attitudes); his awareness of it comes through recognition not of personal needs or personal choices but of attitudes appropriate to that condition. We have seen also that the intellectual formulation of the discovery is more important than the process through which it is made: the experience is narrated and then translated by an explanation. In contrast, consider such truly mimetic discoveries as that in *The Sun Also Rises*—an emotional event in which the possible significances of the experience are never intellectualized— or Stephen Crane's "The Open Boat," in which the intellectualizing at the end goes only so far as to suggest that an interpretation is possible ("they felt that they could then be interpreters"), although it remains unstated. An intellectualized discovery is not necessarily didactic, but intellectualizing a discovery tends to subordinate the experience to the thing disclosed, and if that thing has to do with general social attitudes, these are likely to become the dominant object of attention.

To establish a rhetorical plot, however, we need a new hypothesis capable of giving a stronger account of the novel than is provided by the mimetic alternative. If the analysis starts, as

ours has, with the mimetic construction, the next step is to relate this construction to a thesis—what would presumably be the center of the rhetorical germinal subject. Since the mimetic construction centers in a discovery, we can expect the thesis to be almost identical: the narrator's discovery, generalized, *constitutes* the thesis. He functions in the plot as *didactic spokesman,* his consciousness serving as entry into that of the author. Since the discovery pertains in good part to his own condition, he also acts as *exemplar* of the thesis.

The thesis itself is a generalization, then, of the narrator's "I am an invisible man," with all the consequences and implications we have noticed in this statement. We must ask whom "I" represents in this formulation: who are the invisible men who must learn, as the narrator does, to confront their invisibility in a socially responsible way, to accept the diversity of cultures and affirm the integrity of their own? The protagonist is not the average black man, by any means. He wants throughout to be a leader, and his consciousness at the end is far beyond that of most of his fellows. It is that consciousness which gives him his thesis. He embodies not the black man as such but the potential awakened consciousness of the black man.

Yet the clear implication both in the opening and in the analysis of the idea later is that all blacks and the black race generally are invisible. The narrator differs only in that he understands his condition (though Rinehart and Bledsoe are said to exploit theirs). This can be understood if invisibility is regarded as essentially the inability of others to see one's personal human dignity, to see one as a unique individual, to recognize one's autonomous self. We may ask if characters like Mary Rambo, Ras, and the blueprint man—who seem to have no problems about knowing who they are—are also invisible. The blueprint man asks the narrator, "Why you trying to deny me?"—a sign of his felt invisibility—and it is not difficult to see how Mary Rambo and Ras, both representative in their different ways, are invisible to the Brotherhood as well as to the white power structure.

The thesis includes the assertion that invisibility is a painful and degrading condition. It creates anger. It threatens to blow up society. It is destructive to the black race, setting one member

against another. The implication is that denial of full human identity and dignity is the true source of black suffering, misery, and anger in this century. The argument has thrust for both nonblack readers, who are challenged for their ways of keeping the black man invisible, and black readers, who are challenged to remedy the case by recognizing their invisibility and responding appropriately. A further extension of the whole argument is suggested at the end in the hint that the blacks' condition is shared by nonblacks as well. This extension has not been developed during the novel, but it may be involved in the assumption that the implied reader is neither black nor white yet can share the black narrator's emotions. It lends force to the final affirmation of cultural diversity and autonomy.

The rhetorical plot is thus organized to demonstrate (with much illustration and a variety of support) a thesis about the black man's invisibility. The presentation includes an analysis of the state, a demonstration of its causes, and a judgment as to appropriate action. The thesis is argued by means of the fiction, which functions to this end in at least four ways. Most prominent is the learning process of the protagonist: his story manifests the thesis by teaching it to him, primarily through the College and Brotherhood episodes, as we have seen. But his tale also demonstrates the thesis, or aspects of it, metaphorically—that is, through allegory and symbol, in the various instances we have also considered. Third, to a lesser degree, the thesis is argued by direct explication and assertion—as the narrator, didactic spokesman, addresses the reader, chiefly in the prologue and epilogue, but also in the speeches, whenever these are presented verbatim and for their own sakes. Besides these direct means, the demonstration includes a broad and concrete display of many aspects of black culture and tradition, legend and lore—whose integrity in the diversity of American society is defended by the thesis. Included are a development of folklore in Trueblood's narrative (notice, before his account of the incest begins, how he dwells on such country matters as the river steamboats and hunting), a legend of heroes in Barbee's narrative of the Founder's career (presented as something already known to his audience), a tradition of oppression in such matters as Tarp's chain-gang history, of childhood lore in the frequent references

to folk figures like Brer Rabbit and Jack the Bear, of links to slavery in the background of the elderly Provo couple, of language and other cultural symbols in the numerous vignettes of characters in Harlem, talking and briefly seen.

The organization of the rhetorical plot involves an interweaving of these four elements, often combining two or more of them in the same scene (for example, Trueblood's narrative combines a manifestation of the culture with a step in the action leading to the narrator's necessary discomfiture; the battle royal both manifests the narrator's invisibility and provides an allegory of it). The development of the argument through these means is dialectical: it begins (in the prologue) with a general (and explicit) assertion of the thesis, followed by a symbolic rendering of its causes and effects (battle royal). Then comes a more specific fictional demonstration of the impossibility of finding a responsible black identity first within the white-dominated education structure (College) and then in a revolutionary structure (Brotherhood). Between these demonstrations is an allegorical interlude (factory and hospital) replaying the argument in symbolic terms and offering a symbolic explanation of the causes of invisibility. Running through both sections are the various manifestations of black culture. The argument concludes with a demonstration of the results of invisibility—of individual irresponsibility and exploitation (Rinehart) and deep and violent community emotions (the riot)—followed in the epilogue by an explicit formulation of the appropriate attitude to take, with an emphasis on the value of diversity, social and individual—a conclusion prepared by example and symbol throughout the book.

Such a hypothesis provides a more adequate explanation of *Invisible Man* than any mimetic plot I have been able to find in it. Not only does this view resolve the mimetic difficulties noted above, it strongly, coherently, and consistently accounts for the elements we have seen in the work. In no way does it denigrate the fictional nature of the book—the fiction is, as I have said, the means by which the rhetorical argument is executed, and the argument simply supplies shape, the rationale. The art, the mastery of the novelist, is shown, of course, not only in the formal conception but also most compellingly in the way this conception

pervades the details. We see the art of detail in the scope and range of the fictional world, the realistic focus of which is the black American contemporary world (thirties and forties), ranging from the South to New York and featuring a vivid and concrete view of many aspects of black culture. The most striking feature, however, apart from the general representativeness, is that very flexibility in modal conventions (its relaxations of realism for the sake of symbolic and surrealistic effects) which we found difficult to account for in a traditional discovery plot.

We see the art also in the versatility of the narrative and the style: the first-person narrative and a language adaptable not only to straightforward chronological narrative and events but to a variety of other effects. In addressing the reader and in discussing his own reactions, the narrator's language tends to become emotional, adjectival, rhythmical, reiterative. The speeches develop those qualities to an extreme point, as in the Clifton funeral speech, which builds repetitively, adding incrementally new ideas to the simple original ones with which it starts and which it keeps repeating. Elsewhere the narrative experiments with stream of consciousness and with italicized passages to suggest contrasting and simultaneous lines of thought. There are rhapsodies, Whitmanesque addresses. There is word play at times and frequent irony. One is aware of literary allusions—often (as in the use of the name Emerson) in curious and challengingly ironic ways. The narrative is especially effective in dealing with various linguistic traditions: oral tale telling (Trueblood), ministerial eulogizing (Barbee), and various kinds of black vernacular. Although the narrative style is not always under perfect control (at times it seems a little strident), it provides nevertheless a virtuoso performance.

We see the art most especially in the detailed development of the primary means of the rhetorical plot, in the intensity of the symbolism, the cumulative effect of the implications that pervade all the concrete imagery. And we see it notably in some striking and memorable scenes: in the depiction of the narrator's anxiety before his interview with Bledsoe; or his first walk on the streets of New York; the wonder in his observations of the Wall Street district; the depiction of the first Brotherhood rally; the powerful scenes of Clifton's death and his funeral march, and the brilliant extended account of the riot. And of course, again,

the narratives of Trueblood and Barbee. Such scenes compose the fictional stuff of the book, by virtue of which the didactic argument is brought into being and made so compelling.

As the last point in this analysis, we must distinguish our rhetorical plot hypothesis from another possibility which may be suggested for some readers by the prominence of allegory in the book. Why can we not indeed regard the book as a whole as an allegory? In this case the plot would best be described not as rhetorical or didactic, after all, but as creative. The difference consists in interest and effect. If the work is an allegory, its heart would certainly be the figure of invisibility: if allegory involves most essentially the development of two parallel lines of action, the parallelism would presumably be between the concrete metaphor of invisibility and the mimetic display of the narrator's life which is characterized by that metaphor.

The difficulty with this idea is twofold. In the first place, there seems to be no single developing allegory but instead a number of separate and different ones, nor is there a consistent development of the figure of invisibility to parallel the progress of the protagonist's discoveries. Furthermore, despite the rich development of symbols, the ultimate attention seems devoted to the issues symbolized, the questions of black identity and recognition, rather than to the ingenuity or efficacy of the symbols themselves. Though the ramifications of the ideas of invisibility and blindness are fascinating, even these are subordinate, I think, to the primary interests in this novel. It is the narrator's emotion that gives us our clue: the anger, which he expresses so overtly at the beginning, and which in the end has become the community's rage, dramatized in violence, while he personally has found relief in the act of writing. Anger is the emotional heart of the book, the emotional motivation at the start and the emotional force of the argument. It has little to do with the interests we would expect in a creative plot. It can be of central importance in a rhetorical plot, however. For if the germinal subject of such a plot is based on principles of evaluation, then the anger caused by invisibility is the concrete objectification of those principles in that plot. It is the germinal subject and effect, what the novel as a whole "depicts"—an emotion objectified and displayed, distinct from the joyful artistic emotion which is implied by the successful execution of the form.

[12]

Creative Plot:
Pale Fire

Two problems make Vladimir Nabokov's *Pale Fire* a challenge to the formal critic. One is its unorthodox narrative structure. At first glance there seems to be no narrative at all: instead, a poem (999 lines long, in heroic couplets), and a much longer commentary, the whole preceded by a foreword and followed by an index. What, we may ask, is novelistic about a structure like this, and how can we talk about a plot?

Since both the poet, John Shade, and the commentator, Charles Kinbote, are fictitious, the method suggests parody—possibly of two kinds: parody of a poem and parody of the scholarly enterprise. The reader quickly discovers, however, that parody is only part of the whole. The lives of both poet and commentator are developed, partly in the poem and at greater length in the commentary, and this development makes the work into a novel. It is a peculiar one. Not only are the characters and action embedded in the literary enterprise of poem and commentary, they emerge in an organization calculatedly designed, it would seem, to do away with the sequential arrangement of plot. In an arrangement of poem and commentary, the two parts are usually intimately dovetailed. We would, as we read the poem, pick up the notes as we go along. If we do read *Pale Fire* in this way, its plot is organized by a backtracking process in which the two big sections are read together—simultaneously. The idea is supported by the numerous cross-references which, if followed, would lead us through a still more complex weave, back and forth, in and out and around, with

frequent returns, as we work our way gradually through the text. The whole picture is complicated still more by the astonishing suggestion in the foreword that the reader would do best to "consult them [these notes] first and then study the poem with their help."[1]

As it turns out, the reader's movement isn't nearly so back and forth as my description suggests. Most of the notes in the commentary, except the short ones, relate only very loosely to the poem. Kinbote has his own stories to tell, and he seizes upon any excuse to tell them. Many of the cross-references are to minor connections: they serve the parody and the characterization of Kinbote rather than the actual process of reading. Others become meaningful only on second reading. The natural way to read this text is in its order of presentation, after all—foreword, poem, commentary, index. The organization of these four parts is an order that is *not* interchangeable. The cross-references—notes to poem and notes to notes—make connections explicit, but though every reader will often want to check them, I do not think they reorganize the text or dictate a specific change in the order of reading. They call explicit attention, rather, to links of a kind which exist in all novels and which readers discover, generally, in no determined order.[2]

The progression of the novel is carried by several distinguishable sequences, some implied at the start, others with origins in the poem or the commentary. All are developed in the commentary, intertwined or interwoven with each other, through the so-called notes, many of which are really narrative segments, often quite long. Part of the brilliance of the novel depends on this interweaving, the contrasts and juxtapositions such a method gives rise to, not to speak of the rich range of interests brought together. The formal problem consists, then, in relating these sequences to each other by some unifying principle.

The second formal challenge in *Pale Fire* concerns the nature of the commentator, Charles Kinbote himself. How do we inter-

---

[1]Vladimir Nabokov, *Pale Fire* (New York, 1962), p. 28. Page references in the text refer to this edition.

[2]For other views on the order of reading *Pale Fire*, see June Perry Levine, "Vladimir Nabokov's *Pale Fire*: 'The Method of Composition' as Hero," *International Fiction Review* 5 (July 1978), pp. 103–8.

pret his claim to be the exiled King of Zembla—a "distant northern land," somewhere near Finland, perhaps—in disguise? The claim is central in his commentary; he lives by it and had hoped Shade's poem would be about it. Since the poem is not about it, he has filled his commentary with his claim. The description of his life as King and his escape from the revolution is concrete and circumstantial. If it seems extraordinary that such a figure should end up on the faculty of Wordsmith College in New Wye, state of Appalachia, there is at any rate an explanation for everything—the college trustee with an interest in Zembla; the long-standing literary and pedagogical interests of the King. If Zembla itself seems fanciful, its reality is recognized at Wordsmith: Professor Nattochdag teaches Zemblan there; the Faculty discusses Zembla at the Faculty Club, and one faculty member insists on the close resemblance of Kinbote to the exiled King. Finally, there is Gradus, who comes out of Zembla to kill him but misses and kills Shade instead.

Critics are almost unanimously agreed, however, that Kinbote is mad and the whole story of his kingship is a fabrication. There are good reasons for this judgment—hints that grow strongest toward the end of the book. We know from the start that many of the faculty at Wordsmith consider him a madman. Near the end there is Shade's overheard remark to Mrs. Hurley: "One should not apply it [the word loony] to a person who deliberately peels off a drab and unhappy past and replaces it with a brilliant invention" (p. 238). Though another explanation is offered, the reader cannot avoid concluding that it is a reference to Kinbote. Again, there is the way in which all the witnesses to the activities of the killer are permitted to adjust their stories to make Gradus seem to be really only Jack Grey from the local Institute for the Criminal Insane, who has mistaken Shade for Judge Goldsworth, owner of the house Kinbote was occupying. Even Kinbote himself, when speaking of possible future incognitos at the end, describes a play he might write, about "a lunatic who intends to kill an imaginary king, another lunatic who imagines himself to be that king, and a distinguished old poet who stumbles by chance into the line of fire, and perishes in the clash between the two figments" (p. 301). The name Zembla, he tells us, "is a corruption . . . of Semblerland, a land of reflections, of 're-

semblers'" (p. 265); he refers to his story as a "kind of *romaunt*" displaying a "rich streak of magical madness." Most critics have accepted Mary McCarthy's suggestion that Kinbote is really V. Botkin, "American scholar of Russian descent," mentioned only in the index, and that Zembla is a purely fantasy land. Some have concluded also that Kinbote is writing his commentary not in a trailer camp, as he says, but in an asylum, and even that the commentary is addressed to a doctor.[3]

Yet there are difficulties with these ideas, as we shall see. By no means should we allow ourselves to assume at the start that Kinbote's story of the King is necessarily any less "real" or more "imaginary" than, say, the story of Shade's life or of Kinbote's own during his stay at Wordsmith College in Judge Goldsworth's house. We start with an ambiguity on this point. Our analysis of the plot will have to deal with this ambiguity; the efficacy of the hypothesis will depend to some extent on how well it does so.

Besides the formal problems, *Pale Fire* presents another challenge which for many readers comes first. This is the challenge of details, involving the accurate perception of the parts without regard to the whole they form. We are challenged by the trickiness and game playing that characterize Nabokov's manner and the special erudition he brings to it. The text is full of buried secrets, jokes, traps, riddles. (A good example is the concealment of the source of the title by a misquotation from *Timon of Athens*.)[4] This aspect has given critics for the last nineteen years much work to do. Unlike the riddles of *The Waste Land* or *Finnegans Wake*, however, those of *Pale Fire* do not obstruct a fairly well advanced perception of the form even at an early stage of perusal. The secrets in the text enhance the "progressing visibility of the form," not by heavily blocking the initial view, but by offering new subtleties for continued study. In our analysis of

---

[3]Mary McCarthy, "Vladimir Nabokov's 'Pale Fire,'" *Encounter* 19 (October 1962), pp. 71–84. Nina Berberova claims that after the reference to "doctor" on p. 279, "no doubts are possible" as to the madness and confinement in an asylum of Kinbote ("The Mechanics of *Pale Fire*," in *Nabokov: Criticism, Reminiscences, Translations, and Tributes*, ed. Alfred Appel, Jr., and Charles Newman [Evanston, Ill., 1970], p. 152).

[4]On p. 80 Kinbote translates back into English a passage from *Timon of Athens* previously translated into Zemblan. In the process the words "pale fire," in the original, have been dropped out, though Kinbote is unaware of the omission.

the plot we may assume that these challenges are on their way to being solved but will continue to reveal themselves.

There are other problems, too, in this problem-rich novel: the unreliability of the narrator, the judgment of Shade's poem, for instance. These will show up naturally as we try to analyze whatever the plot must be.

"Narrative in the form of commentary upon a poem" is the primary presentational commitment in *Pale Fire*. It offers a natural starting point for an analysis of the germinal principle. The work gives us two narratives and two narrators, one (John Shade's, the poem) contained within the other (Charles Kinbote's, the foreword, commentary, and index). It combines direct narrative and dramatic method: the former in the poem and many parts of the commentary; the latter in the display to the reader of poem against commentary: the reader can observe for himself the adequacy of the narrator's perception of the poem. The narrative becomes dramatic also when we perceive the various manifestations of Kinbote's unreliability as a narrator:[5] in his strained interpretation of events which invite more natural interpretations (for example, his failure to recognize that he is making a pest of himself with the Shades), in his displays of ignorance of matters familiar to any American reader (for example, that "Chapman's Homer" in an article about baseball would not refer to Keats's poem), in the recognizable language of his various obsessions, putting his narrative objectivity in doubt (the language of his homosexual obsession and of his paranoia, as, for example of the latter, this early warning, in the foreword: "she suddenly shot me a wire, requesting me to accept Prof. H(!) and Prof. C(!!) as co-editors of her husband's poem. How deeply this surprised and pained me! Naturally, it precluded collaboration with my friend's misguided widow" [p. 18]). His unreliability is associated in part with his parodic role as a pedant, his pedantic lack of sense of proportion and, for the rest, in his judgments of himself and others. In abstract matters

---

[5]Barbara J. Eckstein suggests that Kinbote is a parody of the unreliable narrator of realistic fiction ("Conventions of Irony in Some American Novels about Art" [Ph.D. dissertation, University of Cincinnati, 1980]).

such as psychiatry, Marxism, and to some extent art (in theory—though not, evidently, in practical criticism), he is probably trustworthy (that is, the implied author agrees with him), though less so than Shade.

Shade himself as narrator (in his poem) appears to be reliable—at least with regard to what he tells us and how he interprets it. His judgment of his own work may be shakier, since the poem, despite its good qualities, its clarity, readability, vividness, genuine emotion, and good sense, does ramble, does fall into triviality, does fall short of claims it makes for itself ("Now I shall spy on beauty as none has / Spied on it yet" [p. 64]. "Now I shall speak of evil as none has / Spoken before" [p. 67])—unless we are to read such claims not as Nabokov's mockery of Shade but as Shade's own self-mockery,[6] a distinct possibility, to be sure, for the poem is unquestionably self-mocking in many places. In most respects Shade provides a standard of skeptical, good-humored sanity that throws Kinbote's excesses into sharp relief.

We must also note briefly the other primary commitments which the germinal principle covers. The linguistic instrument in both the poem and Kinbote's prose is a flexible, informal, idiomatic, and often colloquial language, conversational in its quality. It is capable in both writers of strong narrative thrust and of vivid concrete descriptive imagery and metaphor. Kinbote's prose shows also some distinctive features: a caustic ironic wit; a tendency to overstate, using epithets and adjectives (as, for example, in the characterizations of Gradus as subhuman); a tendency to reiterate epithets ("my powerful car"); to exploit his

---

[6]Critics differ somewhat as to the merits of Shade's poem. Julia Bader regards it as excellent, for instance; it "can be read alone; the commentary cannot" (*Crystal Land: Artifice in Nabokov's English Novels* [Berkeley, 1972], p. 55). Page Stegner (*Escape into Aesthetics: The Art of Vladimir Nabokov* [New York, 1966], p. 117) finds the poem a "serious meditation on death . . . and the artist's escape from the consequences of physical deformity and decay into the realm of pure aesthetic delight." Richard Pearce ("Nabokov's Black [Hole] Humor: *Lolita* and *Pale Fire*," in *Comic Relief: Humor in Contemporary American Literature*, ed. Sarah Blacher Cohen [Urbana, Ill., 1979], p. 42) finds the poem "neither elegant nor stupid. It is wildly comic but capable of constraining the most ornate diction and the most mundane perceptions, the most sophisticated allusions and the most slapstick descriptions within its tightly controlled meter." See also note 8.

obsessions until the reader recognizes them in the most minimal reminders; and in general to suggest innuendo and irony constantly at work. His language reflects an interest in language as such—in language sounds, as in the alpine scene with the gnarled farmer (a *grunter* [mountain farmer] whose name was Griff, with a guttural call and a daughter named Garh), in names (all the names he finds for Gradus), in word games (see Word Golf), in translation. It is flexible enough to parody the sound of American academics in faculty clubs. It is a language well adapted to dramatize his character (his nastiness, his nerves, his sensitivity, his enthusiasms). And it is capable both of evoking the ecstatic and "magical madness" of his Zembla story and of parodying his own stuffy pedantic quality.

As for the fictional world, in the foreground it is literary: that is, occupied by an explicitly literary text, through which we can behold a middle ground or background realistic and contemporary, though marked by a division into two rather different looking parts. There is the familiar American world of New Wye and Wordsmith College—the world native to Shade, in which Kinbote is a plausible foreigner, a world of college faculties, students, townspeople, nature walks, well within the norms of modern realism. There is also the world of Zembla, not to be found on any real map, lying indefinitely within the real enough world of Europe. It is true that the central places of both worlds have fictitious and sometimes absurd names and are surrounded by places with real names (besides New Wye, in the state of Appalachia, there is New York; besides Zembla, there are the great cities of Europe). One can fly from Zembla to Copenhagen or Stockholm. The oddness begins not with Zembla as such but with the fact that our view into Zembla is through the eyes of its King, and that this King (Charles the Beloved) is none other than the academic Kinbote himself—if indeed he is. It is true that certain northern countries still have kings and queens. The conventions of modern realism do not generally adopt a king's point of view, however; it is contrary to the interest in the familiar, the near at hand, the "life as it is" which is so central to realism. And of course the events in Zembla—the King's escape, with its secret tunnel, its mysterious disguised spies, its secret

signs, its parachute leap, all so squarely in the tradition of high adventure tales—create a distance from New Wye that is more than merely geographical. It is indeed like the division one might expect in a novel about a poem and its commentary, except that it reverses that expectation, since the poem and the poet's world are realistic, whereas the commentary is romantic.[7] The difference between these worlds is of course a reflection of the problematical ambiguity noted at the start, the most important feature of this fictional world, with implications that we shall consider later on.

The first step in the analysis of the plot proper is to distinguish the various sequences which develop through the novel. First, there is the progression of the text itself, through foreword, poem, commentary, and index. It is a movement in which one text (the poem) can be said to give rise to the rest. It is produced by the combined work of Shade and Kinbote, the latter building upon, perhaps to correct or revise or create anew, what the former has done. If the commentary, with its various narratives, is regarded as a "poem" in its own right, the essentials of this sequence might be reduced to a process in which one poem is born out of another.

The other sequences are all visible within this first one, running through it. First among these is John Shade's story—revealed mainly in his poem but enlarged upon and completed in the commentary. It is a life Kinbote calls "singularly uneventful." There are, to be sure, events—most notably the suicide of his unhappy daughter Hazel—yet it is mostly a comfortable, happy, successful life: it includes his growth from childhood and his love for his wife Sybil. There are certain childhood fits, and later a mild heart attack. The most striking feature, apart from the general impression of settled stability and establishment success is the uncomfortable quest, indicated in the poem, for something significant in his life: he looks for signs of life after death and finds nothing. He spies on beauty but is distracted; he con-

---

[7]John O. Stark observes that we tend to read Shade's portion "as if it came from a realistic novel" and Kinbote's "as if it came from a nonrealistic novel" (*The Literature of Exhaustion: Borges, Nabokov, and Barth* [Durham, N.C., 1974], p. 69).

siders evil and finds irritations, certain matters of taste and stupidity.[8] He is wise, skeptical, a lover of nature and his past. He is humane (kind to Kinbote). He finds his hope in patterns of coincidence and in art: "I feel I understand / Existence . . . only through my art, / In terms of combinational delight" (pp. 68–69). In the poem he is "the shadow of the waxwing slain / By the false azure in the windowpane; / I was the smudge of ashen fluff—and I / Lived on, flew on, in the reflected sky" (p. 33). He is driven into art by the need—for life, for beauty—which this expresses. He is in a sense prosaic; his poem, autobiographical and realistic, is more prosaic, despite its skillfully handled meter, than the narrative Kinbote introduces into the commentary. The outcome of Shade's story is his killing by Gradus—an accident, a mistake, whether seen as Gradus missing the King or Jack Grey aiming at Judge Goldsworth—and it is totally unforeseen by Shade. This outcome is known from the beginning, though the manner in which it takes place becomes an increasingly strong question of suspense through the book.

Shade's daughter's part should be noted. She is involved in a quest in some ways similar, though without the aid of art: she seeks and finds possibly evil spirits in a barn, but is unable to persuade her skeptical parents to believe. In view of the resemblance "in certain respects" to Kinbote, which he notes in the commentary, her case—the suicide associated with her social and sexual failures and suggesting some failure or shortcoming in Shade's comfortable fatherly love, some lack of efficacy—points up Shade's possible parallel limitation in relation to Kinbote, not in love or sympathy, to be sure, but in the adequacy of his art—as we shall consider further below.

A second major strand is the story Kinbote had hoped would be told in the poem: the story of himself as King Charles of Zembla—his life and escape from the revolution, culminating with his taking the position at Wordsmith under the incognito of Kinbote. This story is told largely in narrative segments in the notes, mostly in chronological order, with some flash-forwards

---

[8]This point seems evident, even though in an interview Nabokov quoted the lines about evil from memory "without" as Fowler puts it, "any qualification as to their judgment" (Douglas Fowler, *Reading Nabokov* [Ithaca, 1974], p. 105.

and flashbacks. The outcome here, too, is known early in the book. The action unfolds as a great romantic adventure, as we have seen, with conventional adventure trappings. It is enriched by the comic treatment of his troubles with beautiful young women who try to seduce him, a wife whom he can love only in memory or dream, hosts of compliant page boys, and the like. This story rests upon the central ambiguity, of course: is it "real" or is it someone's fantasy? Accordingly, there lurks beneath it, most shadowy, an alternative—a mad inventor, perhaps Botkin, perhaps writing in an insane asylum, perhaps revealing fragments of another life, even an unhappy marriage, with dim clues. The obvious suspense of the King's story concerns the question of how this King finally managed to wind up as professor in such a college and commentator on such a poem. The question is carefully answered before the end. Another suspense, arising out of the shadow alternative, develops the ambiguity itself: it grows as the novel develops and is never answered.

A third sequence, though this could also be considered a part of the King's story, is the approach of the killer Gradus. This, too, is developed chronologically by narratives in the commentary, linked to lines in the poem according not to what they say but to when they were written. As Kinbote points out: "We shall accompany Gradus in constant thought, as he makes his way from distant dim Zembla to green Appalachia, through the entire length of the poem, following the road of its rhythm, riding past in a rhyme . . ." (p. 78). Like the King's story, this, too, is based upon an ambiguity, and we can discern the alternative— Jack Grey pursuing Judge Goldsworth—at the end. The narrative in this sequence emphasizes the process of constructing an action. Thus Kinbote calls attention to the increasing specificity and detail as Gradus draws near: the first note "is the vaguest while those that follow become gradually clearer as gradual Gradus approaches in space and time" (p. 152). The sinister aspect of Gradus's approach is modified by the comic stress on his stupidity and ineptitude, enriched by the wit in the narrator's outrage and contempt. Again, the primary suspense concerns the mistake we know he is going to make: how does he manage to kill Shade instead of Kinbote? Another suspense concerns the

nature of the shadow alternative, which is not revealed until after the shooting itself.

A fourth sequence is the unfolding of Kinbote's relationship with John Shade. This also develops through narrative segments in the commentary, but it is a nonchronological (disclosure) process, revealed through inferences we draw as we recognize the blindness or obfuscation of Kinbote's account. Though it is possible to reconstruct a chronology of Kinbote's relationship to Shade, the sequence is organized rather to break down gradually the initial view of a close and dear friendship. Step by step this reduction proceeds: we learn first that Shade's wife is hostile to Kinbote (so he thinks); then we begin to notice Kinbote's attempts to dismiss with excuses the rebuffs he receives in response to his excessive demands. Then the narratives begin to admit the hurt he feels (clear in the episode of Shade's birthday party, to which he was not invited). Finally we see clearly Shade's efforts to be kind, in response to Kinbote's hysterical need, by taking walks with him; it is during such a moment of kindness that he meets his unexpected death. The most important aspect of this relationship is of course Kinbote's hope that Shade will tell the King's story in his long poem. The frustration of this hope is the incentive for writing the commentary—the creation of the text as a whole. The reader's perception changes in the early stages: only gradually is Kinbote brought to admit that the poem does not secretly tell the Zemblan story or that he was bitterly disappointed to discover that it did not.

Kinbote's relation to Shade is part of the broader problem of his relation to the whole New Wye community. His unawareness of the effect he has on others is a rich source of comedy throughout—again, his plan to surprise the Shades at their summer retreat is a case in point. Yet there are signs gradually emerging that he really does know, that to some extent his behavior is deliberate and provocative. His attitude to most of the people in New Wye is contemptuous. This hostility and self-imposed outcasting are pretty much evident from the beginning. He knows he is being ridiculed. He strikes back.

Still another sequence, of lesser importance, is the account of the actual writing of poem and commentary. The record of Shade's work is fairly detailed; the dates on which he writes are

specified; we watch Kinbote as he spies on Shade at work, following his actions through the narratives in the commentary. The dates are, as we have seen, correlated with the approach of Gradus. The record of the writing of the commentary is not so specific, but we do have some description of Kinbote's life in the Utah motel during the process of composition. This setting, too, may have a shadowy alternative, if those critics who detect the signs of an asylum are not mistaken.

Finally, there is the rich and important sequence of judgments and observations on general matters. Some of these are Shade's, in the poem and in discussions with Kinbote in the commentary; others are Kinbote's, directly presented. They are interspersed among the longer narrative segments in the commentary. As comments, the observations have a closer connection to lines and words in the poem than the others, although even these are for the most part but loosely linked. They cover a broad range of topics. Some deal with literature, some with language, or with language games, or with pronunciation, or names, or aphorisms, or criticism. Some deal with translations, with examples of various kinds. There are examples of other poems by Shade and short lyrics on a variety of subjects, as well as variant lines to those in the poem. There are discussions of prejudice, of religion, of suicide. There are a great variety of judgments on tastes and manners, American trivia and American vulgarity. There are discussions of butterflies and their names and other facets of nature. And there are critical judgments on the poem, appreciations of certain effects, objections to others. A great many of these judgments are parodic or charged with authorial irony, although some (especially those contributed by Shade) appear to be quite straight.

The ordering of these comments depends in part on the other sequences and is otherwise random or arbitrary. It is clear that often they are used to break up the other narratives, set them off in high relief. This purpose is especially evident near the end, where the comments serve a classic function of intensification by delay and by contrast of interests. Often they relate to the other sequences by producing startling effects of juxtaposition and metaphor. They reinforce the literary foreground of the fictional world, keeping the other sequences in touch with this

context and providing a constant substratum of brilliance, subtlety, and wit.

The next step in the plot analysis is to seek the unifying principle. We must consider now the question of the status of the
King, the question of Kinbote's sanity. The prevailing view, as I
have said, is that Kinbote is mad, the story of his kingship (and
perhaps of Zembla itself) a fabrication. By this view (with Kinbote the presumed protagonist) the primary plot process is
probably the victory of the madman over the sane one, demonstrated by his conversion of the poem into the tale of the King.
This process is accompanied by secondary actions whose ultimate function is to establish the fact that Kinbote indeed suffers
from a case of madness. Since the victory consists of Kinbote's
finding a place for his fantasy in Shade's poem and is accomplished by the act of writing the commentary and the rest, the
plot is essentially dynamic (and dramatically represented by the
unfolding of the text itself), though supported or qualified by
some secondary disclosure processes. It is of course a severely
flawed victory, marred by the madness which shows through
despite Kinbote's efforts.

The most obvious difficulties with this theory concern the
limits of Kinbote's fantasy. If, as some claim, he is really Botkin
("of Russian descent") and Zembla itself is fantasy, we are
obliged to extend the range of his fantasy into New Wye and
Wordsmith itself, far beyond the bounds of the obviously unreliable elements in his account of his life there. For as we have seen,
Zembla is known in the Wordsmith College which he presents to
us: there are Professor Nattochdag and the scenes in the Faculty
Club. If these events are to be questioned, we begin to question
everything he tells us: the whole thing becomes "fantasy," and
then where are we? We have at any rate lost the crucial distinction that the madman theory is attempting to set up. Instead, we
may choose to distinguish between Zembla as "real" (in the fictional world, of course) and the King's adventures as imaginary.[9]
The latter distinction casts our Botkin connection in doubt, of

[9]Andrew Field suggests this possibility: "two Zemblas—the thing itself and
the tale as told" (*Nabokov: His Life in Art: A Critical Narrative* [Boston, 1967], p.
294).

course. It is also peculiarly cumbersome, without any evidence I have been able to discover to support it. It gives to Kinbote's madness a peculiar specialized quality (for if there is a Zembla, there must have been a deposed King, too, only he is not, by this theory, Kinbote. Why, then, has Kinbote chosen to identify with him? And why are we given no signs of how this King must have looked to him, Kinbote, as a citizen or admirer?). This, too, makes the line between the imaginary and the real seem arbitrary—as if imposed by us upon the book. In addition to such difficulties, there is the question of the interest which this explanation finds in the plot. It is true, the novel has been described as presenting "the irrational through the rational by probing the world of madness,"[10] and Kinbote has been described as the "bearer of a whole wasteland of cultural fragments which he has shored against his ruin—myths of a decayed and deposed aristocracy, the ghost of the mind of Europe."[11] Yet as long as Kinbote's revision of (or confrontation with) Shade's poem is seen as simply a manifestation of some hallucinatory madness, it seems legitimate to ask to what extent this madness, even creative madness, is an interesting explanation? Is it not a banal explanation, an "unrewarding" one, as one critic has said,[12] a disappointing reduction of this fascinating material?

No doubt for this reason, some readers have attempted to turn Kinbote himself into a figment of the imagination of the poet, John Shade.[13] This interpretation would give us a plot of a completely different kind. It would have the advantage of bringing Shade and "Kinbote" into a more integral relation: it emphasizes the parallels and oppositions between them (Kinbote as alter ego) and implies strongly the incompleteness of Shade in himself both artistically and psychologically. The plot by this view is a dynamic unfolding, through the text, of the inner

---

[10]L. L. Lee, *Vladimir Nabokov* (Boson, 1976), p. 137.

[11]G. M. Hyde, *Vladimir Nabokov: America's Russian Novelist* (London, 1977), p. 177.

[12]Robert Merrill, "Nabokov and Fictional Artifice," *Modern Fiction Studies*, 25:3, p. 458.

[13]Bader and Field see Kinbote as having been created by Shade. It has also been suggested that Kinbote created Shade, but this possibility seems even more difficult to support.

drama of the opposite sides of Shade's personality: the completion of the commentary establishes the needed balance.

The obvious difficulty with this theory is that Shade is killed and lives to tell about it, a turn of events that of course echoes the third and fourth lines of his poem, quoted above. It has been said that "Shade ... has perpetrated his own 'stylistic' death within the novel, and he has then given us a new aspect of himself in the guise of another soul and another artwork." Again, it is a "recurrent idea in *Pale Fire* that the artist momentarily perishes with each of his creations, in order to give life to a work of art." Gradus (the connection to *gradus ad Parnassum* is noted: a dictionary, a "step to the place where the Muses live") is the "final tool used by the poet to complete his work and arrive at Parnassus."[14] Obviously the only way to account for Shade's death is to treat it allegorically—and once again we run into the problem of the limits to fantasy. For it is not only his own death that Shade has presumably invented here; it is also his whole description of life in New Wye, as seen through "Kinbote's" eyes. Has he invented also Kinbote spying on him, Kinbote hurt because he was not invited to Shade's birthday party; has he invented his own kindness to Kinbote to make up for slights? It seems obvious that if once we absorb Kinbote into Shade, we turn everything into fantasy by Shade, and the distinction between Shade and Nabokov himself disappears. And if this happens we are back where we started, and the same problems confront us all over again.

Recognizing this difficulty, some critics have dismissed the controversy as a false issue, insisting rather that all fictional levels in the text are equally real and that the characters Kinbote and Shade are expressions of Nabokov himself.[15] The truth seems to be that the novel does not permit us to decide whether

---

[14]Bader, *Crystal Land,* pp. 31, 39, 34.

[15]Lee: "My point is that each level is quite as true as the next" (*Vladimir Nabokov,* p. 135). Stark: "Any layer inside them [the author and his book]—actually *in* the novel—is imaginary, and none of these inside layers has more reality than any other" (*The Literature of Exhaustion,* p. 65). Eckstein: "Each character's world in the series of worlds which exist in both novels [*Pale Fire* and *The Turn of the Screw*] is at once 'real' and fictional. Each is 'real' because it asserts validity within its own fictional frame" ("Conventions of Irony," p. 181).

the Zemblan exile is "true" or "fantasy," whether Kinbote is psychotically hallucinating or only neurotically trying to preserve some memorial to his past. The hints of madness cannot be confirmed, they cannot be supported in all parts of the novel. On the other hand, the story of the King's conversion into Kinbote can be supported, it does cohere, but it is challenged by those hints of madness and the strange imbalance it creates. The novel moves toward the disclosure not of Kinbote's madness, nor of his sanity, but of the ambiguity, the balance between the two possibilities, which we reach when Kinbote discusses his future incognitos at the end of his final note before the index. The index itself reinforces the point. The suspense of what I have called the "shadow alternatives"—suspense as to the truth of the King's story—ends in ambiguity. We are made to accept *both* the "real" and the "imaginary" interpretations of the King's adventures. We allow to them the qualities of imaginary projection without forfeiting their grounding in the fictional reality of the work. But in so doing we find we have moved into a so-called narrator-controlled fictional world, and the plot, which must incorporate this construction, seems to be a creative plot.

The world is narrator controlled because the integration of the King's story with the others is made coherent, made "probable" in the Aristotelian sense, not by the mimetic principles of the Zemblan world (a King in danger in such a country under such conditions) nor by the different mimetic principles of an unhappy scholar building a fantasy, but by the coexistence of both sets of principles, both sets of probabilities. Two different worlds are brought together and forced to merge, not by resolving the incompatibility between them but by forcing them to coexist—as if by command of the narrator. (For explanation of why I attribute this kind of disruption to the narrator, see chapter 4 and, in the same chapter, n. 14.) By narrator here I do not mean either Kinbote or Shade but the unseen narrator-in-charge behind them both. The discontinuity or incoherence which is the mark of the narrator-controlled fictional world lies here in the fact that *within the fictional world* fantasy is real; the barrier between what is real and what is not real is broken down. (This world is similar to that of *Absalom, Absalom!,* where the imaginings of Quentin and Shreve are taken for real—real and

imagined at once.) Seen in this light, the emphasis on creating Gradus becomes an important clue to our reading of the whole book.

The plot is *creative* because this principle—namely, the collapsing of the real and the imagined—underlies the construction and becomes the chief organizer of the plot. It creates the simultaneous separation and identity of Kinbote and the King. The central action of this plot is the making of the text, the incorporation of one poem (Shade's) into another (Kinbote's); its outcome is not simply the completion of the text, however, but the revelation which emerges from it—namely, the establishment of this unresolvable ambiguity.

Now, if the plot is the making of the text, the protagonist of this plot is the maker. But if the text is made by Kinbote and Shade (a compound protagonist), it ends by questioning its own authorship. The true maker, creator of that ambiguity itself, is this unseen narrator-in-charge, who controls the narrator-controlled world. This narrator is the "latent protagonist." We need the concept of the latent protagonist here, since the ambiguity, the uncertain ontology of the manifest protagonist, can be made intelligible only by referring it to something else, some source from which it arises. (We could refer to an "implied author," but then we would have to find some other way to describe the difference between this and a traditional mimetic plot.) As there is a latent protagonist, so there is a latent, or underlying, plot, in which we can find the principle that unifies and organizes the "manifest" plot. The manifest plot and its manifest protagonist are the creations of the latent protagonist; they are "projections" of his interests. The latent plot is the intelligibility of the manifest plot.

How can we describe that intelligibility? We can discover it, in a case like this, by regarding the manifest plot as an exemplification of a general process. We translate it into general terms, we seek its symbolic significance. We cannot stop with a single symbolic interpretation, to be sure; we must seek all that are relevant. There must be a limit, of course, which we can express by saying that any symbolic reading of the manifest action is legitimate if it increases our perception of its coherence and unity. The underlying plot is an abstract unity of symbolized general

possibilities visible only through the manifest action—so that if the plot gives to that manifest action an effect of unity, it also finds unity, as well as visibility, only in it.[16]

What is the general process exemplified by this manifest one? The novel has been said to be "about the full process of artistic creation," and the essentials have been analyzed in a variety of ways by many critics.[17] This formulation could easily be misinterpreted to imply a didactic or rhetorical plot. The differences are several: one could say that the emphasis is on the exemplification of the creative process rather than the development of the concept, on the latent protagonist's personal perception of it, his struggle with it, perhaps, rather than on an attempt to persuade the reader of its truth. The crucial difference, however, is the multiplicity of possible symbolic interpretations of the manifest process, as we have just observed—the fact that the underlying process, though we called it "general," resists reduction to a formulable statement or proposition, that it can in fact be exemplified only by this one case and can be described only by a combination or convergence of a variety of symbolic interpretations.

In this necessarily abbreviated analysis, I must limit myself, in examining the possibilities, only to those which the construction of the plot renders most obvious. Two aspects of the manifest process seem to be primary. One is the fact that a text or work of art is created from the interaction of the subplots we have noticed, activity which involves, as actors, Shade, Kinbote, the

---

[16]This method of unifying creative plots needs to be used carefully; otherwise we'll find that we have turned all creative plots into didactic ones. Strictly speaking, we begin to generalize just the fictional incoherence that makes for a creative plot, and where we go from there depends on the nature of that incoherence. In *Second Skin*, for example, the significant generalization is simply the recognition that all events are embodiments of Skipper's fears and wishes. Skipper's experiences can then be treated as a projection of a personal vision of wishes and fears. In an allegory (*Pilgrim's Progress*) the generalization is a recognition that all events are governed by a continuing correspondence between two lines of action. The interest of the latent protagonist is creative: to maintain that correspondence as consistently and completely as possible. In the case of *Pale Fire* the incoherence is in the nature of the manifest protagonist, a compound protagonist engaged in artistic activity; our symbolic readings all relate to the question of this protagonist's nature.

[17]Eckstein, "Conventions of Irony," p. 182. See also Bader, *Crystal Land*, Stark, *The Literature of Exhaustion*, and Field, *Nabokov*.

King, and Gradus, and as creators, Shade and Kinbote. The other aspect is the outcome we have just considered: the disclosure in the work of art of the ambiguity between Kinbote and the King, which is finally revealed by the work of art. Questioning the ambiguity first, we see, fairly obviously, that it signifies—it demonstrates or affirms—the power of the imagination (and art) to create reality. It shows the ability of the maker to turn the figmentary into the real by giving to the object (the King) the qualities of both. This point is amply supported by parallels and other suggestions throughout the text. "Once transmuted by you into poetry, the stuff *will* be true, and the people *will* come alive," as Kinbote tells Shade with reference to his Zemblan material (p. 214). The point is driven home in the treatment of Gradus's approach.

If this is the dominant process of the underlying plot, we have a disclosure plot—for the King (in contrast to Gradus) is not dynamically "created" through the processes of the text but is *discovered* as having been so created in an organization which moves toward the revelation of his true ambiguity. This is really a disclosure of the nature of the manifest protagonist which, as we have just suggested, would be the manifest maker of the text: a compound, the unity of Kinbote and Shade. If the outcome, however, is the establishment of the King's and hence Kinbote's ambiguous identity, we will find it more useful to regard the true manifest protagonist (the center into which the latent protagonist projects his vision) as a tripartite compound of Kinbote, Shade, and the King. Why should we add the King to the combination? Because adding him acknowledges the important point (in this novel) that the work of art is created not only by the writers but by the figures they write about—that is to say, into whom they project their imaginations. Shade is both writer and hero of his own poem. Kinbote as Kinbote is unwitting and comic hero of one subplot of his poem; as King he is romantic hero of the other. The tripartite protagonist projects these relationships. It also projects the power of artistic projection itself: Kinbote's protagonist is the King, the latent protagonist's protagonist is the relationship between writer and protagonist.

The other symbolically significant aspect of the manifest plot is the interaction of the members of the manifest protagonist to

create the work of art. This interaction starts perhaps with Shade, the established poet, recognized as such by the others, with all the honors such a poet can receive. As we have already seen, he sees himself as shadow or reflector of beauty. He seems to be seeking a worthy subject for poetry, and looks for strangeness, but the poem he writes is prosaic and realistic and cannot pass beyond his own uneventful life for subject and his sane solid skepticism for attitude. We notice also two visionaries seeking something from him and failing to find it—Kinbote and his daughter Hazel.

In relation to Shade, Kinbote is first of all a reader—commentary and criticism being expressions of reading. He is in a sense a parasite of the poet and is so developed at comic length and in comic detail in the subplot of his relationship to Shade. Still, he is a radically dissatisfied reader. He would rather read about the romantic adventures of the King, a life opposite to the dull shaded normality of Shade's. As "reader" Kinbote identifies with this romantic subject, projects himself into it. His commentary becomes an extravagant "misreading" (anticipating the critics of misreading by a good many years), into which he projects an ideal image of himself.

The simple picture of reader, poet, and romantic hero as compound protagonist is complicated by the approach of Gradus and the killing of Shade. Symbolically it would appear that the poet is killed by the reader's story—that is, by his misreading—an amusing enough idea. If Gradus is also plain Jack Grey, then the reader (Kinbote) has in effect tried to rob the poet of his own death. Here again we see Kinbote's grab for adventure as like a scavenger he tries to absorb into his own life every kind of experience. Perhaps also the attempt expresses his craving for order, for "explanations," since Shade's death is such a mischance. The reader is voracious for experience and for order—that is to say, for story. He appropriates everything of the poet's, his poem and even his death, and makes it express himself. Is this not a kind of madness, normal though it is?

We must pay full attention in this interpretation to the emphasis on Gradus. He is seen by Kinbote at the end as one of the three figures in the story he expects to keep on telling. He becomes almost archetypal in Kinbote's continued expectation of

being pursued by a "bigger, more respectable, more competent Gradus." Who is this Gradus? If he is, in the interpretation earlier noted, a step on the way to Parnassus, he is also, and more obviously, the epitome of the enemy, the destroyer, death. But he is necessary. In terms of the story of which he is a part, he is the cause of the adventure, the incentive, the negative disrupter of harmony, which makes the story go. If there is a protagonist, there must also be a Gradus—the story requires it. He is the motivator of Kinbote and the King; his neglect by Shade (seen also in Shade's poem) is fatal.

The limits of this symbolism appear if we ask why Kinbote the reader is presented as so alienated a figure, a notion concretized in his nationality—he is literally alien. But his distancing from the society, including his homosexuality, as well as his misunderstood relationship with Shade, expresses a general alienation from what is normal and conventional everywhere. There is an inversion of stereotyped notions: here it is the poet, traditionally and romantically the alienated one, who epitomizes the establishment; it is the reader, the commentator, who is outside.

Again, it is Kinbote who wears the masks: his appearance at New Wye is incognito, and his future life, he tells us, will continue incognito—in disguises he will be retelling his story in various ways. Kinbote is the artist here and Shade merely a character in the repeating story.

In a second symbolic interpretation, then, Shade and Kinbote appear as two different kinds of poets. The one is a sane, realistic establishment poet, the other is a mad, neurotic, romantic one. The first cannot see a subject beyond himself; the second can't bear himself and creates another subject, a glamorous exile to glorify his alienation. They are opposites, mirror images of each other—as men (socially, sexually, emotionally), as writers (poem, commentary), and in the works they write. As such they complement each other: neither is complete without the other. When Gradus emerges from the romantic poet's poem to kill the establishment poet, he provides a vindication of the romantic, in spite of his madness—he shows him as close in some sense to the poetic truth—unless (the ambiguity again) that closeness was really only an unfortunate accident of chance. But why, then, is the romantic poem parasitical to the other, attached to it as "com-

mentary"? Does this relationship signify perhaps the necessity of tradition in the development of art? Does the alienated romantic, original though he may be, need to build his original poem on a base of traditional and conventional poetry? The new grows from the old, revises it (and as it does so, the old poet dies).

The two symbolic readings are not alternatives that we must choose between; one does not replace the other. Each is a reasonable analogy to the manifest action, an aspect, a set of implications, by which the manifest becomes meaningful, coherent as a projection of something. They work together. Both are weak, however, in their explanations of Kinbote as exile. And they ignore another feature of the novel which bears on the question of exile, the deliberate exploitation of knowledge of Nabokov's own biography. To be sure, the presence of authorial biography in fiction sometimes confronts formal critics with difficulties. Yet there is really no reason why the image of the implied author might not include some biography, why an author might not include among his conventions some knowledge of himself. The practice is common in poetry. The problem for the reader is to know how much he ought to know. Once again, the best test is probably this: if the introduction of such knowledge into the form appreciably strengthens that form (strengthens, not merely alters—for conceivably some biographical material, so introduced, might undermine it),[18] then it is relevant.

In the case of *Pale Fire*, there are a number of direct Nabokovian allusions—the reference to Hurricane Lolita, to Professor Pnin, to nymphets, for instance—sly references which tell us that knowledge of the author may be pertinent. More significant is the way in which we are reminded of Nabokov the Russian émigré and public personality. The Russian language is prominent throughout: Gradus under pressure speaks Russian; in the entry headed "two tongues," among the seventeen pairs of languages listed, English and Russian form the only pair that is repeated, and it appears four times. The revolution against the

---

[18]The genetic fallacy: if we bring too much knowledge about Lawrence, for instance, to *Sons and Lovers*, we may obscure our perception of the novel—asking the "false question," for example, of whether the novel is being "fair" to Paul Morel's father.

King has Soviet support. There is the allusion to the "old, happy, healthy, heterosexual Russian, a writer in exile," among Kinbote's future incognitos. There are the celebrated Nabokovian opinions on psychiatry and Marxism, projected by Shade and Kinbote. There is Shade's interest in butterflies. Such matters and others bring the figure of Vladimir Nabokov prominently into the form of this work.

Nabokov appears there as an aspect of the latent protagonist—and thereby a shaping force for the fiction. If the Kinbote-Shade-Charles combination projects this latent protagonist's perception of an artistic process, the alienation which is so important in this process may also project the Nabokovian consciousness of exile. Here, then, is a third symbolic reading. Kinbote now becomes a comic (self-mocking? or disguising?) projection of the exile's alienation in the land to which he has been exiled, Charles is a somewhat mocking projection of the glamor and nostalgia of the exile's memory (the exile as hero), Shade is the projection of the exile's view of the sanity and security but confined range of the art of his new home. The exile seeks the shelter of the American Shade, he seeks to find himself (to read himself) in the Shade. He is the exiled poet seeking entry perhaps into the Shade of American literature.[19] This reading, like the others, acts as an implied subplot, metaphor or comment, qualifying the rest and qualified by it: it tells us that the artistic process delineated here is the Nabokovian one, and the discomfort and need that give rise to art, as represented by Kinbote's alienation, consist in the alienation of the Nabokovian exile. The "romaunt" he wants told is the romaunt of the exile. It includes not only the adventures of the King but also the absurdities of Kinbote making a crotchety pest of himself in New Wye. And there is Gradus, of course, destroyer and motivator. In this symbolic reading, the manifest story is "like" Nabokov's own

[19]In his postscript to Lolita, Nabokov spoke of wishing to become an American writer: "I chose American motels instead of Swiss hotels or English inns only because I am trying to be an American writer and claim only the same rights that other American writers enjoy." Also: "An American critic suggested that Lolita was the record of my love affair with the romantic novel. The substitution 'English language' for 'romantic novel' would make this elegant formula more correct" (Lolita [New York, 1955], pp. 317, 318).

story, stringently, sternly, comically depersonalized and projected.

None of these symbolic readings adequately incorporates the
high development of the commentary device itself—the sequence of opinions, judgments, games, in the direct comments, a
separate subplot. Apart from its general function of intensification, which I have already commented upon, this subplot constitutes the most explicit projection of the latent protagonist's general literary interests. Thereby it qualifies all the more specific
narrative and dramatized projections: it distances them and to
some extent undermines the claims of all our symbolic readings,
putting them in a more hypothetical light. The subplot further
establishes a governing attitude, skeptical, playful, wondering,
ridiculing in many aspects—a judgment on the literary enterprise itself, its possibilities and limitations. It provides a context
rich in incidental subtlety and implication, which calls attention
to these qualities throughout and colors everything with its brilliant glow.

Although other relevant symbolic readings may certainly be
added, the three I have considered, qualified by the context of
the developed commentary, seem to me (at this stage of my
perception) to be chiefly responsible for unifying the manifest
plot and for articulating the underlying one. This plot could be
summed up as a creative disclosure plot which reveals a personal
(latent protagonist's) image (projection) of a kind of artistic process, a specifically Nabokovian one. It is creative rather than
rhetorical or didactic because the projection is personal; the
interest is in the creation of the image that projects it rather than
in a concept or judgment served by it. It is disclosure rather than
dynamic because the organization does not unfold the projected
artistic process directly but moves rather to a revelation of the
nature of the compound protagonist—that is, to the nature of
the projection.

The projection gives a vision of certain powers in that artistic
process and of certain conditions giving rise to it. Central among
the conditions is the opposition of the romantic, imaginative,
"mad" vision to the realistic, relatively prosaic, "sane" one. The
incentive for artistic creation arises from the alienation of the
poet (or the reader—the two are ultimately collapsed and col-

lapsed with the critic as well). This alienation (which reveals itself nonartistically in foolishness, vanity, and self-deception) is symbolized in one aspect by the windowpane (alienation from nature) and epitomized in another by exile (from humanity or society). Along with alienation is the necessary consciousness of what Gradus represents—time, change, and death, motivators both within the fiction and outside it, which eventually will kill both poet and protagonist. This vision of art focuses finally on its power to create its own reality (and the probable corollary, suggested in the poem and implicit in Kinbote's desperation, that only through art can reality be made tolerable). Poetic creation is also seen as transcending the misery and foolishness from which it comes—in general through the vitality of the intelligence with which it criticizes that foolishness and more specifically by the combinations of qualities which the true work of art unites. The former is seen in the comedy of the latent protagonist's treatment of Kinbote and in the wit and subtlety of the incidental commentary. The latter is seen in the balance of the two "poems"—for of course the true artistic achievement is not the romantic poem alone but the interaction of the two; though the romantic shows up the limits of the realistic, it, too, is implicitly criticized (as is Kinbote by Shade) by the juxtaposed reality and sanity of the other, and the final poise is between imaginative madness and common sanity.

The analysis is not complete without consideration of the effect. As this is a creative plot, the effect can be equated with the implied attitude of the latent protagonist toward his creation. It includes, first of all, a clear appreciation of the constructional virtuosity which the creative plot displays. This kind of effect, as I suggested earlier, might be called "felicity," generally apparent in the zestful quality of the whole, especially in the interaction of the various sequences, and culminating in the powerful exhilaration of Kinbote's last narrative, where the ambiguity of his role as creator of his stories becomes most explicit. In general, however, the virtuoso aspect is integrated with more specific attitudes attached to the manifest actions as fictions, and the dominant effect is finally defined by these attitudes.

The effect of the manifest actions is, as I have suggested, for the most part clearly and strongly, delightfully and richly comic,

mainly at Kinbote's expense. The potential pathos of Kinbote in the last few pages as he recognizes his possible madness is overshadowed by the evident exhilaration. The potential tragedy in the death of Shade is nullified; the event is kept well within the confines of comedy by its long preparation, the absurdities in its execution, and the way our attention is directed away from it, during and after the moment.

We may ask, however, whether a comic attitude is appropriate to what we have described as the underlying plot—the latent protagonist's perception of the achievement of art, its transcendence of foolishness and misery. If the latent protagonist is laughing at his Kinbote figure, is he also laughing at his compound protagonist and at the artistic process in which it is involved? The implied attitude toward the balanced artistic achievement which this plot projects seems more likely to be not ridicule but appreciation or approval. This, intensified by the unmentioned suffering of the Nabokovian exile and the implied general suffering that gives rise to art, checks the ridicule at the underlying level, limits its scope. Yet the ridicule is not thereby dismissed; the work is not finally a romance in which we find the latent protagonist lost in admiration for what Kinbote-Shade-Charles represent. Rather, that judgment is suspended— ridicule and admiration are arrested in balance, and we have a final effect (once again) of *wonder*. Our attention is fixed upon the strangeness—what is surprising, incredible—of the artistic process which the disclosure plot has revealed, but without judgment good or bad. The comic absurdity is found, as we so clearly see, in the conditions that give rise to art (they must be recognized in the art itself) distancing their unspoken pain; the value of the art does not cancel the absurdity but balances it. The balance—this totally involved and interested perception of distance—is wonder.

Such an analysis finds further support, curiously, in a theory of poetry which is suggested in the text, fragmentarily, in several places. With regard to the supposed likeness between Shade's description of Sybil Shade and the appearance of Queen Disa, Kinbote remarks: "I trust the reader appreciates the strangeness of this, because if he does not, there is no sense in writing poems, or notes to poems, or anything at all" (p. 207). And more clearly:

"By the very act of brutish routine acceptance [of a poem], we undo the work of the ages, the history of the gradual elaboration of poetical description and construction, from the treeman to Browning, from the caveman to Keats. ... I can do what only a true artist can do—pounce upon the forgotten butterfly of revelation, wean myself abruptly from the habit of things, see the web of the world, and the warp and the weft of that web" (p. 289). The dry modern name for the critical idea expressed here is "defamiliarization." The proper effect of art is strangeness, amazement: to see things as we have forgotten how. (Notice how often Kinbote uses the word "magic.") We see the efforts to achieve amazement running through all the ways of this book. It marks the language which fixes attention through wit and innuendo, as well as the constructive tendency to overturn clichés and sterotypes everywhere. Amazement is one of the main effects Kinbote seeks with his narrative of the King; Shade seeks it, too, and tends to miss it, which is no doubt one of the reasons why his poem must be completed by another.

In the theory of this book, the wonder of defamiliarization is a general effect of all art, characterizing the perception of every form until it becomes banal. It is an aesthetic rather than a specific fictional effect and will exist in any good work along with whatever kind of tragic, comic, ironic, or other attitude the work displays. But wonder can be a specific fictional effect, too, an extension of the general artistic attitude into the presented material of the work itself. Wonder itself is held up to display—to be wondered at. We have seen in *The Portrait of a Lady* and *The Sound and the Fury* such displayed wonder applied to fictional characters and behavior. In *Pale Fire* it is directed to the artistic process itself, the absurdity and the magic.

Finally, let us consider just briefly the index, which I suggested at the start was part of the whole. Its most obvious function is to reestablish the distance which has been threatened by the intensities of Kinbote's last narrative. It puts everything in order, bringing narrative progression to a full stop, buried in alphabetical order and cross-reference. In the process the index reviews the subplots. It also introduces new things, enlarged or revised explanations of details indicated only obliquely before.

One of these is Botkin—it thus brings the "shadow alternative" into some dim view and fortifies the final ambiguity. It reveals also that Kinbote has contributed "variant readings" to Shade's poem which in the commentary he had attributed to Shade— reinforcing the distance between Zembla and Shade. The index also distinguishes Kinbote and the King by separate entries, a matter relevant to our conception of the compound protagonist. It contains some games, as we see if we follow the cross-references from Crown Jewels and Word Golf. It clarifies certain relationships, such as Odon's ancestry, and adds other interesting secondary details, such as Kinbote's relations with his neighbors in the Utah trailer camp. Several items in the index have no page references at all. Like the appendix in *The Sound and the Fury,* it is an epilogue; though all essential revelations have been completed, the index brings the disclosure plot to an end by reaffirming the narrator's character as academic and pedant, the ambiguous quality of much of the action, and the dominantly comic tone of the manifest plot. More than anything else it compels us to look closely at the details again. The net effect is to insist on our attention and to remind us that our attention has been demanded all along. In such ways the index reiterates the importance of amazement and surprise and confirms the true wonder of this quite wonderful book.

[13]

The Theory and the Writer

There is another side to the whole question of form—the novelist's side. Kept out of sight, yet felt somehow in the margins, between the lines, it is unseen yet has a voice that I have been hearing all through this book, asking: "Don't you consider yourself a novelist, too, sir? Where is your novel writing in the midst of so much theory and analysis of other people's books? Doesn't it speak to you most intimately of all these questions you have been considering? What does your own work as a novelist have to tell you?" The voice is insistent. Apparently, despite critical decorum and the ideal of impersonality, despite embarrassed personal feelings and the relative obscurity of the novels themselves, I must speak of my own writing, for surely my use of the theory, my understanding of it, has been conditioned by this experience. The discussion would not be complete without considering it.

A patch of autobiography to explain. I started to write fiction first before I began to study literature, and my interest in critical theory grew out of studies in graduate school. My critical interest thus came second. On the other hand, it matured more rapidly, or so it seems, since I completed a book of historical criticism several years before I published any fiction. My impression, however, is that the two interests grew separately, independently—as if I wrote the two kinds of books with the opposite halves of my mind.

There is even a difference in styles between these opposite halves—which a reader of this book who has read any of my novels is bound to have noticed. The difference, I say to myself,

is not deliberate. I ask the question myself: why, when I start to write, does theory or criticism come out so teacherly (add that to Barthes's readerly and writerly), so orderly, so plain and systematic? What happened to the linguistic freedom that I like my novels to have?

I have not abandoned that freedom on purpose—and indeed I do pick and choose my words. Yet somewhere around me is a fence; I pick and choose inside the corral: whoever tells me one choice is better than another here has standards that differ from those of whoever censors my novels.

That difference may (or may not) illuminate the compulsive psychology by which a form controls its writer. In any case it seems to illustrate well criticism's standard explanation of the differences between the novelist's work and the critic's: the old distinction betwee intuitive synthesis and intellectual analysis. The novelist puts things together for direct perception. The critic perceives the result and finds words for it, reduces it to language. Two different faculties, two different skills. No reason to expect the novelist to be a critic or the critic a novelist—nor have I done so in this book. The distinction affords a powerful means for the evasion of responsibility on all sides. It enables the critic to ignore what the novelist has said about his work (good write, no think) and the novelist to avoid nosy questions that students or critics ask (all I do is write the damn things). It enables each to put the other down—the novelist scorns the critic's rationality (parasitical, too), and the critic scorns the novelist's inarticulateness (literature is dumb, says Frye).[1] All the same, the distinction establishes a boundary necessary to keep things clear. Still, when you are both novelist and critic the location of that boundary is a live issue: there is a threatening border war. No theory about the formal principle (about the fundamental integrity of a work, no less) can afford not to look into it.

Although I cannot regard myself as representing any novelist other than myself, I need to test the theory of the formal principle—that is, its usefulness for me as a critic—against my own experience as a novelist. Three questions will focus the

---

[1]Northrop Frye, *Anatomy of Criticism* (New York, 1967), pp. 4–5.

issues involved: (1) How has the conception of a formal principle contributed to the composition of my novels? (2) To what extent does this conception enable me to understand or describe them? (3) How well does it take account of my purposes in writing them?

As for the first question—how has the conception of a formal principle contributed to the composition of my own novels?—when I consider from the viewpoint of critic how my novels were written, I am bound to notice, negatively, that I did not, never did, begin with a classification of forms as my guide—did not begin with the idea of producing a *tragedy,* a *comedy,* a work of *irony.* A *novel,* yes, but not a novel with a specific effect. This fact of life has to be placed against the theoretical contention that the effect, the interest, is the "end," the controlling principle of the form. So it is, analytically, but it was never the starting point in composition. The end had to be discovered as I worked through the novel—discovered and felt, not classified or named.

Similarly negative is the usual absence of a clear originating Jamesian "germ." My starting points were multiple: different ideas brought together. *Camden's Eyes* can illustrate the process. This was my "breakthrough" novel, the first in which I knew what I was doing, in which I felt with a quite sudden surge of confidence like a real novelist. It began, as I recall, with an idea about narrative and point of view, a way to tell a story, and a kind of subject that could be told in that way. The narrative—influenced by critical reading of modern fiction and my understanding of the principles of dramatic narrative—was to be a series of repetitions and retellings, proceeding incrementally, a method in which, as one reader has put it, the topic is exhausted "by finding 'all' the appropriate things to be said on any side of it." This included a free shifting, often within sentences, between first- and third-person narration. The subject, which followed, was to be a character with a corresponding way of seeing and thinking, trying to tell his story. He would have a mind that suited the narrative method (an overwhelming indecision, a paralyzing sense of the complexity and contradiction of thought, of the constantly changing appearances of things both in the present and in the past). Each of his attempts to retell the story would be incomplete or false. Each would reflect his constant

effort both to ascertain and to deceive himself, to make his situation more comfortable for himself. Each effort would be motivated by his recognition of the falseness of the one before. The "truth" would come out gradually, and no single telling could encompass it.

This much was "germinal," yet it could lead nowhere without a third ingredient, a specific situation in which the protagonist's characteristic bewilderment could display itself for all it was worth. Such a situation I found in the idea of a jealous husband, confronted in all his uncertainty with as much certainty as a situation could contain—and still he dissolves it into doubt. Here were the beginnings of a plot, and the complications followed easily: the idea, for example, that the protagonist should have an affair of his own, which would complicate his jealousy. It would also provide an opportunity to display his habits of mind to comic advantage in a second kind of situation. Then I recognized the kinship between this tale and another story I had worked on once about a man who became a voyeur. When I made the jealous husband one, the new aspect quickly expanded as I discovered how it fit and added to the consciousness and feeling and significance of the rest.

Work on that book was sometimes laborious and fussy: I worried about the chronology, for example, trying to keep the calendar straight (how many years were they married before this or that happened? how many children did everybody have?). In addition, I needed to honor the contract I had made with the reader at the beginning, to make sure that I sustained my hero's constant perception of contradictions, that enough suitable possibilities continued to emerge, that I did not fall back into simplicity in the later stages. This aspect was compulsive, exacting, and painful: to maintain the convention I had adopted, upon which so much of the art depended. But I also had moments of exhilaration and feelings of liberation, moments of immodest pleasure in how good it seemed, how funny, vivid, clear, or delicate—new feelings for me as a writer, when I felt as if I were experiencing what other writers have described: the sensation that the work was writing itself or were already written and I just discovering it. The two kinds of processes—the compulsive struggle for detail and the rapid sweep—sometimes

seemed to be almost simultaneous, in the same sitting, on the same page. Looking back, I see in both how a conception of a form was growing, not entirely conscious, goading me at times to dig and scrape and at others giving me a ride of easy invention. Later came the equally compulsive, equally fussy revision, motivated by a sense of how bad my style was in its first draft. No doubt this compulsion also expressed the power of the unconsciously felt form, the knowledge that the first draft was still only approximate (still arbitrary in details) and that the real work of making it visible was yet to be done. The revision worked down into the finest grain: I doubt that more than a dozen sentences of the novel escaped alteration between first draft and final form.

The problem of the ending throws light on how a formal principle may develop. When I started to write, I was undecided among three possibilities: Camden's marriage could break up, or there could be a reconciliation, or the conflicts could go on as before. I chose the second after some thought. It would give the narrator a good reason to "tell" the whole story to himself in the manner I had already decided upon: the novel would be his answer to the perplexing question "How did such a reconciliation happen?" This idea required a new beginning, of course, and now I cannot even remember what the old beginning was. The actual novel, however, takes the ending one step further: after the reconciliation there is a further twist, not revealed until the last paragraph. This twist—a further reversal in the protagonist's uncertain adjustments—did not occur to me until I was far along in the book. Once conceived it insisted upon its superiority to all previous plans, the right inevitable ending to this particular form. Yet I had been working confidently for a long time before this "inevitability" appeared.

One conclusion that I have drawn from this experience (supported by my work on subsequent novels) is that I cannot write without a plan, though any particular plan will surely change. This statement holds on the small scale as well as the large. If I try to proceed without plan, trusting to association or to hope, I stall, I tangle in the limitless possibilities, I sink in the swamp of the arbitrary. I need a plan to establish priorities so that I can decide without anxiety what comes next. I stress anxiety; it is

always there. The process of converting a plan into reality is full of it. Will the plan work? Will I find the detail and the language it requires? The great question about any plan is its feasibility. It is a gamble, a wager of my time against the hope that I shall find within me the stuff—characters, scenes, images, words—to put flesh on the skeleton. Each plan requires not one but two judgments. One: is it a good plan? Two: can I carry it out?

My ability to go ahead with a plan depends heavily upon my confidence, which depends in part upon experience, my knowledge of myself and what I have done before. Most crucial, though, is the intuitive sense that the visible plan has invisible backing. The writer (this one) hopes he has learned to sense the difference between fertile and sterile plans. I know two signs that a plan is probably fertile. First, it keeps working in my mind. It provokes images, details, phrases, and sentences. It invades the world around me, attaching to things I see and hear, insisting on their relevance. A fertile plan keeps trying to materialize, testing its effects on everything it touches. Second, it gives me when I sit down to work a sense of determinacy. I can tell, without having to reason, whether or not a detail belongs. If I am to continue writing, I need to feel that details, words, phrases, scenes, and chapters are not arbitrary, that the choices made are better than the choices rejected. In both planning and writing I need to climb out of the arbitrary swamp, to find the level where indifference vanishes, where I can recognize the right choice that eliminates the others. Perhaps I can't find that right choice for a detail just yet; I'll hope to find it on revision. But if much remains arbitrary, if my decision one way or another seems to make no difference, I will soon be paralyzed and will lose interest.

No doubt these are signs of what R. S. Crane called the intuition of a form.[2] "Intuition"—since the validity of the plan is recognized by processes not on the surface, not reasoned. And "form"—yes: the fertile plan that makes everything right resembles the perceived principle I have been describing here, the formal principle which the work embodies. The abhorrence of

[2]R. S. Crane, *The Languages of Criticism and the Structure of Poetry* (Toronto, 1953), pp. 141-43.

the arbitrary is one sign of this principle, and so is the discovery of detail, the perception of relevance in the world around: the mind's eagerness to grasp such detail is a sign of the form's ability to function. Still, the form does not preexist, complete and intact. It is not there, buried in mind, as if the whole process of composition were a matter of digging it out of the ground. No, the finished form does indeed have to be composed, it has to be *invented,* and while the work is being planned the gambling image still holds: I perceive the form at this time mostly in an abstract shadow—only a few highlights concretely visible. The details that will embody it are largely not yet determined, not even in the unconscious. Nevertheless, when the idea is fertile, I must have a strong unconscious perception of what is possible, of implicit *connections* between the visible highlights, and *this* sense grasps at the details that come to mind and assures me that they are not arbitrary—long before I have had time to work out the relationships.

Thus one of the brightest signs of a fertile form is the ability I find to make wild leaps and to know they will do no harm— extravagant metaphors, strange turns of phrase, totally unforeseen exchanges, scenes—notions that pop into the head while I am in the act of writing, then grow and grow and grow the invisible fibers that weave them into a single entity.

Thus writing seems to confirm the theory of form, along with some important qualifications. First, the intuited form in this account is always a *felt* rather than an articulated principle. Plans may be written out, yet these are not descriptions of the form but sketches or outlines or maybe only catalysts to stimulate its growth. The form itself is felt as a sense of possibility and as a priority-making awareness of relevance and order. Second, although I absolutely need such an intuition in order to compose at all, it will always change during the composition. In *Camden's Eyes* the introduction of a new episode into the plan, and of a new idea for the ending, do not merely make the abstract form concrete but alter the form that I thought I had. The form I am working on is constantly being replaced. I choose its successor because the newcomer more strongly unifies the materials already developed as well as those still being planned. One could say that the new form was potential in those materials from the

beginning but that I did not see it until later. Nevertheless, I did not miss it until I saw it. I thought my conception of form was adequate until I discovered a better one. Some intuition of a form is needed for work, but the first intuited form is seldom the final one. Sometimes changes can mean discarding as much as six months' or even a year's work (yes, that has happened to me). That's why I call it gambling.

My experience does *not* confirm the simplistic formal notion that you have to know the end before you can begin or that you must make a plan and stick to it. It nevertheless does confirm from my point of view as a writer the theoretical importance of the formal principle, conceived as a principle of ordering, of relevance, of interconnectedness—a principle of the first importance. A second question then arises: to what extent does the conception of a formal principle enable me to understand or describe my own novels?

This question really asks if my novelist's experience confirms not merely the general idea of form but also the terms by which it is analyzed. Here as novelist I hesitate, for the specific terms of analysis are the critic's business and the critic's only. But isn't this statement a screen? Couldn't the novelist at least confirm the accuracy of what those terms can say about his work? Certainly the present novelist ought to know how to use the present terms, since he is so intimate with both the present critic and the present novels. The fact is, however, that this novelist suddenly finds himself shy, touchy, reluctant. I must admit, in fact, that for many years I have found myself curiously unwilling to subject my own novels to the same analytical scrutiny to which I am happy to subject others. I think I could make a proper formal analysis of each—tentatively and with some difficulty—and yet I find that I would rather not. The most interesting question, then, concerns this reluctance itself. Why so?

Not to be stubborn, I can make some obvious statements about my novels' forms. I don't mind mentioning that in all three the protagonist learns about himself as he tells the story; the telling itself is a primary revelation, a story over and beyond the actual events described. I can say that in *Camden's Eyes* the plot lies in the protagonist's attempt to organize his understanding of himself in relation to his wife, so that thought is active and reflective

of character; in the process the protagonist reviews every aspect of his case but never achieves a single organized understanding. The reader sees more—he sees the working of the protagonist's mind, with its deceptions, rationalizations, and hopes—and the reader thereby discovers a complex effect, primarily comic. Or I could say that in *The Morley Mythology* the middle-aged protagonist's deliberately adopted self-satisfaction is severely challenged by inner forces that color and even provoke external threats—in a subtle dynamic plot, as the external threat is removed, the inner threat is absorbed and acknowledged to be deep and permanent and necessary.

My reluctance to volunteer more suggests the familiar authorial stinginess: writers are superstitious, perhaps justifiably; they don't want to give too much away. If I attempt a definitive statement, I run the risk (or imagine I do) of disqualifying other interpretations that the reader's imagination may produce. I fear that my plot hypothesis will confine readers more than that of some other critic, since mine is authorized by the "author himself." Nor is it simply that the writer as interpreter of his own work has a heavy thumping voice, more ponderous and crushing than that of another critic. I must make an important distinction here: the very aim of a plot hypothesis is, in fact, to find the limits of a work. This is a fine task for the critic and the reader, but as author I want no part of it. As author, my aim is just the opposite. I would like my reader to discover as many connections and extensions of significance and implication as he can. I would like him to see not only the formal connections that I know are there but also those that (as the work still lives for me) I sense or feel but have not yet articulated, even to myself.

I am also reluctant because as writer of the novel I would rather the form be discovered in the way that I meant it to be, through the process of reading and observing and reflecting on it. Not that I mind the efforts of other critics and interpreters to assist in this process, but for them the possibilities are open, the advantages equal. The novelist's intervention would short-circuit the process of progressive visibility, which we know is so crucial to the effect.

The progression is also involved, probably, in the peculiar difficulty I find when I do ask ultimate formal questions about

my work. Technical questions regarding detail pose no problem, but as for the nature of the formal principle or the germinal principle or the effect—questions about them seem harder applied to my own novels than to others. This is especially true when the novel is new. Eventually, to be sure, the problem does lessen. I used to think of this difficulty as mental inertia—a failure associated with switching from the creative process to the critical. The progressive visibility of the form seems more convincing as a reason, though. The process is as cogent for the author as for the reader. Much of the attraction of a form I am working on lies in my suspicion that it has possibilities which I have not yet grasped. Often I have only this suspicion to tell me that a detail is not arbitrary, and it continues when the work is done—the feeling that more is there than I can see, even after all the months or years of working on it. For this main reason I cannot give a detailed or comprehensive formal analysis of my own novels: because I am more than ever conscious in my own case of the likelihood that anything I say will be superseded sooner or later by something else.

I have suggested that the perception of a formal principle acts upon the novelist as a guide and a restraint—necessary for the process to take place, though unformulated intellectually by him. Now I must ask about motivation—granted that perceiving a formal principle makes composition possible, does it actually drive the novelist to write, and if so, how? This is the third big question proposed at the beginning of this chapter: To what extent does the conception of a formal principle take account of my purposes in writing novels? What does the composition of a form that gradually becomes visible have to do with the deep need, the passionate drive, the obsessive compulsion?

The familiar theoretical answer is that artistic forms are "forms of feeling." History records what men have done, philosophy what they have thought, art what they have felt. We need the more personal answer of the novelist, though, based on his own questionings—an answer difficult to give because of the diffusion of his motives before they are shaped into a specific novel.

Some motivations can be ignored because they are too general: the desire for recognition, for achievement, for money (not

much hope there)—such motivations energize you, but they don't turn you into a novelist rather than a professor or politician or businessman. Some motivations are traps—I call them false motivations—purposes which might tempt you to write fiction but which if seriously followed would prove barren or even destructive (for me, I mean—but this attitude enters into my judgment of other writers, too). Included are various self-serving ends, such as the attempt to use the novel to establish that the author is an admirable person of some kind or to put real people down or to claim membership for the author in some particular group—embarrassing discoveries to make in someone else's work and worse if you spot them in your own.

But what, then, is a proper motivation for this particular novelist? It is not easy to disentangle motives because they all come together in a particular project, forming one aim: my motive is to write this novel now and the next one next. Yet there are general aims, and I can remember that I first thought of writing after reading stories (and later novels), liking them and their effect on my imagination and wanting to create the same effects myself. I read novels and wanted to write books like them—a response to the attraction of their forms.

And this response is still the strongest source. Whatever the psychology, it seems to involve at least three deep-rooted concerns. One I would generally call a "musical" motivation, a desire to capture the reader's attention and take him on a journey with adventure and surprises and an outcome, by which I mean, to take *myself* on such a journey and the reader with me, sharing the experience. I call this desire musical because music does the same thing. Actually it is "formal," because it is really a desire for involvement in a temporal form, a movement that goes from a beginning to an end.

Second is a more specific fascination, as old as my reading of fiction, with the way fictional images look in words and the way they affect my imagination. By "images" I mean every kind of fictional phenomenon that words can effect: characters, events, scenes, speeches, represented thoughts. In part this fascination with the workings of *words* has developed into a wish to use good, modern, varied, expressive prose. I don't know its origin. I have a habit of verbalizing in my thoughts; as things happen to

me, I habitually try to find words for them—an occupational habit, perhaps, intensified by my having become a novelist. Yet I can remember thinking in words as a child, before the idea of writing occurred to me. And I have subsequently learned how excellent a medium words are for focusing and identifying and preserving experience. They constitute a lens and a frame. By stripping from experience everything that they cannot suggest, words concentrate attention, and they present a difficulty to the reader, who must penetrate through them to their meaning and thence to the experience. Every word is a token of formative thought. I was fascinated—I am fascinated—with the way experience looks when so formed, so concentrated.

Third is perhaps simply an extension of the interest in words—a fascination with the appearance of fictional images in the larger structures of fiction, how they look when framed by the fictional convention and fixed in place in the fictional movement. I have always been interested in the power of a story to fix upon concrete specific moments, to control time, as in a scene of two characters talking, indelible on the page, or of a single character at some single moment, his thought full of flux, also indelible in immutable words. But I do not mean to limit this interest to such examples, for actually it is involved in fictional effects of all kinds that are successfully realized. It is the attraction not of the *things* depicted but of the depiction with its concentration and attention, the appeal of the fictional movement—not what is going to happen next, but what is the author going to do next?—and of the sense of exclusion, of what is not shown, to set off what is shown.

Both this fascination and the word interest are also "formal" motivations—interests, that is, in the power of the form. In both cases I am concerned with the capabilities of words and larger structures when they become parts of a fictional form and with the forming or creating power of such words and larger structures (conventions, yes) in themselves. This formal interest seems to precede the interest exerted by any specific thought or image in itself—in fact, an image formed by words may acquire an interest that an analogous image observed in real life (another embodiment) might totally lack.

These "formal" motives all respond to the attractions of the forms of fiction that I felt as a reader. In themselves, such motivations would not enable me to produce anything—nothing but variants of the same forms that had so appealed to me. But there are other motives, too. I eventually developed a respect for craft, for skill in the execution of work, by learning to appreciate it in artists whose work moved me—not just novelists, not just writers, but singers, jazz musicians, others. This motivation, too, is powerful, formal, specifically aesthetic, a desire to create a whole with economy and coherence, even when I do not know what form I want to create. And with time I also recognized the need for orginality: my steadily growing desire to write fiction was not to write stuff the same as somebody else's but to create new, original forms. This need for originality led to my growing interest in narrative and formal experimentation, while my respect for craft made me increasingly fussy (the best word for it) about phrases, sentences, and paragraphs, not to speak of the larger units.

Such motivations, aesthetic and formal, can be assisted by study. The breakthrough in my first novel, mentioned above, depended in part upon a discovery of certain original techniques that I could use and a form into which they could be developed. It grew (not with planned deliberation, but nevertheless quite definitely) from my understanding of the techniques of some other modern writers, and no doubt critical theory helped me understand these writers in terms that enabled me to do some things they had not done.

Yet I doubt that even the combination of these motivations could have led far if there had not been some specifically expressive and communicative drives as well. The communicative need is, to be sure, implied in the musical objective—to take others with me on a ride through a form created by me. Sharing the form with others is implicit in everything I have said about wanting to create one: the form is an experience absolutely my own, and sharing it will confirm me, somehow. The expressive motivation is another matter.

The first "serious" piece of writing I ever did was a twenty-page narrative in which at age fifteen I tried to reproduce a

typical journey on a steamboat line that had gone out of business—a trip I had often made and loved and mourned for.[3] Through the narrative I wanted to "preserve" the feeling, the images, of that journey. This was the earliest specifically *expressive* motivation for writing that I can remember (as distinct from purely formal), preceding (so it seemed) my interest in the form itself, an experience seeking embodiment rather than a form shaping into an experience. Later I began to write sometimes about kinds of experiences that I *wished* could happen. This wish motivation did not seem to endure, however, whereas the earlier desire began to seem more and more fundamental.

In careless and casual thought, I have sometimes claimed that the most compelling underlying motive for my fiction was this desire to *preserve* something, not real happenings, perhaps, but kinds of experience—not in order to write a memoir, not to tie down fact, not even to fasten on my own life, but to catch some quality in events. I am still trying to identify this quality. For a long time I supposed that for me (given my personal bias) the kinds of experiences I wanted most to preserve in fiction involved the processes of perception—of how the world works (how people behave, interact, see, and think), moves (people and things) and, above all, looks. I saw more: a common ground in all my novels was the character's experience of perceiving himself—the general situation of perceiving oneself or of oneself perceiving (not *myself*, not A. M. Wright, but *a* self, any self, a being aware of the distinction between its sentience and the world), recognition that the self is a being that one has created (the self-created self) and that the surrounding world is in some ways a similar creation (the self-created world). The curious thing is that my attempt to preserve the qualities of this kind of experience, this kind of perception, led me not to autobiography, since the demands of fact had nothing to do with it, nor to painting or photography, since my interest lay in movement and change, nor to music, which could do many things but not this. My search led rather to the language of fiction, since evidently my focus was on some very particular kind of mental

---

[3]Readers of *The Morley Mythology* and its prefatory note will know to what I am referring here.

activity and the way things look when subjected to this kind of activity. In the case of my steamboat narrative, for instance: why did I want to produce it in words? If I had had all the resources of the movie maker, and if the boats could have been resurrected from the scrapyard, I could have made a film that did most of what I thought I wanted my narrative to do. Yet I can recall (dimly in this case, but much more concretely in later inspirations) that aspects of the fictional image already seemed inseparable from words, even in that first conception. A written narrative would add to the movie of the steamboat experience the *act* of experiencing it, that is, of absorbing it into an understanding consciousness. I wanted to write not merely to help preserve a memory but to make that memory even more visible than the original experience. No doubt the same motive lies also behind that deeper habit I have mentioned, of verbalizing silently, as a way of understanding and controlling my impressions.

I recognize several underlying psychological needs here, of which the desire simply to preserve memory is the least, although it is a part. There is the desire to master experience that would otherwise be frightening; to bring experience to attention against its becoming stale and familiar (to keep aware of being alive); to defamiliarize things, once again, for the writer as well as the reader, to strip away the "veil of familiarity." The word is the heart of experience, the most intimate part of you that you can bring out into the world.

I call these motives "expressive" because they serve me, using art for expression, as I convert the raw material of my experience into another form so as to intensify and master my own sense of life. This description seems to imply that the force that finally writes the novel is a synthesis between long-standing formal and aesthetic motivations and urgent, specific, expressive ones. They seem to blend in the work, to become one. But were they ever really different, I wonder? It is easy to emphasize the expressive need in such a description because it is so comparatively specific, so much more directly related, seemingly, to the "materials" of the novels, their concrete imitated forms. Yet when I think carefully and recall honestly how my motivations developed and then consider how I work today, I have to recog-

nize that the expressive and the formal needs are not after all parallel and equal: rather, the latter underlie and precede, shape and bring forth the former. By the former I mean, of course, the specific expressive needs (for example, the need to preserve), for one can always speak of a more general drive to "express" which would be indistinguishable from the urge to compose a form. (This *general* expressive need, however, would be less specifically described than the formal needs I have named.)

Apparently I discover what I want to express by learning what kind of form I can or would like to develop. If I have to make changes, the coherence of the form takes precedence over any expressive needs of which I am conscious. I hesitate to say that the form actually invents what I want to express, but I become aware of the expression only after I have recognized the possibility of the form that will create it. The evidence is everywhere. My notion of possible recurring themes, of my deep interest, is changed by each successive novel. For example, lately I have begun to ponder the relationship between one fiction and another: the juxtaposition of fictions, subplot, double plot, some compound protagonists, novel within novel, the way in which two superimposed fictions can become metaphors for each other, each thereby shaking loose many hidden meanings in the other and so doubling or tripling the interest of either by itself. Having discovered this fascination, I see it retrospectively in all my earlier novels—and so find a deeper explanation, as it seems, than my previous attempts to describe what motivated them. This explanation is temporary, no doubt, and still only roughly understood. Do I know what such juxtaposition is trying to express, beyond itself, beyond the great power it has, as a construction, to intensify the attention-making powers of the fictional form? As an expressive motivation, it is still quite obscure, but *formally* it is quite clear.

My statements about what my novels "express" always seem to me quite speculative; I am well aware of the possibility that someone else could describe a novel of mine better than I. The evidence does not even support the notion that the great obsessiveness of writing comes from the need to express anything in particular. The times in writing when I am most driven, most

compulsive, most far gone into intensity, come when I am finishing a draft and when I am putting the finishing touches on a revision—moments, both, when the perfection of the form is most at stake and the hard expressive problems have largely already been solved. Thus I find myself acknowledging the Crocean theory that no knowledge exists unexpressed, that the work of art shapes the expression. The form is not the means to the expression, the form *is* the expression, *is* what the work expresses.

Has this account of my creative processes been influenced by the theory it is supposed to test? Probably. Until it is analyzed, the creative process looks amorphous; the terms of its analysis have to come from somewhere. Even so, I think my account does lend support to the theory. It also brings out certain cautions. For instance, although the creative process I have described shows the importance of the formal principle in the artistic process (a necessary construct to guide artists as they compose, to give them confidence, if nothing else), it does *not* require that a writer be able to describe or analyze that principle nor that it remain unchanged during composition—quite the contrary, in fact. Though guided by a form, drawn forward and checked by it, the writer is at the same time building it, changing and adding all the time, until gradually it becomes firm (especially in revision). Formal visibility continues to be progressive for writer as well as reader, after the work is finished. No doubt for this reason some writers feel that no work is ever finished.

The formal principle is not just a restraint, either, not just a limit. It is a motivation—that is, the desire to concretize it is one—as you see when it begins to consume the world in the writer's mind. To the novelist it does not seem separable from his expressive and communicative motivations. There is the love of the growing form, the *formal process*, as if for its own sake, which does not seem different from the expression of perceptions and the desire to share them with others. And skill, too, is a part, for skill itself is a kind of expression and expression a kind of skill.

What does a work "express" or "communicate," anyway? Feelings, I have said, or experience—but before they take shape in the work itself they are only general, not particular. Nor can

they even be called kinds in the initial stages of discomfort. They are abstract, without embodiment; they can't be named. In the initial stages they can perhaps best be described as a sort of yearning, a seeking to become concrete, to come into being. And the being they want to come into will be, of course, the work itself, the concrete form—a new experience which differs from the fading experiences of life by being defamiliarized, by being preserved, by being mastered by perception.

So the unifying principle, the form, is nothing more nor less than what the work is expressing and communicating. It expresses nothing other than itself. Anyone who would talk about what the work expresses must talk about its form. Form comes first, before any critic can speculate about the abstract elements that may have contributed to the work or motivated its composition.

Index

Allusions to novels by the names of their characters only have been indexed here under their titles and authors.

Index

Index

Index

Index

Index

Index

Poe, Edgar Allan, 133; "A Cask of Amontillado," 158; "The Fall of the House of Usher," 117; "The Masque of the Red Death," 159; "The Pit and the Pendulum," 158-159
Point of view, 27, 76. *See* Narrative
Porter, Katherine Anne: "The Jilting of Granny Weatherall," 73
A Portrait of the Artist as a Young Man (Joyce), 153
The Portrait of a Lady (James), 66, 102, 124, 127, 180n, 192, 195-217, 236, 245, 286; action, 197-208; effect, 210-211, 214; germ, 88-90, 93-96; fictional world, 195-196, 215; imaginary example, 91-98, 114; illustrative points, 53-55, 88-91, 141, 178; language, 196-197, 215-216; narrative, 196, 203n, 215; plot hypothesis, 208-211; problems, 211-214; renunciation, 206-208; revisions, 216-217
Powers, J. F.: *Morte d'Urban*, 151
Praise (effect), 161-162, 164, 168
Predictability, 33-34, 40, 42-43, 51, 103n
Presentation. *See* Compositional principles, of presentation; Narrative
Pride and Prejudice. See Austen
Principles. *See* Compositional principles; Design principle; Formal principle; Germinal principle
Probability and necessity, 67, 230n
Process (part of subject), 96-97, 99; kinds, 127-130
Propp, Vladimir, 108
Prose, in the novel, 61, 63-65
Protagonist, 124-127; compound, 124-126, 128, 165-167, in *The Sound and the Fury:* 224-233, 235-239; latent, 125-127, 133-134, 163, 168-169; in *Pale Fire,* 276-284
Proust, Marcel, 59; *Remembrance of Things Past,* 66; *Swann's Way,* 66
The Public Burning (Coover), 66
Punitive effect, 149-150, 159-160, 164
Pynchon, Thomas, 59, 61; *The Crying of Lot 49,* 126; *Gravity's Rainbow,* 179n, 192

Rasselas (Johnson), 58, 83
Reader's role, 184-185

Reading process, 38, 60, 79-80, 181-182
Realism, as a convention, 43, 45, 50, 174n
Recalcitrance, 37, 48
The Red Badge of Courage (Crane), 153-154
Remembrance of Things Past (Proust), 66
Repugnance (effect), 155, 158-159, 164, 168
The Return of the Native (Hardy), 149
Rhetorical plot, 115-116, 123, 125, 129-130, 133, 168, 277; in *Invisible Man,* 254-257
Richards, I. A., 28, 37
Richardson, Samuel, 59; *Clarissa,* 16; *Pamela,* 16n, 58, 69
Richter, David, 83n, 109, 115
Robbe-Grillet, Alain, 71, 73, 105-106, 126, 143, 185; *Jealousy,* 71n, 116, 143n; *The Voyeur,* 143n
Roberts, Preston T., 148n
Robinson, Henry Morton, 121n
Romance, 152-154, 157, 161, 163, 168; in *The Portrait of a Lady,* 211
"A Rose for Emily" (Faulkner), 127, 159
Rules of art, 43, 49; violation of, *see* Discontinuity

Sacks, Sheldon, 58, 83-84, 109-111, 115, 133, 145
Sanctuary (Faulkner), 159
Sartoris (Faulkner), 66, 239
The Scarlet Letter (Hawthorne), 125, 149
Scott, Sir Walter: *Ivanhoe,* 153
Second Skin. See Hawkes
The Secret Agent (Conrad), 156
"Sentence" (Barthelme), 122
Shakespeare, William, 148; *Macbeth,* 182n
Shared attention, as value, 175, 185
Shelley, Percy Bysshe, 174
Sidney, Sir Philip, *Arcadia,* 83
Signs, 35-36
Singleness, as value, 179
Sister Carrie. See Dreiser
Slatoff, Walter, 218n, 220
"The Snows of Kilimanjaro" (Hemingway), 73
Sons and Lovers (Lawrence), 153, 281n

Index

Index

THE FORMAL PRINCIPLE
IN THE NOVEL

Designed by Richard E. Rosenbaum.
Composed by The Composing Room of Michigan, Inc.
in 10 point Baskerville V.I.P., 2 points leaded,
with display lines in Baskerville.
Printed offset by Braun-Brumfield, Inc. on
Warren's Number 66 Antique Offset, 50 pound basis.
Bound by John H. Dekker & Sons, Inc.
in Joanna book cloth and
stamped in Kurz-Hastings foil.

Library of Congress Cataloging in Publication Data

Wright, Austin.
  The formal principle in the novel.

  Includes index.
  1. Fiction—Technique.   I. Title.
PN3365.W7   808.3   81-70711
ISBN 0-8014-1462-8   AACR2